FINDING A FORM

FINDING
A FORM

ESSAYS BY
William H. Gass

ALFRED A. KNOPF
NEW YORK 1997

THIS IS A BORZOI BOOK
PUBLISHED BY ALFRED A. KNOPF

Copyright © 1996 by William H. Gass
All rights reserved under International and Pan-American Copyright Conventions. Published in the United States by Alfred A. Knopf, Inc., New York, and simultaneously in Canada by Random House of Canada Limited, Toronto. Distributed by Random House, Inc., New York.

http://www.randomhouse.com/

Owing to limitations of space, acknowledgments for permission to reprint previously published material may be found on page 353.

Library of Congress Cataloging-in-Publication Data

Gass, William H.
    Finding a form : essays / by William H. Gass.—1st ed.
        p.   cm.
    ISBN 0-679-44662-1
    1. Literary form.   I. Title.
PN45.5.G355   1996   95-49914
                                                          CIP

Manufactured in the United States of America
Published August 1, 1996
Second Printing, April 1997

To Mary, as always,
and to Heide Ziegler and Marc Chénetier,
faithful lovers of language

ACKNOWLEDGMENTS

All of the essays in this collection have been revised and even rewritten for their appearance here. Occasionally the changes I made were slight, but more often they were extensive, so that these versions should be considered the final and only authorized ones. "Pulitzer: The People's Prize" and "A Failing Grade for the Present Tense" were first published in *The New York Times Book Review*; "Finding a Form," "Ford's Impressionisms," and "The Music of Prose," in *Antaeus*; "A Fiesta for the Form" and "At Death's Door: Wittgenstein," in *The New Republic*; "Robert Walser," as an introduction to a collection of his stories called *Masquerade*, published by Johns Hopkins; "The Language of Being and Dying" and "Nietzsche: The Polemical Philosopher," in *The New York Review of Books*; "Ezra Pound," in the *Times Literary Supplement* (London); "Autobiography," "The Vicissitudes of the Avant-Garde," and "The Baby or the Botticelli" (as "Goodness Knows Nothing of Beauty"), in *Harper's* magazine; "Exile" and "The Story of the State of Nature," in *Salmagundi*; "Nature, Culture, and Cosmos," in *Daphnis: Zeitschrift für Mittlere Deutsche Literatur*; "Simplicities," in *The Review of Contemporary Fiction*; and finally, "The Book As a Container of Consciousness" was given as an address to a conference on the book sponsored by the J. Paul Getty Center for the History of Art and the Humanities, and published, in part, in *The Wilson Quarterly*.

CONTENTS

PART I

PART II

PART III

x   *Contents*

PART IV

PART V

PULITZER:
THE PEOPLE'S PRIZE

t is not a serious novelist's nightmare (the possibility is so absurd); nevertheless, suppose you fancied yourself a serious novelist (a writer, as they say, of the first rank), and a wire were delivered in your dream (the telephone rang, there was a sudden knock), and this were followed by the formal announcement that you, Julia Peterkin, or you, Marjorie Rawlings, or you, Allen Drury or Michael Shaara or Alison Lurie, had been awarded the Pulitzer Prize in fiction for 1929 or '39 or '60 or '75 or '85. Well, what a pleasant supposition: to receive a prize, a famous one at that, with considerable prestige and the presumption of increased sales, as well as other benefits. Why should such a compliment to your art be denied; why should the thought be unlikely, the award embarrassing, the fact nightmarish? Because the Pulitzer Prize in fiction takes dead aim at mediocrity and almost never misses; the prize is simply not given to work of the first rank, rarely even to the second; and if you believed yourself to be a writer of that eminence, you are now assured of being over the hill—not a sturdy mountain flower but a little wilted lily of the valley.

The giving of prizes is a notoriously chancy business. Look at the mistakes the Nobel committee has made. Or shall we amuse ourselves by listing the important works the National Book Awards missed, even before it renamed itself the American Book Awards and brought in movie stars to crown pulpy books at its ceremony, or even after it reformed itself and endeavored to return to respectability again by failing to give Toni Morrison its prize in an oversight so flagrantly outrageous the Pulitzer was forced for once to do the right thing? Any award-giving outfit, whether it is the National Book Critics Circle or PEN, with its Faulkner Award, is doomed by its cumbersome committee structure to make mistakes, to pass the masters by in silence and applaud the apprentices, the mimics, the hacks, or to honor one of those agile surfers who ride every fresh wave.

We must be realistic. The judges are supposed to be notables, not ninnies; consequently they are busy people, a long time in the rackets, with grudges and buddies and old scores and IOUs and other obligations like everybody else. They will have a hundred novels to peruse, most of them so porous even the dense will feel ventilated. They will have to find time for the customary committee get-togethers, which will mean still more debits against an already overdrawn account. The rules for the award will normally be ridiculous, their wording narrow, ambiguous, vague, and overly hortatory. Joseph Pulitzer specified the first fiction prize this way: "Annually, for the American novel published during the year which shall best present the whole atmosphere of American life and the highest standard of American manners and manhood. $1000."

The panel will be formed with the same unfailing dimsight its members will feel obliged to display, and the three judges or the occasional five (for early National Book Awards, for instance, as well as its rejuvenation) will collide like cars at an intersection. Not only will they be partisans of their own tastes—that's natural—each will be implicitly asked to represent their region, race, or sex, because one will have to be a woman, another a black or academic or journalist, old hand or upstart. At least one novelist ought to be on the fiction panel, and a place found for a poet on the poets', as obnoxious as they both often are. The only qualification a judge ought to have is unimpeachable good taste, which immediately renders irrelevant such puerile pluralistic concerns as skin color, sex, and origin. Egalitarians shouldn't give prizes and be too humble to receive them.

It is also likely that the judges will be as conscious of themselves and their reputations as they will be of the books (it adds tone to one's *vita* and authority to the voice). Indeed, power, self-importance, and pomposity will bloom like a garden. The judiciousness of some will extend only to writers who come from the Old South or are politically okay or of a fine family, or who drive with a can of beer between their knees, or who have got old in the service, have been neglected, are awfully nice, and would simply love the honor.

Then there will be members too lazy to do the work, or too busy, and those who will pretend they've read every line of everything when they are ignorant even of the blurbs. There will be quirks and tics and idiosyncrasies brought into play the normal person could not imagine or allow in the bedroom. Some will want to ram their friends and fancies through into the glare of all that glory no matter what (besides, wouldn't Ann or Phil or Billy do the same for them—when that other jury meets next Tuesday?), while others will be so intent on bending over backward all they'll see is sky. Some jurors will try to intimidate others or, failing that, will try to gang up, their cliques meshing like a zipper, and sometimes they'll succeed. A few will be honestly persuasive about weak work, while the most effective will simply be stubborn. Some judges, some juries, abide by their names and treat each work before them as someone accused of a crime.

A lot of writers are disliked and their works slighted because they have been praised by the wrong critics, have sappy photographs on their dust jackets, overly effusive or too bountiful blurbs, made-up, movie-star names. Or are known to have the wrong politics. (I like to believe I could have voted a poetry prize to Marianne Moore even though I know she once wore a Nixon button.) If a work has already won a prize, it is very likely going to be found unfit for another. Oh, yes . . . and publishers don't make the books available to the panel sometimes, even when the prize-givers are willing to pay for them. According to John Hohenberg's history of the awards, *The Pulitzer Prizes*, only five books published in 1916 were submitted to the jury for the first year of the award, 1917, and I have served on juries where repeated requests to publishers brought no response. Nowadays, it costs publishers money for each book they submit to the NBA. Recently, one juror, Paul West, had to ask Dalkey Archive Press to put up Felipe Alfau's *Chromos,* an extraordinary novel, which ought to have won instead of the third-rate work that did.

To complete our descent into the tacky: in some cases the jurors are expected to give the books back. Moreover, publishers have been known to complain bitterly when one of their authors won a prestigious prize—in the first place, because the news would have to be hailed in *The New York Times* (in the same costly box that would announce the writer's demise), and in the second place, because the victory entailed a victory party for which the publishers had no desire to foot the bill, and which, in the third place, they didn't wish to attend because they had no interest in shaking the hand of an author whose merit was an embarrassment to the house.

Someone always foots the bill, of course, and when the outcome doesn't smartly show the shoes, the soles are inclined to squeak, as Nicholas Murray Butler did in the old days when, as president of Columbia University, he oversaw the labors of the Pulitzer Advisory Board, to which the jury makes its recommendation for a final decision. Overseers are inclined to meddle, or to withdraw their moral and monetary support (as the publishers did from the National Book Awards when the modest level of excellence it usually approved was still too elevated to be useful to the concerns of the market).

In addition to these hazards, the fact is that good taste and sensible judgment are rare, and excellence itself is threatening, innovation an outrage. On the other hand, one must be most wary of the jurors who boast that only literary quality guides their selections, because the phrase "literary quality" is a conservative code word these days that means "I wouldn't toss a dime into an ethnic's hat." And "experimental" can be more frankly replaced by "self-indulgent and inept" so often as to cause one to despair of the word. In the face of all these frailties, then, is it any wonder that awards go awry? So complain about human nature if you want to, but there's no need to pull a face about the Pulitzer.

This is an apparently reasonable request. Certainly the sincerity and conscious goodwill of most judges, whether for the Pulitzer or for something else, is not in doubt, nor are the difficulties unreal or easy to surmount. Furthermore, not every outcome is a cropper. Deserved reputations have been made by some awards, and fine writers rescued from obscurity. There have been courageous choices, deeply discerning ones, and quite a few that are at least okay. Of course, you might achieve these results as well by rolling dice. Yes, even pigeon poop is hit or miss—the chances of the skies. Yet the Pulitzer Prize in fiction is almost pure miss. The award is not batting a fine .300 or an acceptable .250. It is nearly zero for the season, unless Toni Morrison's *Beloved* proves to have the qualities of its title. When missing exceeds chance, as in this case; when a record of failure approaches perfection; then we can begin to wonder whether it is really missing the mark at all; whether the Pulitzer, not by design but through its inherent nature, is being given to those it wishes, quite precisely, to award, and is nourishing, if not the multitude, at least those numbers among the cultivated whose shallow roots need just this sort of gentle drizzle.

By the time Joseph Pulitzer's charge to the fiction jury reached it, Nicholas Murray Butler had inserted the word "some" in a discreet though critical spot (he called the addition "insubstantial"), so that the jury's charge read, "novel . . . which shall best present the whole*some* atmosphere of American life . . ." instead of "whole atmosphere," the words that were there originally. The jury could not find a winner the first year, wholesomeness being in short supply even among the mediocre, and they would fail again two years later. Butler also fussed about the word "manhood" because he wanted it clearly understood that women writers would be eligible for the prize, so long, of course, as their work presented "the highest standard of American manners and manhood." "Wholesome" was dropped in 1929 (a poor year for it anyway) and "whole" restored, but "wholesome" answered the bell again the next round, only to be knocked out for good in 1931. Meanwhile, "manhood" and "manners" were also eliminated. In 1936, "best," which had been allowed to wander back in front of "American novel," was softened to "distinguished." Throughout all this, and from the beginning, the short story was given . . . well . . . short shrift. There can be no question that part of the problem with the Pulitzer was the early wording of the award's conditions.

In 1947 the terms were changed once more, "distinguished novel" becoming "distinguished fiction in book form," in order that the coming year's prize could be given to James A. Michener's *Tales of the South Pacific*. If the Advisory Board had really wished to present the Pulitzer to a fine book of short fiction (as W. J. Stuckey notes in his excellent and judicious retrospective study, *The Pulitzer Prize Novels*), J. F. Powers's beautiful collection, *The Prince of Darkness*, was available; but at least a good deed was done —broadening the scope of the prize—even if it was for an insipid reason.

The prize regularly stopped at the wrong station. Having passed all of Faulkner's great novels by with scarcely a hoot of recognition, and Hemingway's as well, and the best efforts of Lewis and Porter and Bellow and Welty too, it would halt and release its steam for lesser works when their writers were safely of world renown. Yet had it not done so, scarcely a novelist of any note would have made the list, for writers like Dreiser, Fitzgerald, Anderson, Wolfe, West, and Flannery O'Connor were ignored altogether in the old days, while Stanley Elkin, John Barth, John Hawkes, William Gaddis, and Donald Barthelme are not honored in ours.

The single outstanding choice of the Pulitzer Prize Committee during its tenure remains *The Age of Innocence*, which gained the palm in 1921 (this is also Mr. Stuckey's opinion). But it restores one's confidence in the otherwise unblemished record of the prize to learn that the majority of the jurors favored *Main Street* (rather astonishing in itself). However, that award was blocked by Hamlin Garland (or possibly by old Nick, the Butler, again), so that it bounced into Edith Wharton's arms instead. Her joy deflated by an account of how she had received it, Wharton referred to the award as "the Pulsifer Prize" in one of her later novels, a name eminently worth retaining for the fiction prize so that it would no longer be identified with the awards in other areas whose records, though spotty, are more nearly awful in quite a normal way, and which continue to bestow on the fiction prize a dignity it has not earned for itself and does not deserve.

Although prize juries are sworn to secrecy concerning their proceedings, leaks are more common than quiet containment. The public loves to read about the wrangling more than it cares about the books or the ceremonial bestowal of the awards; however, winners are frequently denied their pleasure in the prize when judges speak too freely or when the panel's acrimonious and noisy proceedings are overheard, as was the case the first time I was a judge for the NBA. Of course, if you hold your meetings in the public rooms of the Algonquin, you must want to be written up. To find yourself associated with an award given to mediocrity on the basis of sex or race or subject, instead of to literary excellence on the basis of that quality, is, of course, intolerable, and the injustice of having to keep your fist in your mouth when it ought to be in someone else's is understandably galling; yet when you agree to serve, you are risking your pride and the likely defeat of your intentions. Instead of commingling with like-minded goodhearts in a noble exercise (a condition sometimes met), you may find yourself at the same table with incompetence, imbecility, bad faith, and cowardice. You can bet your chair will wear a nasty label, too.

If, on the other hand, panelists hope too strongly for harmony, they may make their decision on the worst possible grounds, choosing the book that offends none but the honor of the prize, and propose that sign of dismal failure, the compromise candidate.

The point of prizes, presumably, is to establish literary standards, honor worthy work and the writers of it, and enlarge the audience for fine fiction by bringing it to wider public notice than its publishers can bear to. The monies involved are now enough to pay for an air conditioner and a case of scotch—a windfall not to be scorned, yet still not the muse's airlift either. Recently, although award amounts have risen, there has been an unfortunate tendency to give prizes to place and show (as if second weren't last), flattening an already skinny purse, but also to succumb to a publicist's desire to keep candidates in suspense, corralling them on award night as if they had written a movie, so that an audience can enjoy the discomfiture of four losers as well as the elation of the lucky duck.

The Pulitzer has perceived an important truth about our complex culture: Serious literature is not important to it; however, the myth that it matters must be maintained. Ceremony is essential, although Mammon is the god that's served. The PEN/Faulkner may toot, but few will hear. Its winners, until recently, could not be made into mass-market movies. Literature, which is written in isolation and read in silence, receives as its share less than 3 percent of the funds available to the National Endowment for the Arts. In my own state of Missouri, by no means the meanest, less than a penny a person is spent per year on arty words. And if you point to the discrepancy between the acknowledged importance of our literature to our culture and the pitiful public support it gets, and decry the injustice of it, you will receive the same response I always have: Those addressed, like a cat, will not follow the direction of your gesture, but will be just curious enough to sniff nervously for a moment the end of your admonitory finger.

So it is silly to give a prize to *Absalom, Absalom!* when you can give it to *Gone with the Wind*, as happened in 1937. It is useless to single out unpleasant books that no one will read or enjoy, like *The Day of the Locust* or *Miss Lonelyhearts*, when so many will love the 1934 winner, *Lamb in His Bosom*, by Caroline Miller. The Pulitzer does not give glory to its choices; its choices give celebrity to it; and that is precisely why it is the best-known and, to the public, the most prestigious prize: It picks best-sellers, books already in the public eye, and if its judges insist on oddities like *Gravity's Rainbow*, the Advisory Board will overrule them, as it did in 1974; and if the judges vote for some dim unknown like Norman Maclean, the board will simply leave the year blank again, as it did in 1977. It is difficult to see why anyone of distinction would want to be like an abused wife and serve on a Pulitzer jury.

It's been clear from the first year that it has never been the judges who needed their consciousness raised, or their moral point of view improved, or their allegiance to American values strengthened, but the Many "out there" who could use such elevation, so it was more than all right if an "all right" book was popular, it was positively a good thing. Indeed, a novel's simplifications could be defended if its message was thereby better understood and more easily lodged in the reader's mind. Hence an award-winning book did not necessarily have to represent the private tastes of the judges or the board; it represented, rather, their judgment that it would be edifying for those who read it. *Strive and Succeed* might have been the appropriate name for most of the winners, since that is what they preached.

These winners have a fruit fly's life span, and oblivion serves their names, but it is beside the point to protest them on this basis, as, indeed, critics have regularly done, sometimes quite scornfully, with no effect whatever. In the last decade the prize has continued its belated ways, finally getting around to John Updike, Norman Mailer, and John Cheever. But the prize understands the public's desires. The public longs to move on.

Suppose the award had really been given to the best work of fiction published each year. Then Faulkner would have won it with *The Sound and the Fury* in 1930, beating out Hemingway and Wolfe (all of whom, in fact, lost to *Laughing Boy*, by Oliver La Farge); he would have won again in 1931 with *As I Lay Dying*, once more in 1933 with *Light in August*, certainly in 1937 with *Absalom, Absalom!*; and he'd have had a good shot at several others. Saul Bellow would have grabbed off at least two, perhaps more, and so on. Well, ho hum, what a bore. It is true that the best tennis players collect cup after cup and carry home baskets of money, but in their case the fix isn't in. In the history of the Pulitzer Prize (leaving out Faulkner, who won twice, though for two less-than-worthy works, A *Fable* and *The Reivers*), Booth Tarkington has been the only double winner. Putting a ceiling on winning was wise, because the literary public will chew its fiction only while the immediate flavor lasts and, when that's gone, spit the book back into its jacket.

But if the award had really been given yearly to the best work, worse than repetition would have occurred. *The Sot-Weed Factor* would have acquired a crown in 1961, and *JR* would have won in '76, and other horrors too dreadful to describe would have happened. The 1974 jury's recommendation of *Gravity's Rainbow* would not have been overruled, for one thing, and Thomas Pynchon would have had the opportunity to turn down a Pulitzer.

While the Pulitzer Prize for poetry has none of the esteem that the Bollingen conveys, it has been spared fiction's shame, partly, I think, because there is no appreciable audience at all for poetry, consequently no reader whose moral and mental welfare the judges must consider their prizewinning poems to improve.

Nothing essential ever disappears. Schlock certainly seems essential. Hence the public and their fiction prize move on, but safely from same to same. For even if the titles change, or the subjects shift slightly as the fads run by, or the authors lean a little this way rather than that, the result is the fading sweet taste of an imagined past. What the public wants, as the Pulitzer sees it (and as Mr. Stuckey correctly concludes, I think), is an exciting story with a timely theme, although it may have a historical setting. The material should be handled simply and delivered in terms of sharp contrasts in order that the problems the novel raises can be decisively resolved. Ideally, it should be written in a style that is as invisible as Ralph Ellison's invisible man, so that the reader can let go of the words and grasp the situation the way one might the wheel of the family car. And since most of the consumers of fiction are women (or they were until women went in for professions and other public works and now return home as tired and weary and in need of the screen's passive amusement as men), it won't hurt to fulfill a few of their longings, to grant, now and then, unconsciously an unconscious wish. Because we have a large, affluent, mildly educated middle class that has fundamentally the same tastes as the popular culture it grew up with, yet with pretensions to something more, something higher, something better suited to its half-opened eyes and spongy mind, there is a large industry of artists, academics, critics, and publicists eager to serve it—lean cuisine, if that's the thing—and the Pulitzer is ready with its rewards.

No, this prize for fiction is not disgraced by its banal and hokey choices. It is the critics and customers who have chosen and acclaimed them, who have bought the books and thought about them and called them literature and tried to stick them like gum on the pillars of our culture. It is they who have earned the opprobrium of this honor.

A FAILING GRADE
FOR THE PRESENT TENSE

Pauline experienced many perils, but none to compare with the perils of the present tense, She was tied to tracks, left to teeter on window ledges, allowed to hang from cliffs by the lace in her pantaloons. Yet in the week while we waited for her bloomers to rip or the train to come, time held its breath as we held ours—in serial suspension; that is, we calmly ignored the pause in her plight as we went about our business, placing our modest cares in a parenthetical phrase; because, when the lace on her undies relaxed at last, when the train's hoot grew cruelly closer, or when Pauline's delicate balance seemed to have slipped beyond refooting; then her peril continued as if there had never been an interruption, not a shiver was missing, or a screech from a scream, and, in order to reassure us of this, the second episode would reprise the conclusion of the first, and so on, right through fifteen plight-packed Saturday matinees.

Later I would be taught to wonder—about the present but not about Pauline—whether anything of which we were normally un-aware might have taken place between one tick and its following tock (molecular doings, quantum leaps), because if you ran past a picket fence at the right speed, you would seem to see the green field beyond, as if the fence weren't there. Walk more slowly, and you might receive nothing but board. Going about at lifespeed, mankind might be missing . . . well, who knew what?

Or maybe, relative to me, the world was moving as the frames of the movie moved, or the pages of those riffle books I fanned to animate Mutt and Jeff in unseemly ways, so that reality was a series of stills, like a solid row of alphabet blocks. There would have to be motion, of course, to produce the illusion, but we would be wrong about where the motion was. Or maybe the present was a continuous whoosh, or an uninterrupted whissh, and had no parts, so that all our divisions of time into eras, decades, milliseconds, advertising spots, falsified its flow.

Suppose I were about to move my queen's knight and, while my hand hovered above the head that, in this case, makes up the whole horse, the frame froze and, freed from that dramatic scene, my opponent and I rushed away during the intermission for a set of tennis played at fast-forward, only to return to the table in less time than it takes to tell: I to lift my knight from its square, my foe to wonder why and where—what then? Take this thought a little further. While one passage of time is dit-dotting along, perhaps others are passing at right angles between the dits like hair through a comb? How could one guess how huge the hiccup in Being was: perhaps, instead of a quick set of tennis, there was a long fall of empire, like that of Rome? In philosophy class, I was taught to ask such questions, and I was cautioned not to smile when I did so, but to appear genuinely concerned and intense. Now I put my VCR on pause and think no more about it. But what if God put me on pause while He spooned up a dish of Heavenly Hash? and slowly, over eons, slowly . . . slowly dribbled across it a sweet excess of chocolate sauce?

When we put a dial on the sun and cut that dial like a pie, we created a mechanical time in which we decided to pass our days, believing in it more faithfully than in Santa Claus, because storetime came in a convenient package—it could be paused, shortened, backed, speeded up, or flopped, enriched, extended, ended—whereas real time simply went *whoo-issh* and wouldn't alter its tune, accelerate, or stop.

The present has many perils. The least of them are philosophical. The heart never stops yesterday, but this instant—on the steps to the bus. Your favorite glass is slipping from your soapy grasp. She says "not now" now.

William James wondered how long the present lasted. It had to have a length, because if you cut every immediate moment into the part of it already over and the part of it yet to come—narrowing your slice from knife to thread—you'd have an edge so fine it had no size. The present would have no presence. Contrary to the clock's analysis, our sensations sustain themselves. James called it "the specious present"—this period we do not appear to pass through but experience as a whole. To taste an entire swallow of wine, to possess all its qualities at once, does not require its characteristics to exist simultaneously. The before and after we perceive in the specious present nevertheless seem equally vivid and there for us, the nows form a row like bricks in a building. None of them are yet a then. In other words, for a brief and variable period, we experience time as we do space.

The present has more lanes than an Olympic pool. My lane is not your lane. In mine, a shirt button is breaking from a weakened thread. In yours, perhaps a sense of wonder at the size of the solar system is enveloping your consciousness like a cloud of steam. The clock's now, nevertheless, swims on evenly, counting and canceling the same number of laps from both our lives, or so we suppose —but are we right? I have sometimes felt that the minutes of others were longer than mine. I have had moments I felt would never end.

Unlike the present, the present *tense* is the condition of a verb. "Is" will remain in the present tense through all eternity, while a day is warm no longer than that day. So the perils of the present tense (and there are plenty) are neither an orchestrated series of difficult movie moments, like those that beset Pauline in film time, nor the normal passage of experience from oops to ouch that often constitutes life time if we're unlucky. Writing of any kind involves the creation on the page of connections in language that denote, describe, and relate events (verbal occurrences that we can call "word time") and within which the only lapse that can count as a crime is a lapse of grammar. Yet the perils of the present tense are real; rescues are infrequent (unlike the case of plucky Pauline, who is always saved from the saw just ahead of its nick); and those efforts to assist that are reluctantly attempted are generally botched. The present tense is a parched and barren country. In the past, writers rarely went there.

The perils of the present tense are pronounced, but as speakers we might now and then avoid them. "What are you doing in there, Helen?" is a question natural enough. "I am mopping the floor around the fridge." (She mops.) "What is Lady Jane saying to Jack Strongthong now?" Helen asks in a moment, carrying on her progressive present. "Come and see the TV for yourself." "I can't stop mopping. This leak is enormous . . . as if the whole fridge were weeping," she says, putting on the subjunctive with the ease of robe and slippers. (She mops.) (Her husband wonders whether his wife actually said what she said, slipping so sexily into the subjunctive, since what she said seems as strange to him as the thought that his thought alliterates.) (The present tense frequently adorns margins in the form of stage directions: She mops.) "Well, hon, Baby Janey ain't sayin' nuthin'," husband answers, shifting into yokelese. "She is slappin' Cousin Jack's slap-scarred face."

Occasionally, without mortal risk, we use the speaking present to sharpen the sense of immediacy in some story we are telling—a story we think is full of giggles, one of them being the tense it's told in. "Let me tell you what happened to me in Altoona last month. I'm standing in front of the local five-and-dime, see, sharpening my musical saw, when this guy comes up to me and says, 'How would you like to make a sawbuck?' 'My name's not Buck, stranger,' I say with a toothless grin, 'but I can try to make one—how's this? *You can lead a mind to matter, but you can't make it think.*' " The present tense is terrific for vaudeville and other turns of phrase. It also lends itself to satirical intentions, usually without much interest.

Why do I warn you, stranger, of the perils of the present tense?

Because there is a lot of it going around. What was once a rather rare disease has become an epidemic. In conjunction with the first person, in collusion with the declarative mode, in company with stammery elisions and verbal reticence—each often illnesses in their own right—it has become that major social and artistic malaise called minimalism, itself a misnomer. This is not the minimalism of Gertrude Stein and Samuel Beckett, or of Anton Webern and Kazimir Malevich, in which a few obsessively selected means are squeezed into a mighty More—that more, as Mies van der Rohe said, which is the large result of less. This is rather the less that less yields. This is modesty taken down a peg. Here we have the simple without the pretensions of simplicity, plainness without the pressures of an Amish or a Shaker ethic.

Minimalism does not really represent an -ism, but a sizable number of -ists. If there is an urban prose, this prose is suburban. If there is an academic prose, this prose is collegiate. If there is a yuppie prose, this would be it, except that it says "nope" more often than it says "yup." Out of Hemingway, out of O'Hara, out of detective fiction and brand-name realism, it is as terse as a telegram. It is as hard-boiled, but not an egg.

One of the virtues of the present is that the present passes. (I should correct myself: the present is the only thing that is always around; what is present in the present passes.) One of the perils of the present tense is exactly the evanescence of its referent. (To be precise: this is true only if the referent is a particular thing or action in the world; if the referent is "mopping," "leaking," "sweating," these Ideas of Action may be as eternal as the Eternal Itself.) One of the perils of writing about any event is, of course, that it will be gone before its verb is well in place and its nouns have had a chance to settle down around it. So if I say: "There is an outbreak of measles at Slimbo's Summer Camp," you, the reader, will smile at this old news, having brought your kid home to get well and rest up several epidemics ago—that would be before chicken pox, before mumps.

How does it happen that I have been alerted to this outbreak of the present tense when, perhaps, you haven't? Not long ago I was asked to select some stories by new writers for an anthology, and my initial survey of the field, taking me geologically about fifteen years deep, uncovered the condition. Further researches at writing schools, the principal source of the contamination, underlined the seriousness of the situation and the extent of its ramifications. (I wrote "underlined" just now—quite wrong; it dates me. "Highlighted" is the right term. A bilious yellow marking pen is run over words as if to cancel them. The face of the text can still be made out, like the figure of someone drowned beneath the phlegm. But for you who are reading this, the practice may have passed beyond your ken—a happy thought.)

There were writing programs in a few universities before World War II, but it was only after that conflict that they began to multiply and flourish. So they've been with us, roughly, a bit beyond a generation, as it is often measured. We are now experiencing the cumulative effects of their operations. You may have noticed the plague of school-styled poets with which our pages have been afflicted, and taken some account of the no-account magazines that exist in order to publish them. In addition, thousands of short-story readers and writers have been released like fingerlings into the thin mainstream of serious prose.

The most distant layer of my excavations turned up pretty much what one might expect: a scattering of subjects, persons, tenses, places. I ran into more males than females, and there were the usual number of initiation stories, family muddles, bittersweet affairs. As I advanced toward the present, however, the number of women writers increased, as did the number of fictions in the first person, and tales in the present tense.

Well, young people are young people, aren't they, I said to myself, so it is only natural that they write about themselves and their immediate problems. Adolescents consume more of their psyches than soda pop, and more local feelings than fast food. On the other hand, these young people are in school, I thought, where they are presumably learning something. Is no indulgence denied them?

What are their mentors doing? Standing in very loco and permissive parentis, it would turn out.

Meanwhile, as I read into the outskirts of the present, the present tense was taking over. By now (that now I neared, not your now, of course), of the 195 fictions I had examined, 81 were in the first person and 52, in whatever person, were in the present tense. I was aware that my sample might be misleading in a number of ways, although it was a good deal more substantial than many telephone surveys reporting on public opinion; but the trend it observed—an increase in women, first persons, and present tenses —went, as my investigations continued, through the roof.

The present tense has singulars and plurals, of course, and persons: I, we, you, they, he, she . . . I mop, she mops . . . you mop, he mops. Back before there was a present tense for writing purposes, if you wanted to risk it anyhow, you consulted the classic case: Katherine Anne Porter's "Flowering Judas," which is in the third-person present. Why would Miss Porter want to put this story of a betrayal, this story of a fat Mexican revolutionary and the woman he wants, into the present tense? Certainly not because everyone else was doing it.

> Braggioni sits heaped upon the edge of a straight-backed chair much too small for him, and sings to Laura in a furry, mournful voice. Laura has begun to find reasons for avoiding her own house until the latest possible moment, for Braggioni is there almost every night. No matter how late she is, he will be sitting there with a surly, waiting expression, pulling at his kinky yellow hair, thumbing the strings of his guitar, snarling a tune under his breath. Lupe the Indian maid meets Laura at the door, and says with a flicker of a glance toward the upper room, "He waits."

William James worried about the size of the specious present, but the present invoked by the present tense, as well as the present referred to by the noun "present," are very elastic. "At the moment, I am mopping the kitchen floor." "Right now, our refrigerator is on the fritz." "We presently live in Santa Monica." "I am a buyer for Best Buy." "*M*A*S*H* is a big hit." "I am a Catholic and don't believe in divorce, so the only way I'll be rid of him is if he dies." "*The Perils of Pauline* is out of fashion." "The jig is up." For how long is this jig up? For Ever. Its overness is never over. Naturally, students of the present tense will learn how to orchestrate these differences, moving from one present to another with dazzling effect. Sure.

In Porter's piece the resources of the habitual present are masterfully exploited. Most events in life come round more than once like Gertrude Stein's ". . . is a rose . . ." does, moving from now to then and back again. Every night Braggioni comes, sits, pulls at his hair, thumbs strings, and snarls a tune. Every night Lupe meets Laura at the door, glances heavenward, says, "He waits." When Porter slips into the past or advances to the future, she does so in order to emphasize the obsessive menace of the present, as repetitive as a firing squad. If something in the story is to occur uniquely, she reverts to the plain past to report it.

> A brown, shock-haired youth came and stood in her patio one night and sang like a lost soul for two hours, but Laura could think of nothing to do about it.

So "Flowering Judas" is written in a thick present, a present made of a deep past. It lingers like an odor in a closed room, and does not dissipate but intensifies with time. This present becomes the story, and its choice, at first surprising, is thoroughly justified. Minimalists don't use the habitual tenses much, however. They like little that is thick. Not carpets. Not cream. Not prose. Thinness is chic.

Our self is split as our pronouns are, and you and I are each and every one of them. There is, first of all, Freud's darkly demonic and anonymous id, or "it," the force to which we grimly appeal when we say, "It drove me to it." Then there is the ego, of course, that most Roman of numerals, Number One, the subjective "I," a consciousness conscious of itself. This inner life has its objective counterpart, the public "me," but "me" is always an "I" turned inside out; otherwise we use "he" or "she." For multiple personalities, "they" and "them" will do nicely, but what about "you"—the faceless, nameless anybody who is almost a thinglike image of the urgent id? When we address ourselves as "you," it is usually to accuse: "Now you've really gone and done it." When we see ourselves as others see us, we become, for a moment, a "me," and when we look back at our imperial "I" from the vantage point of "me," we say, sometimes irreverently, "Hey, you!" The geometry can be confusing. My "me," when observed by another "I," is a "he." And each of the points of view these pronouns name has its own time. The time "I" spent mopping the floor felt like an eternity, whereas for "me" it was five minutes, give or take a tick.

You have told your husband, the sloth, about the leak, about how often the kitchen floor needs to be mopped, but he never comes into the kitchen; it's "Get me a beer, will you?" or a chicken wing. The sloth shifts one haunch, then another. Your time with the TV has become mop time. Flop. Flop. This marriage is a joke. I didn't expect to be fucked by a cliché. Not me. I was expecting a cock of some kind, of course, but not a sloth's dickie. We never wake up in time. We think we are different, and won't make the mistakes other people make. They play the fool. That's the rule. But what about you, now? Now you are as wet and stringy as your mop. Flop. I thought I'd never be one of them, one of those sag-titted, muss-haired, mum-dumb broads. Well, baby, you was wrong. You is in a flat fix. So what shall I do, since I'm Catholic and all? Mope and mop? Flop and sob? Is that it? Yup. Jig's up.

Our fledgling writers, aspiring professionals whose machines beep about their spellings, will make a careful study, naturally enough, of the function of the pronoun, the psychological and ontological import of each, examining such contemporary classics as Juan Goytisolo's *Makbara*, which is almost a textbook of pronoun significance and use. Sure they will. Or their instructors will require them to. Sure they will. When, their mentors rhetorically inquire, do we normally find this brutal "Hey, you?" fastened to the present tense like a horse to a lawnmower? Well, sometimes it happens when "me" says to "I": "You are such a jerk!" Otherwise, it occurs when, as an actor, for instance, we ask the director what we are to do next. "You" becomes the first word of an order—a command or directive. My hubby, let's suppose, has told me to do something with my life, so I leave my place in front of the TV, my place beside him on the sofa, and come into the kitchen. What then? "You imagine a lot of water has leaked on the floor from beneath the fridge, and you mop it up." It may be simpler managing the second-person present in Spanish, but even so, Carlos Fuentes's *Aura* remains a rare tour de force, with its central character utterly in the power of a mysterious, historically determined fate that speaks almost over the shoulder of the writer himself.

You're reading the advertisement: an offer like this isn't made every day. You read it and reread it. It seems to be addressed to you and nobody else. You don't even notice when the ash from your cigarette falls into the cup of tea you ordered in this cheap, dirty café.

Under such an aura, you mop the floor as in a dream; you wonder what is on TV now; you think that your husband is a ten-toed sloth. So forceful is this tense and person, it is as if the café had been commanded to be cheap and dirty. You mop. You think: I wish Roberto Rossellini had thawed me out. Then I could be like this fridge. Aleak. Alas, alack, you are only a frump, a sloth's frump at that.

My survey brings me now to the third-person present, also a favorite of the young. However, the masterwork in this mode is Robert Coover's "The Babysitter," which is written in a series of paragraphs or "screens." We might think of them as windows through which we peep, as indeed plenty of peeping occurs in the story. What is seen in each screen or window is reported to the reader the way Helen's husband—the ten-toed sloth—describes the expression of the slapped face on his set, although we can't expect his language to be lyrical, even when lyricism is called for.

He loves her. She loves him. They whirl airily, stirring a light breeze, through a magical landscape of rose and emerald and deep blue. Her light brown hair coils and wisps softly in the breeze, and the soft folds of her white gown tug at her body and then float away. He smiles in a pulsing crescendo of sincerity and song.

Now, perhaps (now?), we have been given a clue to the popularity of the present. Not only is the present brief, like a small bun to be swallowed on the run; those who live in the present, as we imagine cattle do, expect little from the future and remember nothing of the past. Any sense of continuity is quickly lost, for one present follows hard upon another the way a hard rain falls, and all those things that thicken the present with their reflective weight, that highlight (I hope I've mastered the word) one aspect and darken another, are omitted, because in the thin present what remains of the world is in the center ring, in full focus.

"He loves her. She loves him." How simple it sounds. How simpleminded it is. Not only is love itself complex; it never arrives unaccompanied, but brings its whole village, like a wagon of refugees. Even if we reduce love to a gesture, a look, a kiss, any bald statement of the case risks a smile if not a laugh. "He kisses her. She kisses him." To be exact: he French-kisses her; she fish-kisses him.

If the third-person present has the effect of a narrated film, or the antics of a woman in a window as described by Peeping Tom to Peepless Jerry ("What's she doing now?" "She's still mopping"), the first person is perfect for those who like to imagine themselves in a movie: see me mop. As in a daydream, the "I" projects its "me" into an unsuspecting world.

If you are really passionate about the present tense, you can get it to play every temporal tune. Here is the way Raymond Carver starts a naturally brief piece called "Gazebo."

That morning she pours Teachers over my belly and licks it off. That afternoon she tries to jump out the window.

I go, "Holly, this can't continue. This has got to stop."

It is easy to understand how a snappy beginning like this would appeal to the students. "You should read R. Carver," they'd say at those times when past their workshops I'd drift. So I did, and I was amused and edified. "Let me recommend Proust," I'd say, just to share enthusiasms. Sure. "You should read T. Wolff," they'd say —"where it's at." "Is that the brother of G. Wolff?" I'd wonder. "Dunno," they'd say, "but T is tops." Okay. And I was honestly edified and genuinely amused. Why imitate Proust? "Try R. Musil, won't you?" I'd suggest. Sure thing. Someday. "Don't miss J. McInerney. On all night."

You are not the kind of guy who would be at a place like this at this time of the morning. But here you are, and you cannot say that the terrain is entirely unfamiliar, although the details are fuzzy. You are at a nightclub talking to a girl with a shaved head.

The advantage to writing this slack is that the writer can't hang himself with any length of it.

What's happening? "Me" is doing the talking. This is how it goes: "I" asks "me," "What am I doing now?" and "me" answers, "You are seeing a pink in the linoleum you've never seen before, since the linoleum has never come this clean beneath your repeated mop." I need never leave home. I am in heaven, in holy narcissism, in my present tense. I try again: "How about Colette?" "Hey, you've got to be—aren't you?—kidding." And the writing students hand me a list of a hundred authors each named Ann (or Anne) (or Mary Ann or Barbara Anne or Annie Ann). (Mann's name has an Ann in it, I want to answer.) My enthusiasm wanes—for Musil, for Proust, for Literature. Number 42 of the *Mississippi Review* has been edited by David Leavitt. Called "These Young People Today," it has some stuff in the present tense, of course. After all, it's today. So I read the collection as part of my researches. Reading it is like walking through a cemetery before they've put in any graves.

Some say the movies are to blame, if blame there be. But movies are at best a once-a-week thing, and we all went when we were kids, and ate licorice gummies from a sack and shouted early warnings at Errol Flynn; but when we went to write, we did as the painters did when photos first complexed the scene: we carefully avoided imitating them. (I go too far: there are significant exceptions, John Dos Passos among them, but the students will not have read him; they will read Doctorow instead.) Writers were released from popularity (in a commercial culture, no small thing); they were freed from the tyranny of story and all the trappings of the tale, if they chose to throw them off. Movies may melt the mind down, and they certainly lured many a talent onto the scotchy rocks with their money; however, there was no particular fondness for the present tense until television (and now the VCR) upped our exposure to pictures from two hours a week to six or ten a day, and magazines lay down in a litter of images as though their pages had been blown about in the street.

This fondness for the present tense . . . well, what could be expected from the teenybop scream-jean population: that's what is usually said. Aren't they all—the young—into drugs and thugs, into strobes and films (as that sexist preposition puts it)? Aren't they into video and vibes and cars that go varoom, as well as words like "varoom" from their favorite cartoon balloons? And aren't they into skimpy swimmies and other visuals? And don't they wear brand names on their tops, bottoms, and bumpers, as if they had themselves been manufactured or, like a billboard, rented out? They are definitely not into vocabulary or the pleasures of verbalization; they only like ideas after they have been drawn, and one of their ideas, the idea of history, is exclusively concerned with the passing of fads and crazes, and the instantaneous illumination or extinction of stars.

We should wonder, rather, at the return of the tough guy in this minimalist guise, the guy of few words, of laconic eyes and ears, with a heart of candy, although it is a sweet by this time both stale and hard, cynical in a sentimental sense, weary from the word "go" and half gone, who doesn't defile his feelings with ideas or talk them to destruction. His silences, therefore, are strong. His enemies are no longer red Indians or fierce bulls, nor does he go to war in exotic landscapes. Now his enemies are simply daily life and women. At the same time that we note his triumphant return (as part of a widespread political phenomenon), we should count the number of women, more foul-mouthed and macho than Mailer, who, though sweetly released like pigeons from their cages, have decided to fly like eagles and feed on mice.

The same current that carries Clark Gable and Gary Cooper past Sam Spade and Black Mask dick flicks into our own gun-cocked, blood-spill movies continues through minimalism into cyberpunk and other fashionable celebrations of street life, trash talk, and pop mechanics, until it puddles now in the technofuck film.

The style of these terse, present-tense tales, then, is soft tough. They are stories shorn, not only of adjectives and adverbs, but of words themselves, almost as if their authors didn't know any. Some warriors arm themselves for battle, but these warriors, like wrestlers, strip. They write in strips, too. Sentences are invariably short, declarative, and as factual as a string of fish. Images are out. It is fraudulent to poeticize. I cannot compare myself to my fridge as I mop. Kept simple, quick, direct, like a punch, the sentences avoid subordination, qualification, subtlety. Subordination requires judgment, evaluation; it creates complexity, demands definition. Henry James and William Faulkner had the temerity to put long sentences in their short stories, and these now-old masters thought carefully about the relation of technique to reality, about relative weights of meaning and shifts of points of view, accreditation and authority, pacing and scene shaping, among many other issues, so that even if one seemed to toss one's words into a wordless void, as Samuel Beckett does, those words as they fell would form constellations, and the mind they had been thrown from would have considered them with the same close concern it would give, say, to suicide.

It is obviously much easier to teach the composition of short fiction than that of the novel, so students customarily bring episodes to class—vignettes, shorties, bits written over a weekend or a week. These "stories" are criticized by the teacher, of course, who is often gentle with the psyches of the students, and always looking for a way to say, pleasantly, unpleasant things. The writer's colleagues are under no such compunctions, however. They can be cruel, viciously competitive, clever, and strategic. They can play favorites, form cliques, sandbag like seasoned poker players, use praise to seduce. In short, the students write largely in fear of the disfavor of their peers.

The students do not imitate the faculty; teachers cannot be accused of turning out copies of themselves. The students, instead, write like one another. The teacher is nothing but a future recommendation. Nor do the instructors push their students much. No one is required to do exercises on the practice fields of fiction. No one is asked to write against the little grain they've got. Relations grow personal before they grow professional. And the community perceives each poet as a poet, each writer as a writer, making them members in this social sense, although they may not have written a worthy word. Here they hide from academic requirements and from intellectual challenge. There are always shining exceptions, of course, but on the whole the students show little interest in literature. They are interested in writing instead . . . in expressing a self as shallow as a saucer.

To whom and to what do they look? Not many classes ahead of them was Annie Ann Anderson and Barry Gaylord Linger (about whom there still circulates scads of Workshop gossip), and just see where they are now—with stories appearing in the *New Celeb Yorker*, with a collection out from a prestigious commercial press, with interviews, readings, nibbles from the films, professionally snapped publicity photos featuring glamorous hairdos, a hard-as-nails agent, and a fresh fiction-rich divorce. Because few of the young people I met on my travels had the romantic aspirations my generation had, I decided that they lacked ambition. I was wrong. They have plenty of ambition, but it is of a thoroughly worldly and commonsense kind: they want to make it . . . the way Annie and Barry did . . . they want to be hot, imitated, sought.

The principal perils of the present tense are its limited scope and its absence of mind. It looks; it watches; it sees; it mops. There is one act or felt object, then another. The present tense cannot cope with the present day. As far as the contemporary world is concerned, the present is so full of pus you cannot see the wound.

The present tense with its problems will probably pass. Writing programs, however, are very American and very successful, and will doubtless remain. It has been in every program's interest to feed its students into the commercial world of publishing somewhat as collegiate athletic programs feed their players to the pros. The present success of the short story, like the present success of the present tense, is not merely the consequence of a conservative atmosphere in our country (although it may substantially account for the absence of youthful idealism and general social concerns in this work); it is, in my opinion, the reflection of an established and dominant institution, with its connections, personality, and structure. Times—the cliché has promised—change; scribblers come and go; fads, like that for the present tense, fade; authors, critics, consumers, all eagerly await the next wave; but in the Detroits of our culture, the manufacture of writers continues.

And a general malaise may remain, because where can the young reasonably dream of making a difference? They can recycle beer cans and paper; they can try to save the ozone layer and the rain forests; they can campaign against drunk drivers. Young men can hunt, fish, and sit in bars. Young women can learn how to kick balls and cast votes. But the world is out of all control, not merely theirs. And literature in the grand sense has ceased to matter. What is left is the immediate world around them, its ordinary worries, its ups and downs, the some fun and much sorrow of student domesticity. The past is merely inertia, the future is dismal though unknown, and what is is mostly an image, a flicker, a formula for the eye. Hype is hollow, but so are all the trees.

Weary of the present tense as I am, I shall probably look back at it with longing when the fad for the future arrives (as it periodically threatens to do). After all, Pauline's perils were expressed in gloomy expectations. So as I wait to be run over or cut in half, I wonder what tense I shall be tied to next—where I can hear the buzz of the saw? the "just past" that leaves a slam in the ear like an angry lover? or the canoe approaching the falls?

Weary as I am of the present tense, I have grown quite fond of mopping. I mop. A previously hidden pink appears. At which I marvel. I wring the mop's strings and squeeze water in the sink. If I am large, white, as cold as the fridge, why don't I just let it continue to thaw like an early spring? The puddle grows. My mop makes wide swipes. Back and forth. Up and down. Husband is— has turned—my program off. Cecile's voice went snick in the middle of a groan. Now there are only my sounds, the sounds of swiping, squeezing, draining. So no more cold war. Lukewarm war at last. I splat my mop—splat!—and watch the water spatter. That is/ was fun. I am/was happy.

FINDING
A FORM

The writer, by choosing to write rather than ride Beckett's bike or Don Quixote's nag, is choosing to relate to the world through words. This is as true of a historian or philosopher as it is of a poet. In my case, at least, the choice was an illusory one, for early on in my life I felt overwhelmed by the world (which, for anyone young, is not likely to have borders far beyond the family). It was a world which was certainly no worse than average, not much better either, so it was not one inherently overwhelming, one which would do the strongest of characters in. No. It found in me a weak respondent, a poor player. I was the sort of actor who specialized in exits.

I had a lot of models to follow: first, a father who railed at the world while he listened to it on the radio; who blamed the wops for his discomfort, the bohunks, the spicks, the kikes, the niggers he had to try to teach in the industrial high school where he was a warden more than tutor; a person who took no risks, resisted advancement, remained satisfied to be safely a nobody, who nevertheless would mutter under his breath about it; and then a mother who invested all her savings in bad stock—me—a woman of useless sensitivity and fruitless talent whom my father cowed and bullied, although he offered her (as he offered me) only verbal abuse; still, it was abuse that never tired him, that could be continuous, proving to me what words can do, how words can empower the powerless. As a consequence of these repeated though bruiseless blows, and the fact that for women then there was nothing to do but keep house and suffer hubby and raise kids, so that when I—an only child—grew up, and inevitably drew away as well, she was left marooned in her kitchen and breakfast nook, where bottles of gin washed ashore as though a whole fleet full of spirits had foundered; and she took those bottles in as though they were meant for her womb—children to replace a kid—and that's how she bore her death to its term, for she was drunk more than a dozen years before the blood vessels in her throat burst and she drowned by drinking her own blood.

I had a maiden aunt, too, who had brought Grandma to visit, moving this elderly woman about from relative to relative so each would have an equal share of the burden, and who stayed on after her charge died, discreetly, gradually, stubbornly, secretively, surely, taking over the management of the house, the helpless world of women, from my mother.

Passivity, self-mortification, substitute gratification, impotent bitching, drink: these were the ways of life set before me. Now, when considering the insides of a writer, pondering the psychology of the occupation, I always look first for the weakness which led him to it; because, make no mistake, writing puts the writer in illusory command of the world, empowers someone otherwise powerless, but with a power no more pointed than a pencil.

So in my own situation, where I was taught to deflect my desires from their real object onto another, safer, simpler one; where, when confronted with a problem, like a good Stoic, I strove to alter myself rather than the world, since my self seemed more in my power, and because my aim was usually to relinquish instead of conquer. During this character-creating time, I found I had one facility: I had, on my side, a little language. We do what we can do, and I could do that. Reading and writing aren't arithmetic. I read to escape my condition, I wrote to remedy it—both perilous passivities—and there is scarcely a significant character in my work who is not a failure in the practice of ordinary existence, who does not lead a deflected life. Often, though not always, they live inside a language, and try to protect themselves from every danger with a phrase.

All the world may be a stage, for those who can act in it; and it may, instead, be a game, for those who have the skill and can play; it may be reduced to a square of canvas, redone as a screen full of images; it may be replaced by the sheer shimmer of beautifully related sounds. But for me the world became a page; that, I said, with Stoical acceptance, is the way I wanted it; it is what I would have chosen. It is natural to speak of your own weaknesses so winsomely they will seem strengths, as if everyone else is inadequate if they do not have your inadequacies. We also contemplate what we cannot control. I contemplate the world through words.

The window, in this way, became a central symbol in my work, assuming more and more importance as that work went on. If it were literally true that I saw the world through a window, I would merely be the street spy, peering out on the alley to see what I could see, and making sure nothing went by without my notice, nothing went on without my approval. But when a character of mine looks out through a window, or occasionally peeks in through one, it is the word "window" he is really looking through; it's the word "pane" that preoccupies; it's the idea of "glass," of separated seeing, of the distortions of the medium, its breakage, its discoloration, its framing, that dominates and determines the eye; it is, therefore, the fragility of knowledge that gets stressed, the importance and limitation of point of view, the ambiguity of "in" and "out" that it provides, the range of its examples; the fact that windows are display cases, places where wash is dried, pies are cooled, caged lovebirds hang, where potted plants sit, souvenirs rest from ancient trips, and where light enters only to become a pale patch of warmth for the cat; but above all, the window is a place which waits for that light, endures the darkness, receives each scene; and then, through both the word and its phenomena, provokes reflection; indeed it demonstrates how "pane" permits me to say I am separated from the world by a transparent sheet of cruelty, as though its plane were a piece of paper, as though each word were itself a window through which I could see other words, other windows, as well as myself: always observant, always passive, patient, speculative, so when one at last undertakes an action, as my narrator does in my novel *The Tunnel*, he throws a brick, as others did on *Kristallnacht*, but through a Nordic shopwindow by mistake. He's guilty all the same, of course, but now, by implication, he is guilty of the lesser (though larger) crime of hating the whole of mankind.

Consider the difference between an ordinary fact of experience —a woman's face reflected in what remains of a broken window— and the resonance of the simplest sentence when we listen to the vibration of the words: "Virginia's face was reflected in the broken pane."

It is during these early days of life, too, that the many motives one might have for doing anything are combined and given their priorities. The successful execution of any long and difficult project, especially one done alone and without the support of any social structure, requires the cooperation of every significant desire one has—the theft of their energy, if you like—in order that more determination can be found for the task than its own allure might generate.

Freud's oft-quoted wisecrack, that men write for money, glory, and the love of women, might bestir a banker to his business but will not suffice to account for the composing of poetry and the writing of fiction—fundamentally unfunded, unwanted, and unappreciated enterprises. Of course, writers want glory; they want money; they want to be loved, to be sexually pleased and politically empowered. They also want to play the sage, the moralist, the philosopher, and tell the world where to go. They dream of crowds rushing off at the insistence of their voice to pull down the statues of their rivals. Oh, yes, indeed, they desire to impose their will. But it is a mistake to suppose that the speaking of this or that truth, the display of this or that moral stance, the advocacy of this or that point of view, is, or even ought to be, the principal aim of the artist. That is not to say these values and opinions will be absent. Who can set aside their beliefs, their angers, their greatest fears, as if unfeared at all? Who can fail to praise whatever has given them the most satisfaction, the deepest love: why walk on one's hands when one needs to run?

What is critical to the artist is not the fact that he has many motives (let us hope so), or that their presence should never be felt in his canvases, or found in the narrative nature of his novels, or heard amid the tumult of his dissonances. In the first place, our other aims won't lend their assistance without reward, and they will want, as we say, a piece of the action. No; the question is which of our intentions will be allowed to rule and regulate and direct the others: that is what is critical. It is a matter of the politics of desire, or, as Plato put it when he asked this question of the moral agent: what faculty of the soul is in control of the will?

I believe that the artist's fundamental loyalty must be to form, and his energy employed in the activity of making. Every other diddly desire can find expression; every crackpot idea or local obsession, every bias and graciousness and mark of malice, may have an hour; but it must never be allowed to carry the day. If, of course, one wants to be a publicist for something; if you believe you are a philosopher first and Nietzsche second; if you think the gift of prophecy has been given you; then, by all means, write your bad poems, your insufferable fictions, enjoy the fame that easy ideas often offer, ride the flatulent winds of change, fly like the latest fad to the nearest dead tree; but do not try to count the seasons of your oblivion.

The poet, every artist, is a maker, a maker whose aim is to make something supremely worthwhile, to make something inherently valuable in itself. I am happy this is an old-fashioned view. I am happy it is Greek. One decent ideal can turn a rabble of small-minded and narrowly self-interested needs into an army. I cannot help adding that, in my opinion, one of the most petty of human desires is the desire to be believed, on the one hand, and the will to belief, on the other. Disbelief is healthier, is a better exercise for the mind, and I admire it even when I see someone's disbelief busy disbelieving me.

To see the world through words means more than merely grasping it through gossipacious talk or amiable description. Language, unlike any other medium, I think, is the very instrument and organ of the mind. It is not the representation of thought, as Plato believed, and hence only an inadequate copy; but it is thought itself. Certainly we can picture things to ourselves, but we picture them in order to consider their features, to analyze them, judge their qualities. Even the painter talks to himself as he plans his vacation, he does not draw to himself; the lover speaks of his desire, he does not draw his penis on the bedsheets; even the musician says things to the grocer, he does not hum. The rationalist philosophers were not right when they supposed that the structure of language mirrored the structure of reality (language and reality bear little resemblance and come from different families); but they were right when they identified it with thinking itself. Words may refer to the world (though any finger can point to Paris), but words are also what we think with when we point our finger at Paris and say, "Paris." Literature is mostly made of mind; and unless that is understood about it, little is understood about it.

A sentence, any sentence, is consequently a passage of thought. Dare I give you, as an example, one of mine? A housewife has begun to discover, when she comes downstairs in the morning, the bodies of cockroaches on her carpet—bugs which have probably been killed by her cat.

> Never alive, they came with punctures, their bodies formed from little whorls of copperish dust which in the downstairs darkness I couldn't possibly have seen; and they were dead and upside down when they materialized, for it was in that moment that our cat, herself darkly invisible, leaped and brought her paws together on the true soul of the roach; a soul so static and intense, so immortally arranged, I felt, while I lay shell-like in our bed, turned inside out, driving my mind away, it was the same as the dark soul of the world itself—and it was this beautiful and terrifying feeling that took possession of me finally, stiffened me like a rod beside my husband, played Caesar to my dreams.

There is, in the first place, the movement of the character's mind, which thinks of the roaches as, in a sense, born with the punctures which killed them, inasmuch as she never sees them any other way. Nearby the bodies are little patches of body dust, probably from the punctures themselves, and she thinks, next, of their creation in traditional Christian terms. Her mind returns to the fact that they must have been dead and upside down when born. Next the cat is given a role in their conception. She puts the punctures in. Body becomes soul, because the bony structure of the roach is on the outside, it is the true interior, in a sense immortal because it is bone; it will not decay. Furthermore, its composition is formally beautiful.

These thoughts are part factual, part conjectural, part playful. Their playful nature disappears when the point of the piece comes in view. The housewife thinks of herself as, like them, lying in darkness and, like them, turned inside out, her bones becoming her being. The Pythagorean (later neo-Platonic) phrase "dark soul of the world" completes her odd epiphany. Beneath the traditional Pythagorean triangle of light, given over to the tyranny of the One, the Straight, the Male, is the dark triangle of the Crooked, the Many, and the Female. But now that triangle has been tipped over. Its elements are in plain view. Free. As most wives and mothers, lying beside their sleeping husbands, punctured themselves, are not. When she overcomes her fear of roaches and begins to appreciate the beauty of the bug; when she sees beneath the socially correct arrangement of things its hidden inner order (for which, we have to remember, she has no small responsibility herself), and can appreciate that interior beauty of which she should be the proper mistress, instead of her kids' health or the household laundry, then she will share the point of view of a god—that is, an artist, and therefore a god whose name is spelled with a very small *g* indeed.

Well, the fiction from which I took this paragraph is a sort of feminist piece. That movement of the housewife's mind, however, which the passage at least elliptically presents, is not the same as the movement of the words themselves, and hence is not identical, either, to the passage of the reader's eye and understanding, which begins with "Never," proceeds to "alive," unifies these, continues immediately to "they" ("they were never alive"), and subsequently attributes this absence of life to every previous appearance of the bugs, whether actual or symbolic. After all, roaches wear their skeletons like children at Halloween. Soon the reader's attention is spirited away to theology, and to philosophy as well if he's alert to the reference, but only to select what seems needful from these realms before returning from creation's little whorls of copperish dust to modify these few phrases once again (never alive, forever dust). In short, reading (any reading) is recursive and usually parabolic. While the eye and its attention are shuttling back and forth, the order of the language never entirely disappears but continuously reforms the final amalgamation.

So far, the statically presented structure of the sentence has put two other minds in motion: that of the character whose thoughts are being described, and that of a hypothetical Reader. The former is an active, fictive movement of thought, the latter a devoted process of attention. An additional mind of which the sentence must make us aware is that of the capitalized Author, the constructor, for it is certainly worth realizing that although the character feels, in that sentence, insightful, there is no reason to suppose she feels lyrical. She may feel frightened, moved, unsettled; but the author's mind is in a poetic mode, calm, measured, allusive. The author never thought these phrases in their printed order. The author never thought the sentence the way one might think: What time's lunch? The author did think a great many other things while in the so-called throes of composition. He wrote many more versions, tried numerous combinations, flopped about as awkwardly as a boated fish, said the words to himself time after time in a displeased mumble, but hoped they sang nevertheless; since the sentences he wants to make are like these roaches, firm, immobile, shaped, with their shell the same as their soul—that's what he, the writer, is thinking while he writes—and they are also like a residue the reader will find in the morning; for every sentence allowed to remain upon the page will resemble the dazed survivors of a battle, after the dead and wounded have been carried away, when their alternatives have been rejected and erased, to leave some words still standing on the field, but standing as markers over graves.

Of course, in the case of this particular sentence, written in the first person but in the past tense, the movement of the narrator's mind is itself multiple. There is what she thought at the time—that is suggested—and there is how she has chosen to think about it later, how she now describes it (which might be as lyrically as the author does, but also might not).

In any event, and after many years of scribble and erasure, I came finally to the belief that sentences were containers of consciousness, that they were directly thought itself, which is one thing that goes on in consciousness, but they were other things as well, in more devious, indirect ways. Insofar as the words referred, they involved—through those designations—our perceptions; thus a good sentence had to see and hear and smell and touch or taste whatever it was supposed to see and hear and smell and touch or taste; that acuity and accuracy of sensation was, in those sentences that invoked it, essential. Even in sentences that describe a thought instead of a perception, the thought has to be well seen.

The narrator is writing about the legs of the roach. Both kinds, she says,

> had legs that looked under a glass like the canes of a rose, and the nymph's were sufficiently transparent in a good light you thought you saw its nerves merge and run like a jagged crack to each ultimate claw.

The writer has to be sufficiently accurate about the world, he preserves his authority, but what is crucial is not testability; it is, rather, the precision and clarity of the construction, because what the writer is doing is creating a perception his character is supposed to have, and since the story is about "eye-openers," then the sentence had better seem open-eyed.

In reading what the character sees, the reader sees; but what the reader sees, of course, is not the thing but a construction. Since we know that we are witnessing a perception, we are, in effect, seeing an act of seeing, not merely an object, which might be seen in a number of ways, because in the text there are no more ways than are written. There is no more object than the object which is made by its description. John Hawkes is the American master of the sentence that sees. When his prose perceives a horse, that horse becomes visual as though for the first time. But what makes Hawkes's horse so magical is not merely the way it is made of precise visual detail—any vet might equal that—but the sense of responsiveness and appreciation, relish, worship, in the eye's sight.

The sentence is a literal line of thought, then, but also an apprehension, sometimes of a thought, often of some sensation. It is also aimed. It has energy, drive, direction, purpose. Now we are dealing, in our artificial consciousness, with the element of desire. Some sentences seem to seep, others to be propelled by their own metrical feet. Some sentences are ponderous, tentative, timid; others are quick, burly, full of beans. Consciousness is equally flaccid or energized; or, in more complex cases, some aspects are nearly asleep, others wholly on the *qui vive*. The short declarative fragment, brisk and direct as it is, can also, with its calm assurance and its confident closure, reduce the sense of urgency in the sentence, even introduce a feeling of unsleepy repleteness. For instance, in this brief list of the properties of a place:

> The shade is ample, the grass is good, the sky a glorious fall violet; the apple trees are heavy and red, the roads are calm and empty; corn has sifted from the chains of tractored wagons to speckle the streets with gold and with russet fragments of the cob, and a man would be a fool who wanted, blessed with this, to live anywhere else in the world.

Desire, thought, perception . . . next, passion: each inhabits the sentence it is made from. Feeling infuses the thought, is pleased or confounded by what is heard or touched or seen, is made despondent by what it expects, or eagerly awaits the fulfillment of its needs. Repetition, diction, the way the language is caressed, spat out, or whispered by the writer—every element, as always—combines to create for the sentence its feeling. I think of it as a kind of conceptual climate. Gertrude Stein believed that emotions were the property of paragraphs, not sentences by themselves, though a sentence might often act as uppity as a paragraph. Here is another sample of my own method of mood management.

For we're always out of luck here. That's just how it is—for instance in the winter. The sides of the buildings, the roofs, the limbs of the trees are gray. Streets, sidewalks, faces, feelings—they are gray. Speech is gray, and the grass where it shows. Every flank and front, each top is gray. Everything is gray: hair, eyes, window glass, the hawkers' bills and touters' posters, lips, teeth, poles and metal signs—they're gray, quite gray. Cars are gray. Boots, shoes, suits, hats, gloves are gray. Horses, sheep, and cows, cats killed in the road, squirrels in the same way, sparrows, doves, and pigeons, all are gray, everything is gray, and everyone is out of luck who lives here.

Above all, I believe, consciousness is the residence and nurturing place of the imagination. Without impudent comparisons, without freewheeling fancy, without dreams, without invention, without the transformations of metaphor, the burglaries of meaning that symbols commit: without such aeration, prose deflates, our tires turn on air; flat, they will only leave their rubber on the highway; but, in addition, the other elements of the good sentence— desire, feeling, sensation, thought—require the imagination for their construction. Let us go back a moment to the bugs, whose armatures are their armor, for a comparison of their state with our own.

I suspect if we were as familiar with our bones as with our skin, we'd never bury dead but shrine them in their rooms, arranged as we might like to find them on a visit; and our enemies, if we could steal their bodies from the battle sites, would be museumed as they died, the steel still eloquent in their sides, their metal hats askew, the protective toes of their shoes unworn, and friend and enemy would be so wondrously historical that in a hundred years we'd find the jaws still hung for the same speech and all the parts we spent our life with tilted as they always were—rib cage, collar, skull—still repetitious, still defiant, angel light, still worthy of memorial and affection.

The finest writing is for the voice. There are several good, not to say decisive, reasons for this. No word is a word by itself. Every word is multiple, and not simply because there are homonyms and homophones hanging around, pretending to be friends. A word is made of sounds. A word is made of marks. A word is made of the little muscle movements in the throat which accompany our interior speech—that invisible, inaudible, yet clearly heard interior talk of which Samuel Beckett made himself the master. So there are two spoken tongues to set against the one we write. And if we allow the written word to stand for the spoken one, and silent speech to precede both, then the written word works in three realms at once, not just one.

The mouth is our sustainer: with it our body is fed and our soul made articulate. Orality as a developmental stage is as early as any, near to our deepest and often most desperate feelings. The spoken language is learned at the point, and in the manner, in which we learned to live; when we heard love, anger, anxiety, expectation, in the tones of the parental voice, and later began to find the words we had heard forming in our own mouths as if the ear had borne their seed. Moreover, we still communicate at the daily and most personal level by speaking, not by writing, to one another. If the telephone suggests physical closeness at the price of spiritual distance, E-mail promotes that impersonal intimacy sometimes experienced by strangers. Writing has even lost the kinetic character the hand once gave it, or the portable conveyed through its worn and pounded keys. Prefab letters pop onto a screen in full anonymity now, as if the mind alone had made them, our fingers dancing along over the keyboard as unnoticed as breathing until something breaks or the error beep sounds. As Plato feared, the written word can be stolen, counterfeited, bought, released from the responsibility of its writer, sailed into the world as unsigned as a ship unnamed or under borrowed registry. Suppose politicians were required to compose their own lies, use their own poor words, instead of having their opinions catered—how brief would be their hold on our beliefs; how soon would their souls be seen to be as soiled as their socks.

The sentence—its shape, its sound, the space it makes, its importance to consciousness, its manifestation of the mind/body problem (meaning and thing fastened to the same inscription)—is it in my obsession with the ontology of the word that I find the ground for my own practice? Is that why I emphasize the music of the language, alliterate with the passionate persistence of old poems, wallow in assonance, clutter the otherwise open space of concepts with the clatter and click of dentals and other consonants? Are these the reasons I want the reader's mouth to move as if reading were being in that moment mastered, and the breath were full of chewable food? No. The reason is that I cannot seem to write in any other way; because sound sometimes rushes ahead of sense, and forces such sense, gasping and panting, to catch up. I often think, overhearing myself at work, that I do not write; I mumble, I whisper, I declaim, I inveigh. My study is full of static when it is full of me.

Harmonium, Wallace Stevens called one of his books. *Harmonica*, I'd like to call mine—rude mouth music. That's because every mark on the page, apart from its inherent visual interest, is playing its part in the construction of a verbal consciousness, and that means commas must become concepts, pauses need to be performed, even the margins have to be sung, the lips rounded as widely as the widest vowel, round as the edges of the world. Oh as in "oral."

For that's where every good idea should be found, melting like a chocolate in the curl of the tongue, against the roof of the mouth.

If we insist that we write to be spoken (though no one shall speak us; neither time nor training nor custom incline our rare reader to it), then a concept crucial to the understanding of literature and its effects is "voice." Even when we write in the first person and construct a voice for our invented narrator to speak in, there is always an overvoice in which our character finds a place: the author's voice, the style which tells us, whoever is speaking—Lear or Hamlet or Juliet—that it is Shakespeare nevertheless, in whose verbal stream they are swimming; or we hear the unmistakable tones of Henry James, of Flaubert or Faulkner, in each rednecked, red-earthed farmer, in every bumbling bourgeois or bewildered American lady.

Who better to speak than Thoreau of the sound around one, for he chose the quietest of woods to inhabit.

I kept neither dog, cat, cow, pig, nor hens, so that you would have said there was a deficiency of domestic sounds; neither the churn, nor the spinning-wheel, nor even the singing of the kettle, nor the hissing of the urn, nor children crying, to comfort one. An old-fashioned man would have lost his senses or died of ennui before this. Not even rats in the wall, for they were starved out, or rather were never baited in,—only squirrels on the roof and under the floor, a whip-poor-will on the ridge-pole, a blue jay screaming beneath the window, a hare or woodchuck under the house, a screech owl or a cat owl behind it, a flock of wild geese or a laughing loon on the pond, and a fox to bark in the night. Not even a lark or an oriole, those mild plantation birds, ever visited my clearing. No cockerels to crow nor hens to cackle in the yard. No yard! but unfenced nature reaching up to your very sills. A young forest growing up under your windows, and wild sumachs and blackberry vines breaking through into your cellar; sturdy pitch pines rubbing and creaking against the shingles for want of room, their roots reaching quite under the house. Instead of a scuttle or a blind blown off in the gale,—a pine tree snapped off or torn up by the roots behind your house for fuel. Instead of no path to the front-yard gate in the Great Snow,—no gate—no front-yard,—and no path to the civilized world.

Even so, even when we hear the unmistakable voice of our friend in the next room, find the cadences of Colette on the page (as, once again, Plato warned us), we cannot be certain what part of the soul is speaking (the spoken language, like the soul, is triply tiered); because when desire, or *praxis*, says "love," it is *eros* that is invoked; when the spirited part of the soul, or *doxa*, says "love," it is *philia*, or friendship, which is suggested; and when reason, the *logos*, says "love," it is *agape* or contemplation which is meant.

Of course, every philosophical catastrophe is a literary opportunity. Gertrude Stein finally concluded that the "I" who writes masterpieces had to be the "I" of the transcendental ego, the universal "I," making the text timeless and transcultural. But I am greedy. I like best the "I" that speaks for every layer of the self, sometimes harmoniously, sometimes in discord, as the occasion and the project require. I like ideas best, as I've said, when they are most concrete; when, when you think them, you fry them like eggs; when, when you eat them, the yoke is runny with the softest of dreams.

If words find comfort in the sentence's syntactical handclasp, and sentences find their proper place like pieces of furniture in the rhetorical space of the paragraph, what shall control each scene as it develops, form the fiction finally as a whole?

Well, the old answer was always: plot. It's a terrible word in English, unless one is thinking of some second-rate conspiracy, a meaning it serves very well. Otherwise, it stands for an error for which there's no longer an excuse. There's bird drop, horse plop, and novel plot. Story is what can be taken out of the fiction and made into a movie. Story is what you tell people when they embarrass you by asking what your novel is about. Story is what you do to clean up life and make God into a good burgher who manages the world like a business. History is often written as a story so that it can seem to have a purpose, to be on its way somewhere; because stories deny that life is no more than an endlessly muddled middle; they beg each length of it to have a beginning and end like a ballgame or a banquet. Stories are sneaky justifications. You can buy stories at the store, where they are a dime a dozen. Stories are interesting only when they are floors in buildings. Stories are a bore. What one wants to do with stories is screw them up. Stories ought to be in pictures. They're wonderful to see.

Still, a little story gets into everything. Thank the Ghost of Fictions Past for that.

My stories are malevolently anti-narrative, and my essays are maliciously anti-expository, but the ideology of my opposition arrived long after my antagonism had become a trait of character. Like most kids, I loved the nineteenth-century novel with its wealth of colorful detail, its heroes and villains, its sympathy for the common and the ordinary, its smarmy coziness, its clear-cut characters, its unambiguous values (I was born bourgeois); I lapped up its sweet sentimentality; I allowed to beat in my chest its vulgar material heart. Implicit in much of the novel's melodrama, and explicit in the critics and readers who praised it and made it popular, was the idea that its value rested not on its language, its artifice, its drama, but on its representation of reality. I have no problem with Martin Chuzzlewit as a creature caught in a myth. I can believe in the triumph of the orphan and the importance of "doing good," at least for as many pages as it takes to complete the text.

Early on I learned that life was meaningless, since life was not a sign; that novels were meaningful, because signs were the very materials of their composition. I learned that suffering served no purpose; that the good guys didn't win; that most explanations offered me to make the mess I was in less a mess were self-serving lies. Life wasn't clear, it was ambiguous; motives were many and mixed; values were complex, opposed, poisoned by hypocrisy, without any reasonable ground; most of passion's pageants were frauds, and human feelings had been faked for so long, no one knew what the genuine was; furthermore, many of the things I found most satisfactory were everywhere libelously characterized or their very existence was suppressed; and much of adult society, its institutions and its advertised dreams, were simply superstitions that served a small set of people well while keeping the remainder in miserable ignorance.

Above all, I was struck by the traditional novel's vanity on behalf of man. When I looked at man, l did not see a piece of noble work, a species whose every member was automatically of infinite worth and the pinnacle of Nature's efforts. Nor did history, as I read it, support such grandiose claims. Throughout human time, men had been murdering men with an ease that suggested they took a profound pleasure in it, and like the most voracious insect, the entire tribe was, even as I watched, even as I participated, eating its host like a parasite whose foresight did not exceed its greed. Hate, fear, and hunger were the tribal heroes. In Trollope and Thackeray, as skillful as their satire was, flaws became foibles, wickedness the result of poor upbringing, too much port, and a bad digestion. Flaubert saw how things were and told the truth, as if that mattered.

So I, like many others in every art, rejected a realism that wasn't real and tried to work in a less traditional, less compromised way. I organized my fictions around symbolic centers instead of plotting them out on graph paper; I assigned the exfoliation of these centers to a voice and limited my use of narration, while treating the style and characteristic structure of the sentences that filled the novel, row on row, as microcosmic models for the organization of the whole. I do not pretend to be in the possession of any secrets; I have no cause I espouse; I do not presume to reform my readers, or attempt to flatter their egos either. My loyalty is to my text, for that is what I am composing, and if I change the world, it will be because I've added this or that little reality to it; and if I alter any reader's consciousness, it will be because I have constructed a consciousness of which others may wish to become aware, or even, for a short time, share. The reader's freedom is a holy thing.

My views are what is popularly pictured as "off the wall," but it has seemed to me for a long time that fiction's principal problem, apart from its allegiance to the middle class, was not to be solved by finding a fascinating or outré subject, by maintaining a narrative suspense that was meaningless if you hoped to be reread, or by being blessed for your possession of the right beliefs; the problem was how to achieve any lasting excellence (in philosophy, mathematics, art, and science, always the same)—that is, it was a problem of form. Writers had once looked everywhere to find the necessary regulating schemes. The novel began by imitating nonfictional genres: histories, biographies, collections of letters, diaries, accounts of travel, records of adventure. Later, novelists looked to other arts for suggestions: they pretended to paint portraits of young men and ladies; they composed pastoral symphonies and other metaphorical musicales; or they used their prose to steal from poetry many of its epical methods and effects, and grandly said (as I once muttered) that the strategies of fiction were the same as the strategies of the long poem.

In every case, wonderful stories, great novels, were written, although against the grain, in forms not fashioned for fiction in the first place, with techniques not meant for the novel, but with methods its middle-class audience saw as comfortingly familiar, factual, realistic, acceptably hypocritical. All the while, like the purloined letter, a possible solution to the problem lay in full view, and had likely been in operation all along: first, the solution was apparent in the actual operations of the prose sentence itself; second, it was readily available in scholarly texts, through the nearly forgotten techniques of rhetoric and oratory, contained in those quaintly out-of-date but meticulously catalogued lists of tropes, schemes, arguments, illustrations, and outlines, in those countless unconsulted volumes on eloquence and public address from Aristotle, Longinus, Cicero, and Quintilian through Priestley, Adam Smith, and De Quincey to Emerson, Hugh Blair, and Edward Channing; and third, in the efforts of linguists and logicians to discover the secrets of syntax and to explain its regulating power.

George Saintsbury's admirable *History of English Prose Rhythm* told me more about the art of writing than a hundred literary critics, each eager to light like a fly on the latest fad, and soon, predictably, to be abuzz with the energy so secondarily received.

That is, if we understand how prose is put together, not only logically or grammatically, but rhetorically and esthetically as well, then we might understand how an entire tale could be uniformly wagged, or how a whole novel could be unified. Moreover, philosophers have frequently ascribed metaphysical significance to propositional forms, and considered them to be the structural essentials of any conceived world.

This is not the place to dwell upon the course of development of my idiosyncrasies, but it is perhaps appropriate for me to conclude these remarks by looking at some of the reasons why such interests are so rarely shared. There are four dimensions to the writer's realm, and few occupy all axes equally. If a Realist were lucky enough to begin a piece: "When Gregor Samsa awoke one morning from an uneasy sleep, he found himself transformed into a gigantic insect," he would be distressed indeed if we disbelieved him, and thought he was deconstructing *The Faerie Queene.* He would be calculating, as he wrote the line, the matter-of-fact effect such an event would have on the other characters Gregor Samsa would be plotted to encounter, on the consciousness of Gregor himself, and even on the mattress and the springs of the bed. The Idealist would immediately wonder what the event meant, and would be concerned to render it in such a way that it would resonate as the writer wished. The night before, as Gregor's head hit his pillow, he was merely being treated like a bug, living and acting and feeling like one (as the Idealist might interpret his behavior), but now, this a.m., he was a bug, and the Realist had taken over.

Nothing prevents Kafka from being both, as he undoubtedly is. *Moby-Dick* presents us with a similar tension. Every paragraph of data about the whale—its hunting, its capture, its cutting up— insists on the solidity and importance of daily life, its traumas and its tasks. A whale is a whale, here, white or not, and a big bug in a bed is a bother, especially if it's your brother. What'll you feed him?

what will friends think? how will the family fare without the funds the brother/bug brought home? The Realist pores over the world like a lover, and learns to render its qualities to a tee. When the Realist's "I" perceives, what matters is what the ego sees. The Idealist will insist that this story is not "about" Gregor Samsa and his family, but about sibling rivalry, for if Gregor is transformed into a bug in the beginning, Grete becomes a butterfly at the end. Let the Realist worry about bedbugs and their bite; the Idealist will study Jewish family relations, and he will see that the name "Samsa" contains "sam," that is, seed, or the cock's roach.

Meanwhile, the Romantic will have understood the sentence to be really about the author's own condition, for isn't he the put-upon person who has to work like a menial when his spirit would be free? Kafka writes about Kafka principally, and only secondarily about Gregor Samsa and his plight; or, if you insist on some theoretical intent, also about the anxieties inherent in the human condition. But of course I have gone too far. *The Metamorphosis* does not reveal Kafka; rather, it delivers to us the consciousness presupposed by its creation. This consciousness is a construction, it must be admitted, and its distance from its swearing, sweating, farting namesake is substantial. This distance—this difference—is also the reason why we often admire an author whom, as a citizen or a biographical subject, we can scarcely endure; or, to point to the problem from its opposite end, why we occasionally wish some dear sweet friend were a better writer, even at the expense of their sweetness, and even if the friendship were to bend.

A fully felt fictional world must be at least three-dimensional, and bounded by the Real, the Ideal, and the Romantic. But there is, as we know, a fourth dimension, and I tend to emphasize it, not only because of its neglect, but also because it is the country to which I have fled, and that safe haven is the medium itself. There, if we are a Methodologist (my term for my type), we shall have found the other dimensions in miniature already, since the word rests nowhere but on the pedestal of its referent (Gregor Samsa, the bedded bug person); there it measures its mass by the number

and nature of its range of meanings (all the definitions of "metamorphosis," for instance: the scientific, the poetic, the philosophical, the religious); nor is any word spoken without a speaker, or
written without a writer (at least it has a human source); consequently every utterance has a cause and, one presumes, a reason
as well, so if we are content to explain the nature of any particular
part of a text by appealing to the rest, we nevertheless have to turn
to the author for the answer: why did you write *The Metamorphosis*
when you could have been engaged in something harmless like a
game of golf?

A Methodologist (for whom the medium is the muse) will re-
formulate traditional esthetic problems in terms of language.
Crudely put: in this milieu point of view has to do with the deploy-
ment of pronouns, character with the establishment of linguistic
centers to which and from which meanings flow; themes are built
with universals, and their enrichment depends upon the significance of a text beyond its surface sense; perceptions will appear to
be fresh and precise if denotation is managed well; energy is expressed by verbal beat, through sentence length and Anglo-Saxon
or Latin vocabulary choice; feeling arises particularly from such
things as rhythm and alliteration, although every element of language plays a role; thought is constructed out of concepts and
their interconnections; imagination involves the management of
metaphor at every level; narrative reliability rises or falls with the
influence of modal operators; form can be found in the logic of the
language—its grammar, scansion, symmetries, rhetorical schema,
and methods of variation; and each of the qualities I have just
listed, along with many others, can be used to give to a text its
desirable complement of four dimensions.

So even if you hope to find some lasting security inside language,
and believe that your powers are at their peak there, if nowhere
else, despair and disappointment will dog you still; for neither you
nor your weaknesses, nor the world and its villains, will have been
banished just because, now, it is in syllables and sentences where
they hide; since, oddly enough, while you can confront and de-

nounce a colleague or a spouse, run from an angry dog, or jump bail and flee your country, you can't argue with an image; in as much as a badly made sentence is a judgment pronounced upon its perpetrator, and even one poor paragraph indelibly stains the soul. The unpleasant consequence of every such botch is that your life, as you register your writing, looks back at you as from a dirty mirror, and there you perceive a record of ineptitude, compromise, and failure.

A FIESTA
FOR THE FORM

When I was a child I was frequently forced to entertain a malicious little boy two years beneath my notice. He was loud, rude, undisciplined, and entirely too intelligent for his parents, whom he ruled with incontinence and screaming. I remember the time when, at dinner, he spat in the mashed potatoes, and how my father sat in silent smiling fury through the whole affair, since it was the little snot's house we were visiting, and it was the little snot's mum who had mashed the spuds he'd spat in, and it was their gold-rimmed dish that continued, untaken, around the table, so that a proper punishment was far outside his jurisdiction. One afternoon, both his parents having to sing in the matinee of something by Gilbert and Sullivan, the Kaiserling (as my father called him) was fobbed off on me. We were playing with trucks and trains in the living room, just at the feet of my father, who was trying to read and at the same time obliterate our presence by opening the evening paper widely across his face, thus disappearing behind its sheets. Suddenly (on what provocation I cannot recall, if there was one) the Kaiserling hurled a cast-iron dump truck through the headlines, piercing them the way a trained tiger leaps through a circle of paper flames, and raising a red welt the precise size of the barrow on my father's brow, before the entire toy fell against the base of a floor lamp with what seemed to me a terrible crash.

My father rose groggily with the Kaiserling's collar in his fist, for he knew without need of knowing who had so directly expressed himself, and his reflexes in those days were still those of the athlete he had been. He swung the brat back and forth by his shirt until, alas, the shirt tore—creating, of course, *evidence*. It was one of those eminently satisfactory incidents that now and then, and always without warning, grace one's life; for I should have dearly loved to have thrown the truck myself; and the breaching of that wall of indifferent dislike was more than appropriate, as was the thwack of the truck on my father's forehead, a thump so long deserved, I thought . . . by fate so long postponed. The comeuppance of the kid, who was no longer sure, as he dangled, of his immunity; the frustration of my father, who could not commit the crime the occasion called for; the quarreling among mothers, fathers, husbands, wives, and friends that was soon to come: all were causes of the deepest pleasure for me like a fizz of fine grape soda through the upper nose.

And I'm reminded now, perhaps in a manner not unlike the elaborate, large, and densely populated metaphors of our latest Spanish-speaking novelists, of the appearance in our provincial northern world of other singular movers of earth, of tough heavy untykelike toys, missiles hurled at the brow of a petty almighty. When I consider the image, rather as if Father Freud had designed it, I see how my own point of view shifts, and how I am in all roles like a raisin; for I have scarcely fed a fresh sheet of paper into my IBM and begun some decorous composition when *The Autumn of the Patriarch* bursts through the page, shattering a delicate tea-fumed sentence like a china cup. This is another kind of news, and I am dazed. Or I am sitting quietly in my study, perhaps, considering a bit of brittle characterization (a photographer's assistant, I think, with hair like the camera's hood), when I see *The Obscene Bird of Night* perched above my chamber door, or when—*caramba*, as we used to exclaim as kids (*Donnerwetter* and *caramba*, we cried before we learned to roll our r's and growl, *merrrrrde*)—so, *caramba*, then, and *Conversation in the Cathedral* crashes through the pane of my plans like a rioter's brick. They come from everywhere, these massive, burning books; new masterpieces hatch like chicks and reach maturity in a matter of weeks. No use to shake the terrible volume till the jacket tears (whichever one it is), not a word will fall out (and I have given *Three Trapped Tigers* a good shaking, I can tell you), although almost daily I receive the galleys of my compatriots from which words, presugared and sufficient for every minimal daily requirement, spill like Cheerios from their cereal box. Perhaps when the books are bound and cleverly promo'd, with testimonials from *The New York Times* on their flaps and backs, the words stay put. I haven't looked.

It wasn't long ago that literature, at least the novel, seemed safely in gringo hands; we could look down along the slope of the world with the arrogance of the higher climber at the silly specks below: those clumsy countries not even the Balkans would have borrowed for their operettas. Let them have their Hemingway as he had their bulls; let them follow Faulkner if they liked. The wiser among us would do neither. Besides, Spanish was the language of etiquette and euphemism, and to follow Faulkner through his narrative loops and ellipses merely by inverting his question marks; to sing the heart dark, as he had, in a sweetly melodious and lisping Latin, was to leave the soft nest of your lady's lap to yap after the hounds . . . misguided, hopeless, absurd.

All the same, prose went secretly south. Prose, the cold northern art, began to journey like the Germans to Venice, or wash up, like blond Scandinavian girls are supposed to, on the shores of the Aegean; even Spain had its Mexico just across the straits, as France its several Egypts. It proved always possible to go south, to Tangier, into some interior, up a Conradian river as we once went west; but how different those old expeditions were, because our wagons, our wants, our humble household wealth, our hardy women, always went *out* in that west they went to; it was seen as a place to replace life, to alter both circumstance and nature, to begin anew; whereas to go south was to go dangerously downhill, as Malcolm Lowry's metaphors persistently suggest. We went there only for a visit, for we knew that if we ventured far enough, down south became deep.

With the way west blocked by the Pacific, it was still possible for us (it proved necessary for us) (it was our fate) to turn left and make the descent. If Africa went endlessly *in*, Central America went endlessly *down* like some twisted pipe driven angrily into the continent below, or conversely like some whirlwind rising from a lower land to suck the heavens in. First there were the deserts, and then the jungles began: the heat, the snakes, the carnivorous fish, the orchids, the butterflies, the blowgun's bite. There was fecundity, and the fear of what that implied; there was raw life like a split-open fruit, the sweet taste of death in a soft chocolate skull. Space slowly became time, and around that different clock customs collided like car and cycle in a traffic circle. As though they were Semites, each tick fought its following tock.

One found oneself in noisy fumeous bazaars, beggar-crowded, dream-strewn streets, such as those we've been transported through in Juan Goytisolo's unequaled imagery; or, going south, where cultures, like transvestites, swap one another's clothes and clichés, we might stroll in ancient worlds one hour and hurtle down new-laid highways the next, through cities that are like a great stage, everything not alive the same pale age; or yet encounter pagan Christs and Negroid Marys; hobnob with savage Christians, crosses of dried bones tied about their waists; to shout, hold it! and catch seven contradictions in one snapshot like a shark; or vomit from a bus and buy (what luck!) the sort of shrunken head with which Virginia Woolf so dramatically began *Orlando*. Yes, going south we could find the whole cheap crazy gimcracky paraphernalia of our advertised life transformed: Andy Warhol, Coca-Cola, rock, and religion, blue jeans, movies, comic books, and cars, mingling madly like auto horns and strummed guitars with the crude clay pots and garish colors of the Indians; down there where everyone wears serapes and too many rings, and writes upon the dry adobe walls with penis piss, and feathers metal roosters with wings of hammered tin, and fights cocks, foments revolution, cooks and eats corn and black beans exclusively, with calamitous effects, including black teeth; where all ambition has melted in the heat, and sleep is sought under any shade—tables, trees, and hats, clouds, skirts—and waking is slow and deliberate, the way a bandito shakes the scorpion from his summer sandals before going forth in bandoliers like trouser braces to grin a toothy untrustworthy grin at the plaintive tourists or brisk corporation agents he's about to rob, the ungrateful wretch; in countries where poverty is an art, and wealth (whoopee! as we exclaimed when we were kids; *olé* and whoopee), wealth is what of that world *we* own; and isn't that the detritus of Disney out there washing about like swill against rotting jungle-river wharves? civilizing, although slowly, these lands of magic and mystery and brutality and decay, even of "coffee and oranges in a sunny chair, / and the green freedom of a cockatoo"; down south where we might sample exotic alcohols and pleasure-promising drugs, and then return home with an altered consciousness like a duty-free souvenir, our sensuality aroused like the princess from her woodsy sleep, our sex upset like Gide's; going down—with all its sexual suggestion—to fall at the feet of the world, eventually to reach the floor of Dante's hell, the heartless Antarctic ice, the cold still lifeless eye of the inferno which, while falling, we took photos of.

I have just recited a list of myths, of course, made by movies mostly (that light of darkness in a palace of liars), yet it is a list containing real fears, a few flat-out truths, some honest hope . . . dreams of a place where prose might loosen its pants; and now, indeed, it has sprung up at us; it has come back to us in a series of powerful orgasmic bursts. Having tarried in Paris, perhaps, like Odysseus with Calypso, it has returned to the new world, having circled the old, in the guise of symbol and allegory, transmogrified history, felt fact and passionate observation, colorful tapestry, subtle arrangement and thunderous rhetoric, or more purely and completely, to calculate the sum, as exuberant, exact, and angry poetry. It is a literature of exile, as often happens, but an exile forced, not chosen, as ours were chosen for a time. Americans often attended Europe as they would a college. Their leave-taking was not a bloody severance, like a lost limb. Yet paradoxically, it was as though the language had to be roughly sent away like an intractable child to grow great, for nothing could be more dialectical than the way the Spanish-speaking people have objectified themselves and their carefully duenna'd inner life by driving out their artists. What petty bourgeois princelings and corporate connivance could not anticipate was the overall effect of this distance, this view of the homeland, in effect, across some strait; and that language which ancient religious certainties and royalist pretensions had made stilted and stuffy, which foreign interference had abused, internal tyranny had stilled, and death had chosen, has wonderfully revived; because there is a substantial body of novels now that constitute what I want to call, in grateful celebration, the miracle of the risen word.

Perhaps we readers who are writers in the United States today are feeling a little of what the British novelists felt when (through the mediation of devoted translators, too) the Russian novel appeared in all its misshapen majesty, and Dostoyevsky, Tolstoy, and Turgenev swept by Scott and Thackeray and Trollope like a swift train through a vacant station.

They were long, those damn books; they were full of strange unpronounceable names: loving names, childhood names, nicknames, patronyms; there were kinship relations that one can imagine disconcerting Lévi-Strauss; there was a considerable fuss made concerning the life, sorrows, and status of the peasants, the *oblige* of the *noblesse*; and about God, truth, and the meaning of life there was even more; moods came and went like clouds, and characters went mad with dismal regularity. Oh, they were long, those damn books. And they were extravagantly admired for their worst, or most irrelevant, qualities. Must we do that again?

The admiration of the literate public for *One Hundred Years of Solitude* doesn't count either (*ahito ta!* as we cried when we were kids and the rain kept us in; *ahimè* and *hélas*). It doesn't count, not because *One Hundred Years of Solitude* isn't a literally dazzling book, so that the eye blinks repeatedly as you read; but because it permits, perhaps even encourages, a nostalgia for the old forms and functions of the novel; consequently, it is loved for its brightly colored characters, its fascinating storytelling, its exotic setting like *Nostromo*'s, its controlled release of the reader from realism, its Mary Poppins magic. It has slid backward in time to become one of the books we loved when we were kids. *The Autumn of the Patriarch* does not encourage that kind of pleasant regression; it has less philistine appeal; its hate is a hot iron, its language like a noose about the throat.

Are these, then, the true Friends of the Forms of Fiction, who just adore *One Hundred Years*, as it is familiarly called, but who find *Hopscotch* just another fancy contrivance; who are baffled and finally worn out (as who, reasonably, might not be; as who, emotionally, must not) by the proliferating prose of Lezama Lima's *Paradiso*; who are bewildered by the multiplicity of techniques employed in these novels, their metaliturgical fusing of history and fiction, fact and superstition, which produces a far sturdier alloy than the merely wet mix of journalism and melodrama we opportunely use in this country to disguise a lack of artistic intent and want of talent? Gosh! (as we used to exclaim in a less forthright age, gosh and by golly) what are we to make of those who refuse to lose themselves in Vargas Llosa's artful mazes and many minds; who falter in front of the plasticity of place, the penetration of times by times, as they occur in these books, occluding and combining the way color enters color; who reject the interplay of tapestry and torrent, as if music were carving stone like blown sea waves, of moonshade in daylight, reality rendered as dream, dream delivered up on the beach like a half-drowned refugee? phenomena that are fundamental (as are all these elements and others) to Carlos Fuentes's *Terra Nostra*, a towering achievement few Americans, I fear, will ever climb to the top of.

For these are the fathers who are hiding behind their daily papers, to alter the sense of the image again; and who bitterly complain, when struck at all, of pointless complexity, needless difficulties, and abnormal artifice, of cold contrivance in the execution of the blow (all qualities life can be accused of having, but never fairly these fictions); but, they say, the novel is worn out anyhow (though, of course, there is *One Hundred Years*; however, look at *Letters*, John Barth's broken time machine, or William Gaddis's *JR*, as disagreeably oral as Cabrera Infante's *Three Trapped Tigers*, both as discolored and distempered as a spew of chewing tobacco); there is no optimism in them, no uplift, just genius; and isn't Goytisolo as bitter as Céline? which isn't nice; Lezama Lima as luxuriantly self-indulgent as the jungle? Cortázar as cute and nihilistic as Sterne? Why do they so stubbornly seek for alternatives to the world?

But our Spanish-speaking, novel-writing friends have demonstrated that although some readers may be weary and fast weakening, they are not, nor is their art. The novel, so far, now, from being played out, if we look about the world at the company it keeps, is holding a fiesta for the form: whether we read Handke, Bernhard, Gadda, or Calvino, whether we stand before the Goytisolo triptych as before a glorious Bosch; whether the work is in Polish, German, or Japanese, concerns itself with Peru or making money or Tidewater Maryland, USA; for language, the instrument of the *logos*, the soul itself, is everywhere alive and kicking, creating a world that, for all I know, may be real; for all I care, may be purely imaginary; and the writers who serve this art share, I think, at least this belief, and are prepared to honor the commandment that *Terra Nostra*'s El Señor so urgently utters: "Take paper, pen, and ink; listen to my story . . . write: nothing truly exists if it not be consigned to paper." And when Cabrera Infante conceives a rumba dancer in the middle of a sensual gesture:

> . . . as the music stopped every time he switched off the jukebox, the dancer remained in the air and made a couple of long delicate steps, her whole body trembling, and she stretched out a leg sepia one moment, then earth-brown, then chocolate, tobacco, sugar-coated, black, cinnamon now, now coffee, now white coffee, now honey, glittering with sweat, slick and taut through dancing, now in that moment letting her skirt ride up over her round polished sepia cinnamon tobacco coffee and honey-colored knee, over her long, broad, full, elastic perfect thighs . . .

we easily understand how any man might love such a limb and long to sip that creamy coffee with his lips; but, even more completely, how the writer loves the language that gives that leg its life; since this sentence, or any one well wrought, is not simply a significant series of signs, but a judgment, a stone in a wall, a brick in a paragraph, a house, or a palace like the Escorial, which figures so importantly in *Terra Nostra*; and the consciousness it contains visibly distends it the way a serpent who has just swallowed its supper is swollen; both the rodent in the stomach and the snake are real, as is the snake's slick skin, its cautious cressential slither, its warning hiss, the sun it sleeps in, the warm rock and sandy ground around, the slowly liquefying flesh of the rat.

Going south. After all, reading these works is a lot like that. Going south. The excitement I feel when I enter the world of an author I have never read before, and I realize—from the opening lines of *The Green House*, for instance, which launch me up a steaming river in the company of some soldiers, several nuns, and a thin shadow of gnats—that I am in godlike hands, and that these people are being well-served—saved—even if they are damned; well, my excitement is not unlike that produced in people by a dancer's shapely limb, because a good reader is not merely being informed that parrots give you diarrhea (as the book soon does) (and something good to know if you contemplate eating one), because this "fact" is a piece of poetry, and then I hear the words the parrots use to fly from the village; so that this reader, who is also a writer, can consequently take heart for his own weak art: it is worth it; Fuentes's remote black beach, the hawk whose claws cuff the wrist—they are worth it; the construction of the Escorial—again, syllable by syllable—is worth it; the pain, the worry, the discouragement, well spent; it can be done; it is being done; do it; and you are ready to proceed once more; to chew up and swallow another page, as if it held secrets; to swallow your shame, the sentences you've slain and left to rot; you are ready to get on with it; become drunk again on the glories of creation, on the long low sounds that omnipotence makes in its sooty vertiginous throat as a way is cleared to let the word "light" burst out.

Well, here's to happy days, as we once said, tossing back our bourbon in the years before Beckett's unhappy play (well, bottoms up and happy days); which was how I felt, myself, when my father put the Kaiserling down because his collar was tearing and evidence was accumulating. The little shit stared at me in wonder then, in amazement, for he'd seen me throw the truck myself after taking careful aim; so that the comeuppance of the kid, the justified trick I'd played, I thought, the bump on my father's brow, so perfectly deserved, so long delayed, and the Kaiserling's attempt to shift the blame to me, which I knew would be bootless, and surely still to come like the main feature—recrimination and quarreling among the adults: all were causes of the deepest pleasure to me, like the slow melt of one of those waxy chocolate skulls in my smiling mouth.

ROBERT WALSER

They found Robert Walser's body in the middle of a snowy field. It was Christmas Day, so the timing of his death was perhaps excessively symbolic. I like to think the field he fell in was as smoothly white as writing paper. There his figure, hand held to its failed heart, could pretend to be a word—not a statement, not a query, not an exclamation—but a word, unassertive and nearly illegible, squeezed into smallness by a cramped hand. It would be a word, if it *were* a word (such doubtful hesitations were characteristic of Walser), which would bring to an end a life of observant idling, city strolling, mountain hikes, and woodland walks, a life lived on the edges of lakes, on the margins of meadows, on the verges of things, a life in slow but constant motion, at a gawker's pace: sad, removed, amused, ironic, obsessively self-absorbed.

At least three of Walser's seven siblings were successful. Success was something Walser studied, weighed, admired, mocked, refused. He had a grandfather who was a journalist, a father who bound books. He would write for periodicals himself, and author novels. He was born in Biel, by Bieler See, in northwest Switzerland, but left school at fourteen and worked briefly in a bank; with the desire to be an actor, went to Stuttgart, where he found employment in a publishing house; turned up in Zurich in 1896 to begin his odd-jobs life in earnest; and managed, by the time he was twenty, to get his first poems in a Berne newspaper.

He was a kind of columnist before the time of columns. So many of his pieces are brief, reflective, simple enough in their syntax and diction to be columns, deceptively ordinary in their observations, a little like those cozy nature notes that prop up editorial pages still, a little like some letters to the editor, too: the signature HARMLESS CRANK could be appended to quite a few without discordance or much malice. And yet, reading them, one is astonished that any were ever put in print, because Walser matches trivial thoughts to trivial subjects—as rug to drape—with relentless insistence; so concerning ladies' shoes, for instance, he dares to believe that they are either brown or black; moreover, his transitions are abrupt as table edges; non sequiturs flock his pages like starlings to their evening trees; the pieces turn, often savagely, against themselves, or they dwindle away in apparent weariness and, unable to find a reason to cease, cease for want of a reason for going on.

Walser passes nine quiet years in Zurich; eight in Berlin, where he lives for a while in his brother's apartment and cares for the cat; eight more back in Basel, near his sister this time; twelve in Berne (eight years go by there before he has himself institutionalized after several possibly suicidal episodes and his sister's insistence); then, finally, the remaining removed and silent twenty-three in the asylum at Herisau, taking his walks, busy about the idle business of being mad, waiting for the blank which would blanket his attendant blankness (such wordplay was characteristic of Walser), and finding it, we might say, when his heart failed in a field full of snow.

Throughout this time, he's been an inventor's assistant, worked in banks and insurance offices, as an archivist or the secretary of an art dealer, attended a school for servants, and become a butler for a bit, before he accepts insanity as his true profession.

Lightly attached to people, to the formalities of society, to any work which lies beneath another's will like a leg beneath a log, and more in love with localities and their regularities (like the seasons) which do not require him, Walser draws a borderline near poverty for himself and lives his increasingly frugal life in little rooms, in donated leftover spaces, in otherwise unoccupied attics, in circumstances straitened to the shape of his thin frame, shrunk to the size of his microscopic script, a miniaturization perhaps too suitable to his status (such patterned repetitions are characteristic). Walser is always the dog beneath the dogs, a ne'er-do-well and a nobody. He pens lines for which he receives small recognition and less pay. He composes novels that get lost or are so artfully mislaid they might have been murdered. He stays out of other people's way, posting his innumerable ruminations to publications that not infrequently publish them—surprising even themselves. Most float back, leaf after leaf, to pile up eventually into books.

His is the perfect stroller's psychology. To his eye, everything is equal; to his heart, everything is fresh and astonishing; to his mind, everything presents a pleasant puzzle. Diversion is his principal direction, whim his master, the serendipitous the substance of his daily routine. I think that Walser most loved his long peaceful walks in the woods, and in particular that moment when a clearing came into view like sunshine between clouds, or a lake rose from its labor of duplicating mountains to drench the spaces between trees. In any case, his characters run away to the forest as often as creatures in fairy tales, and more often than not with similar results.

Walser's prose frequently reads as if it had been lifted from a tourist brochure, because his narrators almost never see things with Kafka's scrupulously realistic and coolly dispassionate gaze: they look upon a commonplace world in terms of conventional values and received opinions. Things are therefore said to be "lovely," "dear," "sweet," "charming," "little," "clever," "perfect," or "enchanting." Things are tritely characterized as beautiful and good, deliciously tempting, absolutely true to their type; they are as pleasing as can be imagined, as delightful as anywhere can be found. Things are meant to be presented to us exactly as they appear to smug, assured, accepted, and acceptable estimation. Walser paints a postcard world.

A farmer's market is bright, lively, sumptuous, and gay. . . .
Sun-splashed sausages have a splendid appearance. The meat
shows off in all its glory, proud and purple, from the hooks on
which it hangs. Vegetables laughing verdantly, oranges jesting
in gorgeous yellow heaps, fish swimming about in wide tubs
of water. . . . This joyful, simple life, it's so unpretentiously
attractive, it laughs at you with its homey, petit-bourgeois
laugh. And then the sky with its topnotch, first-rate blue.
["Market," in *Masquerade and Other Stories*, Johns Hopkins
University Press, 1990, p. 35.]

His narrators consequently split their point of view, merging
their removed and alienated angles of vision with the way the observed believe and wish themselves to feel: at weddings, happy as
all git-out; at funerals, sad as Niobe or Job; enjoying their gluttonies
without anxiety or future pangs, exercising their tyrannies without
guilt or fear of overthrow. His narrators' noses are pressed to the
window: surely those are goodies there, beyond the fogged glass.
The young servant thinks: Look at the family eat—how delicious
the food must be; listen to their laughter—how happy they are; how
nice it must be to be beautifully dressed, to own a fine carriage, to
live in this house I work so hard and helplessly to keep clean.

And the food *is* no doubt delicious. It *is* pleasant to be well got
up and possess a closet of consequence. It *is* certainly lovely to
look down on the soiled hats of passersby when wheeling through
the park. It doesn't take a tired proverb to tell us that between high
life and low, high is higher. But it is also true that the wide sky is
the property of rich and poor alike; that the broad lake will not
refuse the body of any bather, even one cockeyed with care; that
the massive range of mountains will stare indifferently at good and
evil equally, at fortune or misfortune, at noble and knave; that
each—sky, lake, peak—that surrounds and shelters us is honestly
serene, and cool and blue—first-rate in every way.

If Kafka's neutrality widens our eyes with horror and surprise,
Walser's depictions, always working within what is socially given,

are equally revealing. The effect is complex, and always wholly his own. No writer I know employs the adjectives and adverbs of value so repeatedly, with such real appreciation and conviction, with such relentless resentment. Standing alongside the lunching patrons of a Berlin bar, his word-making voice can genuinely claim that "it's a sincere pleasure to watch people fishing for frankfurters and Italian salad."

If his narrators sometimes seem to be ninnies, it is because they are beguiled by surface, by the comfort of commonplace persiflage. False faces frighten them, yet they entrust themselves to strangers whose smiles are matched by the ninny's own grins and good feelings. They fall for any startling detail like those who are fated to stub their toes on the beach's single stone. Watch "the good," "the true," and "the beautiful" dance hand in hand while a reassuring lie unfolds, a jolt gets delivered, in the following characteristically shrewd sentence: "Carefree and cheerful as only a true pauper can be, a good youth with a ridiculous nose wandered one day through the beautiful green countryside." Yet the ohs and ahs of these innocent souls cynically amuse the very mouths that make them, because the extent of every narrator's self-deprecation is at the same time a measure of the congratulations they will shower on themselves—superior in the form and fullness of their inferiority like a simple paperclip or tack or pin beside the welder's torch or the rivet gun.

The effect of such writing is complex and contradictory. It is as if, holding in one's hand a postcard picturing, let us say, a pretty Swiss scene—perhaps an inn at the edge of a snowy village with the Alps (as they ought to be) above, blue lake below—one were in the same look to sense behind the little window with its painted pot the shadow of a weeping woman, while in another room of the inn there was loneliness as cold as the window glass, cruelty in the severely scraped and shoveled walk, death in the depths of the lake, a cloud of callousness about the mountain peaks; and then, with nary a word about what one had seen—about bitterness, sadness, deprivation, boredom, defeat, failure added to failure—yet having seen these things, sensed these things, felt them like a cinder in the shoe, one were nevertheless to write (and Walser is the writer to do it) an apparently pleasant description of the pretty Swiss inn on its pretty site, colors as bright as printed paint, surfaces as shiny and slick as ice, smoke as fixed and frozen in its coils as on the quarter-a-copy card, with its space for any message, provided the message is trite and true, gay and brief.

So the prose strolls, and what it reports primarily qualifies the character and color of its concerns, not the character and color of things. As it strolls, observing what it wishes to observe, it dreams: so that about the figure of a young woman who is cutting roses in her garden it may place its usually decorous yet desirous arms; it selects: so that an overheard remark will be passed around like a snack on a plate; it ponders: and in the face of some innocuous scene, it can nevertheless hem and haw itself into revelations. If Walser is a descriptive writer, and he is surely that, what he is describing, always, is a state of mind . . . and mostly the same mind, it would seem.

To say that the prose strolls is to suggest that it follows the contours of its subject. There is no narrative because there is no thread. The text stops before this item, ruminates a bit, then it stops before that; it thinks one thing (who knows why?), then another; but there is no continuity, for the cat will not be followed in its flight up a tree, only caught with its back bowed and its fur erect. A shade is pulled, a pitcher sits upon a table, someone is met, the narrator is addressed, he gives banal advice, but each of these is a moment only in the arc of a life quite accidentally intersected. Nor is a thought, which might have been provoked by the drawn shade or the scared cat, allowed to grow others, to flower so far as theory, or to link up and chuff on down a track like cars connected to form a train. Nor will the narrator act on anything, however violent and effective he has been in his fantasies. If he says he has kissed, doubt it; if he says he is drunk, don't believe. Not even nothing does he do.

The formless look of many of these pieces, then, is only a look, because the prose does imitate the shape of its subject. If the narrator takes a walk, so does the tale; if the narrator is nervous, so is the prose. An early piece, "Lake Greifen," for instance, is already characteristic of Walser's art. Here, a very self-conscious description of a lake is set in the text the way the lake lies in its landscape. The doubling up of the language reflects the mirrored images of trees and sky on the surface of the water.

> But let's give the description itself, in its traditional effusiveness, a chance to speak: a wide, white stillness it is, ringed in turn by an ethereal, green stillness; it is lake and encircling forest; it is sky, such a light blue, half overcast sky; it is water, water so like the sky it can only be sky, and the sky only blue water; sweet, blue, warm stillness it is, and morning; a lovely, lovely morning. ["Lake Greifen," p. 3.]

The narrator, who has left a large city lake to seek out this small hidden one, swims far out with the greatest joy, but perhaps he has swum too far, for now he must struggle back to shore, where he lies panting and happy on the beach. What will such a swim be like, he wonders, when the lake is dark and the sky is full of stars? The story says no more (the story is over), but we can guess the rest, including the prose for the missing part: as calm as slate, composed of starlight, water, and drowning.

Walser is no ordinary voyeur, consumed by the secrets he feels have enraptured his eye, because quite prominent in any of his observations is the observer himself, and that person, too, Walser is watching. He follows each thought, each feeling, from the time one arrives on the scene to the moment it leaves, with a fond but skeptical regard, so that it is the seeing of the thing seen, he sees; and then, since he is also an author composing a page, in addition to everything else he must take into account, he watches the writing of the writing itself (both the walk through the woods and the corresponding walk of the words), until a person who has been simply encountered in *this* world becomes a person perceived in *his*, and until, in turn, this complex, pale, increasingly imaginary figure is further transformed by words into further words; words which talk about themselves, moreover, which smile at their own quirks and frills, and wave farewell while a substantial and often painful world dwindles away into this detached, multiphenomenal, pleasantly impotent, verbal object.

How absurdly philosophical we have become, Walser might exclaim at this point, and threaten (it would be characteristic) to drop our entire subject, lift my pen and his abruptly from the page.

The world he views should not become a view to be framed and hung in his attic room, or exposed to the morning amusement of casual people. He feels guilty when he turns a lovely woman into words; when a longed-for caress becomes a sentence perhaps shaped by that yearning. Walser's lyricism, which is intense, attempts to revivify his verbal world, often with images that burst like bullets from the text. In his extraordinary novel *Jakob von Gunten*, which exploits the author's experiences as a butler-in-training, he has his narrator remark about Fuchs, a fellow student, that he "speaks like a flopped somersault," a metaphor that would turn anybody's head. In a piece called "Comedy Evening," translated in the collection *Masquerade*, he writes: "In the mezzanine beneath me, an elderly lady blew her nose with a ferociously lacy handkerchief. I found everything beautiful, enormously bewitching." In "Tobold," an important story, he tells us that "With both swiftness and, understandably, great ceremoniousness, I bore the beverage to the beautiful woman, who appeared constructed and constituted entirely of fresh milk." Had there been a woman whose soft pale lucent skin had given rise to this witticism, would it be fitting that all that is now anonymously remembered of her is the milk a fictional servant felt she was made of?

In this same significant story, there is a small speech that I call a "blurt," because the author's usual reticence is lifted and Walser speaks directly about one of the contradictions which disturb him: that between the surface of the well-off world (to which he has devoted so many flattering phrases) and the interior gloom beneath —a gloom resembling the gloom of the poor and ugly, a resemblance which is deeply troubling.

Can princesses cry too? I've always thought it impossible. Such high-placed women, I always thought, would never insult and sully their pure, clear eyes, the pure and sparkling sky of their vision, with soiling, defiling tears, which disfigure the unchanging expression of their faces. Why are you crying? If even princesses cry, if wealthy, powerful people can lose their balance and their proud, imperious bearings, can be depressed and overcome by a profound weariness: then what can one say and how can one be surprised to see beggars and beggar-women bent over in suffering and misery, if one sees the poor and the humble wringing their piteous hands in despair, at a loss as to what more they can do than bathe themselves in unending, miserable sighs and moans and in torrents of tears. Nothing, then, is certain in this world shaken by storms and afflictions. Everything, then, is weak. Well, if this is so, I'll be glad to die someday, I'll gladly take leave of this hopeless, sick, weak, troubled world to rest in my relaxing, dear, good grave from all my uncertainties and hardships. ["Tabloid," pp. 98–9.]

The page is the dear, good grave where everything that lasts will finally rest. For Walser, this conclusion was never quite comforting enough.

Thomas Hobbes described the State of Nature as a state of war, with every man's hand against every man's, and argued that only the mutual relinquishment of rights, along with their implementing means, could guarantee peace. He furthermore wrote of the paradox of power, which meant that as any man obtained power, he would need still more power to protect what he had acquired, because envy of him would increase along with the fear; and this consequence was clear, since in the customary state it is the sovereign who is most perilously placed. If you were, however, a nobody, a nebbish; if you had nothing that could be desired; if you were dismally undistinguished; then perhaps you would be ignored and could go about the little business of your life unnoticed, invisible as a servant is supposed to be, performing small services quietly, unthreatened and serene.

To hold a priceless vase in your hands may be pleasing, but you are at the same time in danger of dropping it. If you possess any authority over others, you are in a position—through indolence, incompetence, or spitefulness—to injure them. Success survives on success; the higher you rise, the dizzier you become; obligations weigh, moment by moment, more heavily upon you; others begin to rest their limbs, their lives, upon your limbs and life, which the postures of sex not even secretly symbolize. Thus what Robert Walser fears, and flees from, is power when he feels it in his own hands. The power others possess is something that, like a great outcropping of rock, may fall upon you; but it also makes a shade under which you may find shelter.

His mind pleads incompetence. Asylums *are* asylums. There he can guiltlessly surrender his fate and pass his days at the behest of others. He will no longer need to write in such a way that its public obscurity is assured. He will no longer need to write. The daily walk will suffice.

Among Immanuel Kant's many important distinctions is the one he made between willing something to happen and wishing it would. When we will an end, he said, we must necessarily will some means which will be effective in obtaining it. If you hear me speaking of my love of boating and the sea, of my dream of one day owning my own yacht and sailing the Chesapeake as if it were my private lake, you will be quite properly disabused of your belief in my desire when you notice that I subscribe to not a single boating magazine; that I do not follow the Cup races in the papers; that I have not set aside any sums toward the purchase of so much as a jaunty cap; that, in fact, I spend my vacations with my family in the desert Southwest. In short, I may wish for such a luxury, but I have never willed it. When I wish, my means are dreams. Each evening, before sleep and in place of love, I imagine my vessel parting the waves: I cry to the sky the salty orders of a shipmaster and eat heartily without any fear of sickness from the rolling of the sea that lies around me like my cool, uncohabited sheets. As a people, as a race, Kant observed, we always will war; we only wish for peace.

Walser's narrators (and we can presume, in this case, Walser himself) have become will-less wanderers, impotent observers of life, passive perceivers of action and passion. Only on the page will the will risk the expression and exercise of its considerable means.

And when the circumstances of life—my six children and my fruitful but frigid wife, perhaps my boringly repetitive work as an insurance adjuster, my rascally relatives and a harsh climate, the painfully pushed-forward designs of those who would exploit me— when these force me (as I think) to give up my own aims altogether, then I shall find myself in a classical state of powerless resentment, aggrieved because existence has become a broken promise; and my head shall fill with willing women, my yacht will always find the best breeze, I shall dream of flames while I stir my ashes, and my soul will swell like a balloon to float over the world, touching it only as a shadow.

The details of the disappointment will differ; the site of the defeat will shift; the resistance to one's fate or one's readiness to accept it will vary in their strength; but the pattern is plain enough, its commonness is common indeed, its dangers real. Switzerland is a prison. Consequently the world is one.

If I were then to try to save myself through writing, how difficult it would be for me to maintain the posture of a realist, for I should have had little acquaintance with the real (indeed, less and less), rather more with the subjects of my wishes than the objects of my will. In order to confer the blessings of being upon the small, hollow dreams of my soul, these harmlessly private elaborations will have to achieve somehow the heartless powers of the page; yet my characters must be inventions, and how quickly these inventions will feel my disdain. What value could they have if they remain so utterly in my power? So much for the story, too, which can be pushed and pulled this way and that, or dropped, suddenly, like a weighted sack into the lake.

Through a course of such "thinking," if I read him aright, Walser became a postmodernist well before the fashion. The painfully beautiful, brief "essay" "A Flaubert Prose Piece" deals with the way a successful fiction fictionalizes its author, so that both his invented woman, and the author's *moi* she was, eventually "glided and passed among the people gliding and passing by, like a dream vision within the vision of a dream."

As Walser's final confinement nears, his writing seems increasingly made of dissociated sentences. To turn time, like an hourglass, abruptly over, so that its many days fall the other way, his feuilletons resemble the work of Donald Barthelme, almost collagelike in their structural juxtapositions. Not a few, like the brutally disturbing "Salon Episode," have a genuinely surreal surface. The detached, desperate "inhumanity" of his work remains. It has been many years since a figure in one of his fictions has had a real name. And if one had a name, it would be generic, like Pierrot. But it is easier now to follow the inner flow beneath these scraps of language, to appreciate the simple clarity of the sentences he has constructed, to recognize that these meditations (for they have never been anything else) move not in the manner of events or in the manner of a river or in the manner, either, of thought, or in the "happy hour" fashion of the told tale (each brought so beautifully together in "Boat Trip," one of the triumphs of Walser's art), but in the way of an almost inarticulate metaphysical feeling; a response to the moves and meanings of both human life and nature, which is purged of every local note and self-interested particularity and which achieves, like the purest poetry, an understanding mix of longing, appreciation, and despair, as if they were the pigments composing a color to lay down upon the surface of something passing—sweetly regretful—like the fall of light upon a bit of lost water, or a brief gleam caught in a fold of twilit snow, as if it were going to remain there forever.

FORD'S
IMPRESSIONISMS

I t has always been a dreadful word: that is, one which promoted imprecision. This is in itself odd, because originally an "impression" stood for something distinct, something involving a rather vigorous assault, a pressing of one substance upon another with such severity as to make a rather definite dent. The signet ring leaves its stamp; the press runs off its copies; a beautiful form keeps its shape in the iris of the eye. The protean character of clay, however, the openness of paper, the normal receptivity of sight, can be carried too far, for the tree in whose bark a heart is carved must be trunked and roughly scarfed before it can be cut. The sword that Cuchulain waves at the sea will not impress it, nor will my weight much worry a rock, nor my whistle bore a settled passage like a pipe's through the air. In impressment, one element is imperious, the other slavish; one acts and is off and shortly out of sight like the foot with its footfall, while the other retains the step like a print in wet sand, or discloses on a disobedient back the cruel mark of the lash.

If I am born with a crack along my length, I have not been impressed; I have been badly born. That is: impressions do not eternally exist; they must arrive; they can also be effaced and disappear. Thus an impression is that lingering result of an action which functions as a sign. An impression can take place only on a larger, unaffected field. A piece of paper upon which I have printed a black dot bigger than it is has not been impressed, it has been blotted out. An impression, then, has very definite limits in both space and time, and these limits suggest that there are regions within these two dimensions which they do not impinge upon, traipse through, or occupy.

Upon that which is blank, the impression is often an enriching sign; upon that which is already full and formed, it is a scar. For John Locke, the surface of the soul was, at birth, like a washed slate, ready to receive whatever life might write; so when Hume introduces the word into philosophy to designate a dot of sensation, there is a certain singularity and hardness to that *pointillisme*. It is, like the atom, inviolable. Yet the ring's image is made of the space where it was, as is the foot's step—an outline that's all edge; while the printer's sheet is flat and yields the picture of a width. On the other hand, the Humean impression, as we approach it, seems as solid as a brush daub, a bean even—a bead—a being quite complete in itself, as though both ring and wax had been removed to leave the somehow solid image of the stamp behind like a con-gealed area of atmosphere.

The impression is, like the atom, also invisible, for it is lost among others, just as Seurat's little dots are. Our experience con-sists of immense aggregates, which occupy even the most self-effacing and slimmest moments. Only an act of philosophical anal-ysis can hope to pry one elemental chip from this complex and constantly shifting mosaic.

In short, because they are neither *of* anything, nor stamped *upon* anything, nor *about* anything, Hume's impressions are misnamed. Yet the word casts an impossibly perfect shade: behind it lies the ghost of the material world; before it, that of the mind.

If Hume's impressions are definite enough, our understanding of them is not. They pale like colors in the sun and soon have quite gone out. It is never impressions which we bring back when we recall the past, since some fading is implicit in their nature—a little at least is always lost—although they live on a bit longer in the guise of immediate recollections. The popular image is that of the ash-covered coal which we can revive for a bit with our breath and cause to glow again. But these memories consume themselves, grow cold and are forgotten finally because, among other reasons, room must be found for a fresh stock. Of course, we remember as we must, or wish, or need to, yet each time we beckon some former figure, it returns paler and more fuzzed than before, as though anticipating the widow's weeds it will one day wear.

Words, so much more readily remembered, gradually replace our past with their own. Our birth pangs become pages. Our battles, our triumphs, our trophies, our stubbed toes, will survive only in their descriptions; because it is the gravestone we visit, when we visit, not the grave. It is against the stone we stand our plastic flowers. Who wishes to bid good morrow to a box of rot and bones? We say a name, and only a faint simulacrum of its object forms itself (if any at all does)—forms itself in that grayless gray area of consciousness where we put imaginary maps and once heard music; where we hunt for lost articles and diagram desire. Are these the referents of the name? these photoprints? cinders of old sensations? But the stories we tell in the name of that name may be handsomely detailed, alive, and complete. Generally, there are several events in our life which are slow to go and continue to burn in our souls beneath their protective layers of ash, but on the whole we retain what we verbally repeat: it is the life we relate that constitutes our personal history. We are in great part what we tell ourselves we are.

Locke thought our minds at birth like a slate washed clean as a seal's back. Such a surface would not resist the world's writing. When a word was set down there, the pad would make no objection, the grain would not fight the knife, the ink wouldn't run, the message smear. The mind could be counted on not to interfere, to insert its own phrases in the normal spaces between the names of things, turning a sentence of experience, for example, into one of calamity and accusation, as if "Whoops, I've dropped that old pot" were suddenly to become "My god, I have carelessly broken the priceless Ming vase of the Empress."

Hume provided for impressions of reflection as well, so that it was expected that a sensation would be accompanied by a feeling, an apprehension, or even a belief; but just as Hume remained unconcerned about the demise or replacement of impressions, he also ignored the fact that some impressions alter others—jostle, inflate, distort, destroy. For Hume, impressions do not act, they *are*, and fly by like notes, no more under their own power than the components of a trill. On the other hand, they cannot be accounted for the way we find sources for the sounds of music, or the way the cow's bell leads us to the cow.

Hume's simple ideas, which are for him faded impressions, as well as his complex ones, which are groupings of memories in various ways to form more general notions: these are present in the exotic mishmash of impressions that make up our experience, too. Consciousness is in a condition of chaos: desires, anxieties, sensations, moods, thoughts, pains, beliefs, passions, disappointments, resolves, exist in a jumble that Ford Madox Ford understands far better than Hume. Simplification is Hume's aim. Complication is Ford's. Despite the name, then, Hume's impressions are not impressions of anything. In themselves, they are never "from," "of," or "about"; yet they are what we remember when we remember; they are what we think about when we think; they are seeing, hearing, touching, tasting, smelling in itself; they accompany all that we do. And though they come and go like the Cheshire Cat's grin, they are each as obdurate as nails.

Seurat's divisionism at first admirably reaffirms Hume's analysis, but it then goes on to suggest quite different things. The painter's dots mix and vibrate in the eye, which Hume's impressions never do because they are not objects of experience; and Seurat comes away from his site with sketches that constitute a kind of sensory manifold, which he orders, as Kant would, by means of the complex and elegant architecture of his art. Form and peace are one. And when yellows and oranges are used to suggest the excitement of the circus or the high-kick, they are employed to promote a gaiety in which no nervousness exists. As in Ingres or Poussin, a classical calm controls and directs an ardent sensuality, the deepest passions.

The distortion of the word continues. Why not? Wonderland and wilderness surround us like a text of trees. Everywhere there are walls to fall from, and arrogant Humpty Dumptys perched atop them ready to brag before they break.

> The history of literary impressionism remains to be written. It will have to take into account eighteenth-century British empiricism, romantic theory, positivism, French realism, French impressionist painting, pragmatism, and phenomenology—at least. It will need to make precise distinctions among the various impressionisms of Dickens, James, Crane, Conrad, and Ford. It will need especially to remain lucid about the intimate connections and contradictions between literary realism and literary impressionism. It will probably never be written. [Thomas C. Moser, *The Life in the Fiction of Ford Madox Ford*, Princeton University Press, 1980, pp. 123–4.]

When the painters who are to be called impressionists discovered, as they are presumed to have done, that the monocular perspective of Leonardo, Piero, and the Italian Renaissance was actually not expressive of experienced space, they began to dissolve the clear outlines of objects in classical painting and mix them with light and shade and air and atmosphere and even the uneasy flicker of the eye itself, moving their art, as they thought, from object to act, from known to knowing. They painted, the critics said, *seeing as such*, even though, as the simplest test will show, their work, when lined up alongside its so-called model, looks very little like the world looks, and even less like the world. In that sense, they are as far off on their tack as Poussin was on his. And as another moment's reflection will demonstrate, you simply can't paint perceiving, you can only diagram its mechanics, because seeing is not something seen. You can only paint the surfaces of things, or signs suggestive of the surfaces of things, or signs themselves as if they were things or surfaces, or you can give all that up and paint paint.

But the impossibility of the procedure was not the point. When the impressionists gave up one convention for another (or for sev-

eral others, as it would turn out), they persisted in supposing that
they were capturing the real world—not, of course, the real world
thought, but the real world *seen*. And soon not simply seen, but
seen like a report in the paper: by X, at Y, in Z. Nevertheless,
Claude Monet's *Haystack*, or his chillier *Haystack in Winter*, or his
bluish pair of *Haystacks at Sunset*, or his identically named but
rather more redly empurpled *Haystacks at Sunset*, said to be *near
Giverny*, are no more nearly haystacks than Ingres's enameled
nudes are naked ladies. Monet may have felt he was painting the
instantaneous, but if he had really been painting immediate moments and no more, his work wouldn't be worth now the twit of
time it takes to take it in.

(Paradoxically, the camera records a sliver of experience so small
we never experience it either.)

As Monet's later lyrics celebrating his beloved waterlilies indicate, the impulse of the impressionist is to obliterate or at least
transmogrify the object. If we compare an impressionist canvas
with those of a master of realistic suggestion like Qi Baishi, this
impulse is as clear as its outcome. Baishi's brush depends upon an
intense prior study of its subject (as Monet's surely did), but of its
subject as such, of its subject as it must appear as it passes un-
scathed through life's various occasions, within but external to its
circumstances; and it reveals that enduring subject to us by elimi-
nating everything but its visual essentials. The essence of phenomena is this painter's aim: *the* garden rake, *the* overflowing bowl of
cherries, *the* precise moment a bird leaves a branch, or the bird
alights. Yet to be *the* quintessential bowl, it must manage to be *a*
particular and quite ordinary bowl as well. When Baishi undertook
the painting of a shoal of prawns, he raised these crustaceans at
home in order to observe them, sometimes provoking their movements by the gentle pressures of his brush. Two bold strokes were
enough to hover a dragonfly above a lotus; one stroke could give
an entire backbone to a buffalo.

The economy of these means suggests for their object an intense
simplicity and innocence of nature.

But the many brush strokes of the impressionists bury their object beneath a flurry of color like a heap of fall leaves: all that is left behind is the mound where they lie. The light which normally enables us to see is employed now to screen things from easy view. A curtain comes down like a scrim in front of the Rouen Cathedral; the Doges' Palace dissolves in a mellowed fog of sunspew. In Qi Baishi, on the other hand, there is no light at all; there is only the sign, sitting like the mynah among the winter sweet, in the center of a purity like that of white paper.

The word "impression" implies an incompleteness. The foot, the shoe, the step have been removed. Only their "impression" remains. Yet even here we can see how the impressing object refuses to identify itself and occupy a single location. The edge of my thumbnail leaves a crease in the paper, but I shall sometimes say that the crease was caused by my nail and not simply by its edge, or I shall say the thumb did it, or my hand, or after all confess that it was I and my intentions, my plan, which was responsible, for my plan was to leave a secret message on the sheet and so foil my captors. But to whom is my little thumbnail sketch such a call for help, and not just a few happenstancial indentations? Only the nail's edge makes the immediate physical impression. So it is the knowledge that another mind possesses which allows it to perceive these remoter connections; it is Holmes who knows his mystery man must have red hair; it is the anthropologist who sees a civilization's shape in a few shards. We often make our inferences so automatically, with such rapidity, and take them to such lengths, that we are scarcely aware of the actual crease or scratch or dent or little design which first sent us off to unravel a long skein of relations. When we read we scarcely see the ink, or often even the words, lost in the world we believe we see beyond the page.

Life, as represented by a collective noun, and standing for a large array of distant causes, cannot crease the paper and leave its line upon us; at least not if we mean by "impression" a definite bit of experience, for "life" is hardly that. The sum of these experiences, however—picked over, lied about, seated like dignitaries at a banquet—can leave an impression upon our judgment. So when we say, as we sometimes do, that X gives us an impression of life, we may mean it confirms our opinions; and when we say that Y struck us with the force of the real thing, we may mean our feelings were similarly stirred. It is not merely what the world writes, then, that determines our impressions, but also where it writes, for I suspect that if we are in any way a tablet, we must be made of many differently tinted sheets, each capable of receiving messages, so that what is written in one place is mainly equations, or aphorisms, or graffiti.

Consequently, when I maintain that a novel has given me "an impression of life" (something I would no more say than "nertz" to a bishop, but which we shall imagine my saying so that the point can be made), I mean I have compared the impression it has made on me with the one which life has, and found their shapes to be essentially the same. It is as if the fall of the word "foot" were to make the same print as the shoe.

But if I meant "shape," "structure," "form," or "outline," it is not at all clear that others would have "pattern" in mind, rather than "tone," "color," "effect," and general excitement.

Impressions are both distinct and vague, particular and general, pure and mixed. When we recall some occasion in our past worth recollection, we often add more of ourselves and our reactions than our memory alone can manage. True, the event and its agents and object are gone, and we cannot impress them, but we can impress the substitutes we have imagined. Here, in our heads, they receive our blows, suffer our wit, are scalded by our sarcasms. Here, what we call an impression is really our impressment, and now things can begin to happen as they should have the first time, since they are at present under new management—no longer ruled by chance or God or nature but by ourselves and the malice of our wisdom. A pleasant afternoon, which treats us like our favorite uncle, may give us a balloon, but it is we who will have to blow it up. Then, as we expand upon events and witness their disappointing outcome, we say, well, life's like that, or life's like this: it is a folderol; it's hit or miss; it's puff 'n' bust.

We have already seen our word slip like a stealthy Indian from tree to tree. It can only be bent on mischief, as we know from the movies. But it is precisely mischief which its employers wish to make.

(1) It is an atom of sense, the rose's "red red," hence it is clear, untroubled, unitary, definite, objectlike, and in the present tense. Experience is a mosaic made of such impressions, random as a dappled pond.

(2) It is the mark in memory of such a sensation, the red of last summer's rose; hence it is faded and fuzzy, and only grayly represents the color. Experience, of course, combines the present and the past in every measure: real red, remembered red, the red expected—which is the remembered red thrown straight ahead.

(3) It is the representation of the activity of the senses themselves, the eye as it reddens the rose into its redness; hence it deals with the momentary and the fleeting, for the head turns and time turns too. Scenes weep from the corner of the eye. This activity is so complex, however, that the impressionist will be unable to render all of it at once: the central area of focus, the hazy penumbra, optical illusions, light as if it were the air itself, or secondary effects of its action, such as shadows, glints, and other reflections.

(4) It is the effect this full red rose, presented as a token of love perhaps, has upon an impressionable mind; hence it is indelible and enduring but much mixed with emotion, with other images and associations, and liable to set an entire train of feelings going —often out of its own station. All aboard that's going ashore.

(5) It is a vague general attitude or feeling based upon a few rather fleeting perceptions. "I haven't been in Paris long enough to have more than an impression of the city." These are often described as *first impressions*, i.e., uncorrected ones.

(6) It is a confused understanding which is the result of sensory overload, a multiplicity of strong experiences, some canceling others out. "I carried away only an impression of my dinner at the White House." The excitability of the receiver is implied.

(7)   It is a general judgment about a single experience, concentrating not upon the experience for its own sake but upon what it means or portends. "It was ıny impression that the rose was a bit wilted and had probably been clipped from an old bouquet." From this we can infer enormities. "It was my impression that Gladys's suitor was a bit of a cheapskate, even a bounder." The more distant and daring the inference, the more it deserves to be called "an impression."

(8)   It is a general judgment about a vast number of related experiences. "It is my impression that romantic types don't make good husbands." Hume would call this a complex idea. If it were the report of a team of sociologists, it would be called not an impression but a fact. Here, however, it represents just one person's opinion.

(9)   It is something the well-bred say in order not to appear too opinionated, pushy, or argumentative, and which allows others an equal, if even opposite, point of view. "My general impression was of a man immodestly in love with himself. What was your impression?"

(10)   The tenth sense is like the ninth, but it functions to produce an exactly opposite effect. The word becomes part of the vocabulary of a vague, roundabout manner of speaking that genially assumes the willing complicity of the listener. In this completely social mode of speech, negatives or double negatives are frequent ("I shouldn't care to be among the uninvited"); assertions are posed as questions ("Don't you find it a bit chilly in here?"); and code words abound, usually among adverbs, such as "wonderfully," "dreadfully," "frightfully," "oddly," "awfully," and so on. If you have a cold, you say you are dreadfully indisposed; but if you are dying, you claim to be only a little under the weather or a mite short of top-notch. So if you have lived in Paris for five years, you say you have rather an impression of it; whereas, if you have been visiting Provence for a fortnight, you say you've fairly covered the country (you mean you've been frightfully busy gadding about). Here, certainty, arrogance, and prejudice disguise themselves as

fallibility, modesty, and liberality. When Henry James (whose language this is) says that the novel is "a personal, a direct impression of life," he may mean it is like a blow between the eyes. He certainly means it to be a most carefully considered judgment by someone who knows what he is talking about.

"Impressionism" might have been a useful word to describe one's first impressions of Monet, Degas, Bonnard, and the somewhat similar art of others like Toulouse-Lautrec and van Gogh, but its uses altered almost immediately. Originally it was an attempt to define a group of painters; but soon groups of painters began to be studied in order to define it. This turnaround is characteristic of deleterious critical terminology. Think of the endlessly expended anal energies that have gone into determining the meaning of the Renaissance, the true nature of Baroque, Mannerist, and high and low Gothic styles, the definite durations of the Classical and Romantic periods, the exact nature of the Modern Movement with all its Neo-'s, Pre-'s, and Post-'s. Close the covers on such works; there is nothing in them but a self-promoting darkness. When a word is encouraged to become as ambiguous as our specimen, and when it is used without wariness or the least hint of scrupulosity or rigor, we can wonder whether concealment rather than clarity is its advantage, and whether it is more filled with feeling than with sense, since its various meanings annul one another like doodles drawn nervously on doodles, or the play of progressively more powerful trumps.

When, in 1911, Ford Madox Ford uses the term in a P.S. to his dedication of *Memories and Impressions* (he was Ford Madox Hueffer then), he is excusing his inaccuracies in advance by appealing to a blend of #4, #6, and #10.

Just a word to make plain the actual nature of this book: It consists of impressions. When some part of it appeared in serial form, a distinguished critic fell foul of one of the stories that I told. My impression was and remains that I heard Thomas Carlyle tell how at Weimar he borrowed an apron from a waiter and served tea to Goethe and Schiller, who were sitting in eighteenth-century court dress beneath a tree. . . . It [the anecdote] was intended to show the state of mind of a child of seven brought into contact with a Victorian great figure. When I wrote the anecdote I was perfectly aware that Carlyle never was in Weimar while Schiller was alive, or that Schiller and Goethe would not be likely to drink tea, and that they would not have worn eighteenth-century court dress at any time when Carlyle was alive. But as a boy I had that pretty and romantic impression, and so I presented it to the world—for what it was worth. [New York: Harper, 1911, pp. xv, xvi, xvii.]

Ford goes on, in this rather devious afterthought, to stress the exaggerated (and hence socially acceptable) character of the report of his impressions. They are, that is, hyperbolic. "My impression is that there have been six thousand four hundred and seventy-two books written to give the facts about the Pre-Raphaelite movement," he writes at one point, by way of illustrating his use of the term. With regard to our topic, four things are striking about this preemptive defense. First, the impression is more informative concerning the state of mind that receives it than about its source or object. Second, the value of the impression, as imprecise as it may be about the world (in this case, mightily), is greater than the facts it defiles, on the ground that *this is how it felt or seemed or was experienced* and is, therefore, if sincerely reported, more humanly true and honestly real. Third, Ford's examples inadvertently betray him by their contradictions, because there is no room, among the range of meanings of "impression" he is invoking here, for this sort of numerical precision (six thousand four hundred and seventy-two books). And fourth, since there cannot be any such statistical impression, we are confronted, instead, by a daunting account; and we know that these reports, however grotesquely overstated, have to be vague and general (six thousand, perhaps, but why six?), and even stereotypical (a million is usual—any rich, round sum), because the impression being reported is simply one of "quite a lot."

In 1913, when Ford wrote about impressionism for the magazine *Poetry and Drama*, he again revealed a bias in favor of temperament. For the mere purveyor of facts he has but ironic praise.

> The Impressionist gives you his own views, expecting you to draw deductions, since presumably you know the sort of chap he is. The agricultural correspondent of the Times, on the one hand—and a jolly good writer he is—attempts to give you, not so much his own impressions of a new grass as the factual observations of himself and of as many as possible other sound authorities. He will tell you how many blades of the new grass will grow upon an acre, what height they will attain, what will be a reasonable tonnage to expect when green, when sun-dried in the form of hay or as ensilage. . . . Mr. Hudson, on the other hand, will give you nothing but the pleasure of coming in contact with his temperament, and I doubt whether, if you read with the greatest care his description of false sea-buckthorn (*Hippophae rhamnoides*) you would very willingly recognize that greenish-grey plant, with the spines and the berries like reddish amber, if you came across it. ["On Impressionism," in *Critical Writings of Ford Madox Ford*, edited by Frank MacShane, Lincoln: University of Nebraska Press, 1964, pp. 34–5.]

(Ford, who should never be trusted alone with a trusting reader, manages to vulgarize his tone when talking of the journalist, slip a little Latin in when speaking of Mr. Hudson, as well as introduce a slyly sufficient description of false sea-buckthorn into his allegations of insufficiency, revealing a good deal about his own temperament along the way.)

The ordinary public world of the naive realist, or the positivist's more accurately formalized and measured one, is rejected on behalf of doubt and dissolution, in favor of a movement into memory, a memory frail and shaken. It is not simply that Locke's blank tablet is replaced by a mind which, in typical Kantian fashion, actively participates in the construction of experience; it is rather that each individual is encouraged to draw, as personally and privately as possible, the peculiar features of his phenomena. It is not the vertical or transcendent significance of things depicted that matters anymore (once the painting of a woman with an infant in her arms was the painting of a mother and her child who were the Virgin and baby Jesus, who are the mother and son of God and represent the arrival of redemption and one's only shot at salvation); neither is it the representation of the things themselves that counts (a jug, a table, a woman at a window) or the homey horizontal connections (with rug and floor and furniture store); nor is it the realization of the conditions of observation that is of central interest (sunlight, haze, rain)—the halo of regard. Although it is expected that the eye and its object will remain, it is the viewer, and neither viewing nor the view, that predominates; the emphasis is not upon experience, with all its affinity for the external world, but upon consciousness and its inveterate habit of self-regard.

This pattern of development is by no means confined to painting or even literature. If Gaston Bachelard is right, the sciences seem to follow the same course. This tendency doesn't stop with Ford's impressionism either, but continues in a kind of recursive arc that contains too many stages to be simply called dialectical. However, let's examine Ford's case first, before looking at the epistemic loop.

Ford likes to argue by example, and perhaps his best-known one occurs in his book on Conrad (*Joseph Conrad: A Personal Remembrance*, Boston: Little, Brown, 1924, pp. 192ff). It concerns a Mr. Slack, and tells us how, in 1914, Mr. Slack erected a greenhouse and subsequently painted it with Cox's green aluminum paint. Some years back, Ford imagines, we were witness to this event, which may have transpired over several weeks. Nothing is that continuous in memory, and our mind will naturally break this nevertheless small affair into still smaller portions, some of which will really belong outside it altogether. "If you think about the matter you will remember, in various unordered pictures, how one day

Mr. Slack appeared in his garden and contemplated the wall of his house." (This is the application of Impressionism #2 to Impressionism #5.) We associate rather freely with the event in order to remember its date (as if anyone would normally care): "You will then try to remember the year of that occurrence and you will fix it as August, 1914, because having had the foresight to bear the municipal stock of the City of Liège you were able to afford a first-class season ticket for the first time in your life." Then we recall that soon after, we saw Mr. Slack in the company of a pale, weaselly-faced fellow whom we shall later be able to say did the work. (There is just a dash of Impressionism #7 here.)

To remember Mr. Slack is to remember much more about him than his appearance on that occasion. He is the Mr. Slack of that moment, of course, but he is also Mr. Slack as we knew him before, as well as the Mr. Slack he will be afterward—each image at rest in our memory as if our encounters made up his bones. ("You will remember Mr. Slack—then much thinner because it was before he found out where to buy that cheap Burgundy of which he has since drunk an inordinate quantity, though whiskey you think would be much better for him!")

Here comes Mr. Slack with Weasel-face in tow. Mr. Slack points at the wall of his house—here, there—and Weasel-face touches his cap. (We have been, in this fashion, *shown* his civility—or we have been shown his servility, depending upon our point of view.) At this point our mind slips into the slough of its customary narrow personal concerns as, the implication is, it always does, especially when it is occupied with memories that have no particular magnetism of their own. Mr. Slack is momentarily forgotten while we remember how our daughter Millicent was behaving at the time ("Millicent had not yet put her hair up"), or possibly misbehaving (". . . you will see in one corner of your mind's eye a little picture of Mr. Mills the vicar talking—oh, very kindly—to Millicent after she has come back from Brighton. . . . But perhaps you had better not risk that"). Indeed, memories without a strong emotional charge, like this one of Mr. Slack, are easily pushed aside by more

powerful ones with which they have had the bad luck to be associated; on the other hand, the powerful ones are often unpleasant,
so that other mental forces must be brought up in order to drive
them off and let Mr. Slack occupy a more peaceful stage.

Beyond our little cottages and half-lots, however, peace is not
the play, and although our context in this example is neighborly
and familial, and although the fact is not invited in by Ford himself
(who is, nevertheless, and in part because of this discretion, a habitual slyboots), we cannot fail to realize that war was declared
during the first week of August 1914; that General Max von Hau-
sen's Third Army was massed opposite Liège—soon to be beleaguered and then destroyed—the city whose bonds we were so
fortunate as to hold; that the narrow circle of our concerns tells
upon us, especially, perhaps, on Mr. Slack, whose name is a poor
one to wear during wartime.

Now imagine Monet being asked to paint this kind of impression.

By this method any occasion is dissolved into its elements (act,
agent, object, qualities, and temporal successions—first this, then
that); its various modes of apprehension are marked off (detailed
close-ups, distant overviews, vague general effects); and all of these
are stirred about, apparently higgledy-piggledy, until not only order
but many actual bits are utterly lost. This mess is mixed with all
sorts of memories and associations, some longer and more detailed
than the central memory itself. The writer then rebuilds the event,
as it were, by means of sidelongs and fractures, obscure details and
elaborate digressions, surprising omissions and untoward simplifications.

The fit is loose, but this method more nearly resembles the working habits of the cubists than those of the impressionists.

Of course, the real chances are that the writer began with the
bits and let the words feel their way toward some absent whole the
way a sketch suggests a face or a landscape, rather than commenc-
ing with a complete and disciplined design and then scrubbing
things out and messing them up.

The impression we are after here, and which we wish to give to the reader, is that of a consciousness, not of a thing. Things arrive in consciousness from every direction: through sensation, thought, memory, desire. A world in ruins dumps its contents into a pot that leaks. "Modern life is so extraordinary, so hazy, so tenuous, with still such definite and concrete spots in it," Ford writes, "that I am forever on the look-out for some poet who shall render it with all its values" (Preface to Ford's *Collected Poems*, 1911, and revised for publication in *Poetry Magazine*, July-August, 1913, in Mac-Shane, p. 142). Mr. Slack's greenhouse is such a solid spot. What makes it tenuous is the fact, on the one hand, that the Germans are overrunning Belgium and that after this war no one will touch his cap with such alacrity, while on the other, that "we" are mixing Millicent's indiscretions at Brighton with Mr. Slack and Weasel-face and Cox's aluminum paint ("You remember the half-empty tin that Mr. Slack showed you—he had a most undignified cold—with a name in a horseshoe over a blue circle that contained a red lion asleep in front of a real-gold sun"); we are also congratulating ourselves on our season ticket; we are thinking this and that, but thinking nothing through; and these other vagrant occupations distort, disrupt, and diminish the clarity, solidity, and completeness of the "greenhouse affair." In fact, when Mr. Slack began to eye the side of his house, we were probably not thinking of Millicent or of municipal bonds or of Mr. Mills, the vicar, at all, but were simply wondering what was up. And when we remember these circumstances, we probably do not have so clear a picture of the label on Cox's aluminum paint cans, though we may certainly have had at the time. Impressionisms #2 and #4 predominate, but instead of a romantic rose whose presentation turns the head, we have a dull Mr. Slack and his little household addendum obviously substituting for and consequently obscuring some tawdry, quite personal, and distressing thought.

You cannot have an impression of another consciousness as if it were a train shed, a bright sail, or stretch of beach. Although we might have impressions *in* our consciousness, to say we had an impression *of* our consciousness during any particular present would be odd indeed. We can have an impression of life *as it comes back to us,* and as it comes back to us it is incomplete and thoroughly confounded with other elements which it certainly didn't possess originally; it is distorted and rearranged and treated like a table on which we lay out our obsessions.

The fact is that the painters were taking their art in quite another direction (toward a goal *it saw,* if they did not, and one which Kandinsky and others reached), but they were unable to give up the traditional (reactionary and bourgeois) belief that the aim of their art involved, in some essential sense, fidelity to nature. Art and nature had been long wed. Together they were to bring forth a country full of likenesses. Even Kandinsky is forced to spiritualize truth and confer it upon lines and planes in order to continue this charade. When the Old Testament prophets, one remembers, realized that the Kingdom promised them in their contract with the deity was going to be withheld—they weren't even going to get its dust in their eyes—they similarly spiritualized the laws and dematerialized the many meadows, milks, and honeys they really hungered for. The ultimate such refinement of the physical (i.e., the actual) was called "circumcision of the heart." Ford makes the same concessions to the conventional doctrines while smoothly subverting them. Life does not narrate, Ford says, and indeed it does not; it takes a teller of tales to disentangle the story, but most people continue to believe the tale is there and describes the main road, the true course taken; for how else could we make sense of byways and forks and high roads and digressions? There is a thread to thought, too, and there is honest dialogue as well, pertinent question and actual answer—so what if no one correctly responds or bothers to listen, as Ford seems to suggest is the actual way of it —because if the exchange is shattered, the bits will still continue to belong.

When the traditional painter persists in drawing firm lines which define the limits of objects and the boundaries of their being; even when he sets them in a pure perspectival space, when he washes them clean of spook and shade; he is merely disclosing the real as it rests there, holding the reins of things and directing their travel. I am convinced that this is what the ordinary reader believes, and if you want to achieve in your work the illusion of reality, it is best not to trust to appearances. Since life contains stories but does not tell them, no one minds the truth: that this or that story is being *told.* Furthermore, that's how, daily, we receive news, anecdote, and information: we are *told.* And the teller often puts in observations of his or her own, goes off on a tangent or has a bad cough. The listener has to find the tale in its telling the same way the teller has to find it in events. We are quite comfortable with these conventions, and it is simply not true that the palpable presence of the author puts people off or makes them feel the text is representing something to them that is artificial and unreal.

A conventional manner, then, never hurts the illusion, for when we are told something (although the teller may know more than we do, and in that, or even in some other ways, be superior—and who wants to hear a story you know better than its raconteur?), we are standing or sitting side by side in the same world, and her comments or his asides (supposed to break the illusion of life that the tale is creating) encourage our complicity in events, reassure us about the common plane upon which author, characters, and audience live; and this collusion completes its rhyme: the illusion —if that is what you want—is secure.

Impressionism, when applied as a method to the memoir, suggests the supremacy of sincerity and standpoint over objective truthfulness and historical fact, and means, in fiction, the rendering of a withdrawn fictive consciousness rather than any publicly thrown-open world of agony and act. It is the subjective side of things that counts; it is the subject's idiosyncrasies, the subject's special situation, that is central. If you like, it is Dickens moved indoors. "This is called egotism," Ford says, "but, to tell the truth, I do not see how impressionism can be anything else." On the other hand, the author must be at pains to remove every trace and presence of the guiding pen. Thoughts and actions must seem to be shown, not told. Because life does not narrate, Ford argues, there should be no narrator, unless the narrator is differentiated from the author and made a member of the cast. The reason for this recommendation is that the illusion of life is lost if the conductor's hand can be observed in the midst of an imperious wave. When we can see, quite plainly, a pipe in the picture, we do not care to be told that "this is not a pipe." We know it's not a pipe, and we're not about to puff it. Ford forgets that our knowing that something is an illusion does not necessarily disturb our enjoyment of it—on the contrary. What is annoying is having our elbow jogged, our ribs nudged. The magician does not say, each time: "Now let me show you another *trick*."

And consider what happens when we do make the narrator a member of the cast: his authority diminishes; suspicions shade his figure; reliability is lost; and we are uncomfortably set adrift in the middle of *The Good Soldier*, which might be an instance of Impressionism #8, but hardly otherwise.

I have given some reasons, already, why I don't think illusions are created or destroyed by the methods Ford approves of or warns us against; but the principal problem for the impressionist, who wishes to create "an impression of life" rather than of something else, is that the practice of impressionism is not suited to it. We know only one consciousness directly—our own—and we do not share that knowledge with anyone else. It is the world of objects and actions which we share, and which we feel we know as others know them. Madame Bovary is a person to us the way our aunts and uncles are, and we prefer to see her from the outside just as we see and know those aunts and uncles. Their reality is not diminished for us just because we cannot look straight into their thoughts and smell their smells. Actually, such a project is odd, the idea belongs to the "fantastic," and the ability would be unnatural. The only way you could make another's consciousness seem at all real to me (in this illusory sense) would be to cause that person's thoughts and feelings to jump around in the same sudden inexplicable manner mine jump, establishing a kind of dynamic similarity (which is what Ford's example purports to do); but I would be happier encountering another consciousness as I usually encounter it: indirectly and by inference from appearance and behavior. We must not forget who the writers were who were so successful in creating for their readers a vivid, richly populated world: Stendhal, Tolstoy, Dickens, are writers who accomplish this most wonderfully, writers like Trollope and Thackeray. Painters like Velásquez, not Sisley or Pissarro, or like Vermeer, not Monet. If you want the stench of reality and the sweet illusion of life, their way is the way to get it. Write, for example, like this:

> But there sat Tietjens, in his grey tweeds, his legs apart, lumpish, clumsy, his tallowy, intelligent-looking hands drooping inert between his legs, his eyes gazing at a coloured photograph of the port of Boulogne beside the mirror beneath the luggage rack. Blond, high-coloured, vacant apparently, you couldn't tell what in the world he was thinking of. The mathematical theory of waves, very likely, or slips in someone's article on Arminianism. [*Some Do Not*, from *Parade's End*, New York: Alfred A. Knopf, 1960, p. 15.]

You give the page a few blows of prose, and it will remember even if the reader will not: "The nose like a pallid triangle on a bladder of lard! That was Tietjens' face." Much of the time, as far as Ford's own literary practice goes, his impressionism seems to have consisted simply of intercutting, time shifts, and rows of dots . . . while the sort of impressionism his theory recommends is more satisfactorily instanced by passages like this one from Dorothy Richardson (from "The Tunnel" section of *Pilgrimage*, vol. 2, New York: Popular Library, 1976, p. 96; Miriam has just had her stroll interrupted by a man who has approached her with dubious intentions):

> Miriam marched angrily forward with shaking limbs that steadied themselves very quickly . . . the night had become suddenly cold; bitter and penetrating; a north-east wind, of course. It was frightfully cold, after the warm room; the square was bleak and endless; the many façades were too far off to

keep the wind away; the pavement was very cold under her right foot; that was it; the broken sole was the worry that had been trying to come up; she could talk with it; it would not matter if the weather kept dry . . . an unright gait, hurrying quickly away across the moonlit sheen; just the one she had summoned up courage and anger to challenge, was not so bad as the others . . . they were not so bad; that was not it; it was the way they got in the way . . . figures of men, dark, in dark clothes, presenting themselves, calling attention to themselves and the way they saw things, mean and suggestive, always just when things were loveliest.

Yet even here there is not enough diversionary activity, and Miriam's worry about the broken sole should have simply "come up" without any explanation or remark. The words in this passage have a habit of repeating themselves, not a trait followers of Flaubert could approve; but why should Flaubert be the model for an impressionist (as Ford claims he is)?

There is reason to believe that the impression we are pursuing is really an effect of the prose upon the mind of the reader; that if, for instance, the writer writes of what can properly be called "real life," then the reader will receive its impression, in which case the impression will not be in the score or on the canvas or the page but in the beholder's eye or ear or head. There is further reason to believe that, since the impression we are to sustain or endure is usually "of" life (a life that has been presumably unable, at least while unaided by the arts, to have much effect), writing will be the act, not of writing, really, but of impressing life upon someone alive. Sometimes the word "illusion" is used as if writing worked upon the reader the way those lines rushing off to vanish in a pure point work upon the viewer of the painting—a little triangulation and it's there: a boat upon the Thames. Impressionism is thus a branch of rhetoric. In order to move the masses, it studies the psychology of the masses. Yet I doubt that Ford had any such thing in mind. In any case, how can impressionism of this sort succeed when life itself has failed? I suppose because it selects, condenses, and sets life forth in a disorderly yet intelligible way.

This theory's regard for its readers is tender indeed, but Ford himself is aware of how vastly the backgrounds, skills, attitudes, and interests of readers differ; how low the average level of patience is, how short the span of attention, how well-held every bias; and he is working in a period during which the audience for the novel is melting away like life savings. He is also aware, to the point of being worried, that this lovable ruffian is in charge of the performance and must turn the page if the events depicted there are to continue smoothly; but Ford's insistence that the function of style is to blow through the reader with a force sufficient to (in effect) riffle the sheets is simpleminded and leads him to suggest a few rules for keeping things moving which would sound today overly commercial even in a writers' workshop.

The first business of Style is to make work interesting: the second business of Style is to make work interesting: the third business of Style is to make work interesting: the fourth business of Style is to make work interesting: the fifth business of Style . . .

Style, then, has no other business.

A style interests when it carries the reader along; it is then a good style. [*Joseph Conrad*, p. 208.]

(The repeated, almost subliminal banker's metaphor, the grandiloquent capitalization, the pidginish "to make work interesting," the crude simplification of thought and its loud reiteration, the consequent populism of the entire passage, laid against Ford's own level of performance, lead me to doubt the sincerity with which he holds this position.)

Mr. Wouk, Mr. Wallace, Mr. Follett, Mr. Michener, Mr. Robbins: they carry the reader along. They carry thousands of readers along. "A style ceases to interest when by reason of disjointed sentences, overused words, monotonous or jog-trot cadences, it fatigues the reader's mind" (*Conrad*, pp. 206ff). We mustn't fatigue the reader, who is probably already winded from a three-mile jog through the park. "To say that a face was cramoisy is undesirable;

few people nowadays know what the word means." These, and
other rules that Ford cites in this section, have long been admired
by the same meretricious writers and editors to whom, one must
now imagine, they are addressed. Yet they are not so addressed,
and they do not mean, I am convinced, what they now say. That
much, *the times have changed.*

What are these rules to Joyce, to Proust, to Thomas Mann,
Conrad, or even Ford himself? It is, in truth, when Ford tries to be
"interesting" that his texts slide away into vapidity. Again, what is
important for our purposes is the fact that impressionism tends to
make it hard, not soft, for the reader. When the narrative flow is as
vital as blood through the heart, then one properly worries whether
the reader will faithfully man the pump, but nowadays (that direction toward which impressionism leans) texts expect halts, stum-
bles, skips, rereads, reversals, rests. If one is concerned, as Ford is
in his book on Conrad, to recommend the use of simple language,
even simpler imagery, and simply tell his story, then he should
adopt the methods of the earlier masters, as I've suggested; they
always smooth things out; and they really make reading them the
pleasure that millions remember as they remember the other pleasures of their youth, and receive now from the movies.

If our term "impressionism" slips about and is, indeed, a thief of
thought; and if the impressionist's practice similarly shifts; if the
theory's rationale is weak and even inappropriate; I think we can
reasonably suspect that something else is up; that technique, as
Ford extols it in his essay of that name, has seen new possibilities
in the art and is trying to realize them at the same time that the old
allegiances to Victorian reality and Social Truth remain, pulling in
the opposite direction—a pull that, unlike taffy, isn't much fun
and cannot be expected to improve the product.

Ford's views are caught in a transitory phase of an epistemic loop
—a series of stages through which we can normally expect both
science and art repeatedly to pass. If we begin, for example, with
a period in which the things represented in paintings possess a
transcendental significance, pointing beyond themselves to higher

matters, then we are in a stage in which the world itself is a sign and allegory is inevitable. But as things descendentalize, as those higher notions lose their validity, holy virgins turn into sweet young things, and Christ-childs become merely bawling babies, their halos replaced by teething rings. Bunyan gives way to Defoe. At this point, the actions that the novelist describes, the objects the painter paints, establish their own community and lines of signifi- cance. Plate, knife, fork, cloth, bowl, and table: these are cities in the same state. A Dutch interior maps an entire domestic life. In the next stage, attention turns toward the act of attention itself, and considers the nature of perception with all its aids and impedi- ments. At first, we still think of sensation as a process that reveals an object to us, and we wonder how that happens, but the chances are we shall eventually understand it the way we previously under- stood the light that managed to enter an open window, or a door left ajar, to bring a tiled floor to view.

Imagine that we are pouring tea into a cup. Should we really concentrate upon the cup? What will it tell us about pouring? We could pour the tea upon our shoe. Pouring would be pouring. The suggestion is that sensing is like pouring. So we back away from the object, and the utility of perception, and begin to enjoy our senses for their own sakes. We begin to pour the way show-off waiters pour—with an admiration for the length of the trajectory. Of course, at first it must splash down into cup, bowl, shoe— whatever is aimed at—but trajectories are trajectories. Just ask the gunnery officer.

But what are we doing? We are studying the operation of the senses. With what? The mind. So sensation supplies the mind its material. Now a new relation, very like the old, appears: that be- tween a subject—the knower and the knower's ideas, life history, bilious character, obnoxious aunt—and the process of knowing what is known, an object again, though dematerialized. Not *a* hay- stack, but Monet's.

We should be prepared, by now, for thought to do to itself what perception did: back up along the relational line that connects the known with its knower. Instead of examining the sensuous medium of perception, we interest ourselves in the medium of the mind—which is language. Here we are—home at last. But the word has its halves: the world of the referent, and the realm of meanings or ideas. The loop has looped, and we are ready to begin again. Or we are not ready; we are dizzy from the last ride; we refuse to board.

Ford's impressionism, as is true of impressionism in general, is caught between the forward thrust of the art of fiction toward its own internal coherence, independence, value, and validity, and the pull of the bourgeois past—the Catholic past in Ford's case—where, in a perfect imitation of the social structure, the old supplantation of literature with reality, or with morality, or with spirituality, was a simple fact, as slavery once was. But impressionism is the last bow the old order is likely to receive. Monet may make Kmart's pasteboard walls, but never Kandinsky.

There is an immense nostalgia in Ford, a large looking back, and his impressionism is the blur a double-vision sometimes makes. I suspect that many critical theories exist to deny and obscure this tension between local stages in the loop, and that makes an ambiguous critical terminology essential. I am one thing, and a peaceful whole, the theory says, when in fact it is plural, and in quarreling pieces. Ford does not employ an academic jargon, nor does his language Heidegger a holiness his vision does not have. He does not willfully obscure his case, yet he has the nineteenth-century novel in his blood and admiration. At the same time, his art, his unrivaled technique, his skill of finger, as we might say, his thorough sense of himself as an artist (again, in the old sense), requires him to go as his artistic skill and artistic conscience require. Which direction is the blood to run? hither? or yon?

The theory of Impressionism (I now dignify it with the capital letter it has become accustomed to) is a wonderful theory. It makes no sense at all—in Hume, or James, or Ford, in Monet or in Bonnard—but it allows subversion to go on with the approval of the subverted. "The Impressionists taught us that snow is sometimes purple," a teacher of mine once said, and apparently it was important for us folks to think so—which we did. We do. After all, if the practices of these writers and painters are a little peculiar, they are still pointing out to us truths about the world it is vital for us to know: like the way the sun's rays blow into straw, the way our memory of Mr. Slack betrays our dismay about Millicent.

THE LANGUAGE OF
BEING AND DYING

Danilo Kiš was born in Subotica. To my Western ears, the name seems that of an imaginary city. However, Subotica is located in Yugoslavia, a country once put together out of bits and pieces like Dr. Frankenstein's notorious experiment: impressive when it walked at all, but making any move with difficulty. Kiš died before the monster began devouring itself: eating its own heart with its own teeth.

Subotica is near enough the Hungarian and Romanian borders that I can easily conceive it drifting into either country like a cloud: a dozen languages intermingling, languages rearranging their vowels to resemble one another the way politicians alter their allegiances. "The story I am about to tell," the narrator of A *Tomb for Boris Davidovich* begins,

a story born in doubt and perplexity, has only the misfortune (some call it the fortune) of being true: it was recorded by the hands of honorable people and reliable witnesses. But to be true in the way its author dreams about, it would have to be told in Roumanian, Hungarian, Ukranian, or Yiddish; or, rather, in a mixture of all these languages. Then by the logic of chance and of murky, deep, unconscious happenings, through the consciousness of the narrator, there would flash also a Russian word or two, now a tender one like *telyatina*, now a hard one like *kinjal*. If the narrator, therefore, could reach the unattainable, terrifying moment of Babel, the humble pleadings and awful beseechings of Hanna Krzyzewska would resound in Roumanian, in Polish, in Ukranian (as if her death were only the consequence of some great and fatal misunderstanding), and then just before the death rattle and final calm her incoherence would turn into the prayer for the dead, spoken in Hebrew, the language of being and dying. [Translated by Duška Mikić-Mitchell, New York: Harcourt Brace, 1978, p. 3.]

Back and forth over this land, during Danilo Kiš's childhood, armies and ideologies washed with the brutal regularity of surf. As a small boy and a Jew, in such circumstances, he was naturally surrounded by death and lies. There were the lies of hope and the lies of fear, the lies of love and the lies of hate, the lies of cynicism, the lies of faith. Lies were like the leaves the bombs blew from the trees. Any language, even the death rattle, can express them. What signs might point the way, might save anyone lost in a forest of deceit? Perhaps only an innocence which lends the eyes wonder without soiling the soul with belief. Danilo Kiš's novel *Garden, Ashes* (his first to appear in English) describes the early life of such a boy, who, to escape small horrors as well as huge ones, crosses the borders between dream, daydream, and reality like a fugitive from each.

The second of his books to appear here, *A Tomb for Boris Davidovich*, although described as a novel, is a collection of short stories, each of which concerns a Jewish revolutionary enmeshed in fatal ontological as well as political difficulties. The tomb of the title story is a cenotaph, a grave without an occupant, because Boris Davidovich has too many personas to possess an identity and, just as Empedocles did into Etna, leaps into a vat of hot metal, disappearing without a trace like a repatriated god.

Boris Davidovich is born in 1891 or 1893 or 1896. The vagueness is precise. A few coins will falsify a record. Bureaucracies survive on the quality of their corruption. Born of a brief encounter, Boris

Davidovich's name is never firmly in place. He is shortly also known as Bezrabotny, as Jacob Mauzer, and as M. U. Zemlyanikov, although B. D. Novsky is his predominant alias. One of his pseudonyms—B. N. Dolsky—is mistakenly understood to be that of a certain Podolsky. He employs numerous noms de plume, particularly Parabellum, Victor Tverdohlebov, Proletarsky, and N. L. Davidovich. If his name ("son of David") will not fix him, neither will his occupation, for during his brief life (much of it spent in prison), he will be a smuggler, a butcher's apprentice, a dishwasher, a legal clerk, and then, in a military arsenal, a cataloguer of artillery shells. He's a dockworker too, the employee of a box-and-cardboard factory, as well as another which makes wallpaper. In France, he is arrested while harvesting grapes. He is also a fireman's helper on a steam engine, a practicing engineer, a barge dispatcher, a journalist, agitator, terrorist, sharpshooter, soldier, student, political commissar, and diplomat—each for a period brief as a blink. The otherwise complete and thorough *Granat Encyclopedia of the Revolution* does not mention even one of his names— omissions which Kiš's "story" intends to remedy—and even though his death can be exactly dated as 4 p.m., November 21, 1937, when he was transmogrified into a wisp of smoke above the hissing vat, he was reported to be alive by the Western press as late as June of 1956—in Moscow, where he was seen leaning like a shadow against a Kremlin wall.

Davidovich—Dolsky—Novsky (whoever he really is)—passes a sizable portion of his life in flight, in prison or in jail, in sanatoriums and hospitals recovering his wits or his nerves, in the editorial offices of fly-by-night revolutionary papers where he pens exposures and denunciations. An unspecified ideology seeps through the spaces of his existence like an unacknowledged pollutant, since every political faith is ultimately fatal. His actions are equally indeterminate in the sense that their aims are obscure, especially when violent, and seem bent on preserving some wholly imaginary purity. The language that most adequately depicts this life is interchangeably political and religious. There are heresies and their persecution; there are denunciations, inquisitions, confessions, tortures, confrontations, crimes, criminals, and their investigators; there are betrayals, murders, assassinations, hoaxes, plots, cover-ups, smears, innuendos, allegations, fears, suspicions, mistrust.

We find him—Bezrabotny—Zemlyanikov (whoever he is)—living on the streets, in tenements and public baths, with a distant relative, a momentary friend: without a certifiable name, a fixed address, a permanent position, and, although supposedly subversive, without an identifiable belief. How many truths may we imagine he has denied in order to survive? how many lies has he been forced to affirm? how often can he have known which was which —lie or truth, affirmation or denial?

Yet this life, elusive as a vapor, can be constructed from the very gaps in its chronology, its lacunae and erasures, from documents no longer available, from possible forgeries and illegible letters, from the depositions of traitors and fanatics, the footnotes of plodding scholars, and the suspicious testimony of a conveniently invented sister.

This brilliant tale is characteristic Kiš, not only because of its subject matter (in this case, Jews who are destroyed by their very passion for justice), or because of its ironic yet factually deadpan tone, or on account of its apparently misplaced lyricism, so much like a songbird singing in a storm; but also because of the story's tug of war with history—its total reliance on, and lack of belief in, texts.

(Indeed, several paragraphs back I wrote that Novsky, although definitely dead, had been seen in Moscow "leaning like a shadow against a Kremlin wall." However, all that the London *Times* reported [according to Kiš's possibly prejudiced account] was that he had been observed "near" that wall. Nor did the newspaper capitalize the word "wall"—clearly an anti-Communist slur. Nor do shadows lean: they are cast; they fall. The misleading elaboration should have read: "seen like a shadow thrown against a Kremlin Wall." It is the noxious accumulations of such slightly skewed details that undermines the veracities of history more certainly than even its invented facts, its poisonous biases, its outrageous omissions, its hypocritical objectivity, its illusion of causal connections, its pretentious claim to have explanatory power.)

Behind Borgesian concerns of this kind lurk two dismaying realizations. The first is that the force of individual events—even cataclysmic ones like the Lisbon earthquake of November 1, 1755, which shook a poem from Voltaire like a pippin from a tree, and then continued to trouble him during the composition of *Candide* —is but a cough in a clinic compared to the trauma of its descriptions, which conveyed the earthquake's horror to more distant climes than the trembling earth was able, and tumbled it into *Candide* itself. Egregious errors of translation ("a virgin shall conceive" for "a maiden, or young woman, shall conceive," to cite a notorious instance) alter history more powerfully than the simple, explicable truth. Falsified documents, qualifying emendations, misleading interpolations, clever deletions, can reshape events, not in their own region of reality, but in the characteristic way they reach men's minds. Furthermore, texts, because they duplicitously repeat themselves each time they are read, and because they are subject to interpretation and commentary, belong to a more powerful realm of Being than the world of unrecurrent events, aging people, and transitory things.

The second, saddening realization is that unless, consequently, you can insert yourself into some account, unless your history has a History, you might as well not exist, so paltry are the normal powers of the present; and yet, if you manage to make your way into a text, or become defined by a set of documents, you will become a different being altogether; your proofs will rest in a file folder which will resemble your grave. Bureaucrats will burnish one medal, tarnish another, or strip you of both. The city which was given your name by removing another's will regain in time its former designation. Or, tortured, you will tattle on yourself, and that tale, too, will be attached to your dossier and become your identity, your passport to history. Yet what is history but other eyes in other ages, arranging the data to suit their own policies, salting their grievances with your tears, advancing another false cause? If your text serves the interests of some institution, of those who would be stronger, then your folder will fatten, will be frequently consulted, will be protected, imitated, polished like a rifle. Fame is, under these circumstances, your frequency of citation.

The title story of Kiš's collection *The Encyclopedia of the Dead* is based on such melancholy considerations. It imagines that there is a Book of the Dead for nobodies compiled by a religious organization (resembling the archival activities of the Mormons, as the author's notes observe). After the French Revolution proclaimed the equality of Man (true enough for corpses), subversive scriveners shelved these "This Was Your Life" biographies in alphabetically laid-out lower rooms of the Swedish Royal Library: a textual catacomb and historical Hades. As George Eliot remarked, history is really made by the myriad little people who lead hidden lives and rest presently in unvisited tombs. (I suspect that these bookish spaces mimic and invert those occupied by the Nobel Prize Committee, whose collection is, of course, largely of also-rans.) (The activities of this necrological society are as secret and multifarious as those of Borges's now famous encyclopediasts, whose volumes create the countries of Tlön and Uqbar, and whose facts are so persuasively imagined that they begin to supplant the complacent realities of our own dessicated compendia.) (Indeed, much of Danilo Kiš's "essays" and fictionalized memoirs seem as if they might occupy shrewdly placed parentheses within the Argentine master's work.) (In the Swedish Academy's peevish eyes, Borges is himself an also-ran.)

The narrator, finding herself locked in this dusty, chilly, familial place, looks for the life of her recently deceased father there, and finding it—complete as a warehouse inventory—takes highly condensed and hurried notes, notes which allow her to compose the present tale, a recollection of her journey to the Underworld. The entire trip turns out to have been a dream—alas, a moviemaker's ending—which the body of the text suggests through montage and other visual devices, but whose alleged nonverbal origin leaves me unconvinced.

Inside this retold dream is a freeze-dried life—a list, really, of

one man's coming and going—and like ordinary existence everywhere, its singular events are made of summarizing facts. It is a
life composed of kinds, in which a characteristic catastrophe is
surrounded by typical trivialities—incidents of outstanding ordinariness—while every region of reality is ransacked for examples
of this and that which will be locally convincing yet symbolically
vast: one more day of labor, one more wedding night, the tools,
the flowers, the hot sun, the sheets, the weariness of love and work,
always the same, though different, too, in the amount of dust, in
the frequency of passion's noises, the quality of surprise in the
bride, the length of a chewy lunch; each variable, of which life at
any moment is composed, as common as a word right out of the
dictionary, repeatable as corn flakes, and the many sentences we
make the same as well (good morning, Al—hiya, George—how
they hangin', Frank?), but none, in a context in which they rub
one another (cold cream and skin, torn shirt, slipped disk), creating
the same stridulation, the same significance, precisely the same
result (an allergic rash, an embarrassed blush, a cry of pain like
one of pleasure, or a rush of blood to the belly when fear is felt).

> After all—and this is what I consider the compilers' central
> message—nothing in the history of mankind is ever repeated,
> things that at first glance seem the same are scarcely even
> similar; each individual is a star unto himself, everything hap-
> pens always and never, all things repeat themselves ad infini-
> tum yet are unique. (That is why the authors of the majestic
> monument to diversity that is *The Encyclopedia of the Dead*
> stress the particular; that is why every human being is sacred
> to them.) [Translated by Michael Henry Heim, New York:
> Farrar Straus Giroux, 1989, p. 51.]

Uniqueness in such a vast ocean of similar otherness loses its value,
however, for what is the worth of so many hen's teeth, though
they enable dentists to furnish police with the identities of the
mysteriously deceased? Unique combinations of the most common
words can, during the run of even a few lines, be discovered: (1)

the plumber has lost my latchkey; (2) twins were born to the Tolli-
vers in a speeding Tip Top taxi; (3) Dollars will defeat Doughnuts
by the length of a cold nose in the one-legged sack race. The list of
facts and features, people and occasions, that constitute the narrator's father's life is a carefully selected one, with much more omitted than included, for if nothing were excluded and no decision
made as to what mattered and what did not (since, if every person
weighs on the scale of history—each unique as a droplet in a
sneeze—so does every ant at the picnic and every loon in the lake
and every coasting cloud and every breeze), then even a short life
would receive an endless recital, and have a heaviness which would
break the pan of every balance. Uniqueness needs numbers, and is
no idle pursuit.

Moreover, although a mouthful of chilled wine on the tavern's
cuff may be a one-of-a-kind occasion in terms of the wine's wheaty
color, oaky taste, and nasturtium-heavy nose—combining to make
it singular in its swallow—no listing will lend that fact any further
interest unless the interest were to lie in the quality of the description of such a mouthful, in the choice of its moment to appear in
some larger narration, and in the significance, then, the wine's
golden nature can receive from the chronicle as a whole, as well
as whatever feeling the music of the language or the pace of its
disclosures, can generate, or gain from an imagery that may revive
its taste. In short, only the style of the description will be capable
of imbuing the event with a value that extends beyond the one of
merely existing, since existing is easy to do (anything that *is* at all
has done it). It is as easy to be as not to be (for not being is also the
mildest form of exercise). Nevertheless, few of these examples of
the world's bric-a-brac have their existence realized in language;
fewer still in language that lasts, language that lives through the
dying it describes; that outlasts the endings it observes and cele-
brates; language like that which Danilo Kiš has contrived for the
list that is this biography, and the death, too, that the story suggests
grows like a noxious flower from the soil of life itself, even as that
life is led.

The fact that, while working at the Milišić Refinery as a day
laborer my father brought home molasses under his coat, at
great risk, has the same significance for *The Encyclopedia of
the Dead* as the raid on the eye clinic in our immediate vicinity
or the exploits of my Uncle Cveja Karakašević, a native of
Ruma, who would filch what he could from the German Officers' Club at 7 French Street, where he was employed as a
"purveyor." . . . By the same token, and in keeping with the
logic of their program (that there is nothing insignificant in
a human life, no hierarchy of events), they entered all our
childhood illnesses—mumps, tonsillitis, whooping cough,
rashes—as well as a bout of lice and my father's lung trouble
(their diagnosis tallies with Dr. Djurović's: emphysema, due to
heavy smoking). But you will also find a bulletin on the Bajlo-
nova Marketplace notice board with a list of executed hostages
that includes close friends and acquaintances of my father's;
the names of patriots whose bodies swung from telegraph
poles on Terazije, in the very center of Belgrade; the words of
a German officer demanding to see his *Ausweis* at the station
restaurant in Niš; the description of a Četnik wedding in Vla-
sotinci, with rifles going off all through the night. (55–6)

However, the life whose tale is told in this story has had to rise
from the world in which we presume it was first enacted through
the language of these secret encylopediasts until it reaches the
daughter's astonished notes. There every layer is transformed by
being dreamed (for these assiduously compiled volumes are not
"real"); whereupon, on waking, the dream is remembered, with all
its texts, and finally, for the reader, is recomposed and recited.

The allegory, now, is obvious, because the passions attributed to
the society of chroniclers are, in fact, traditionally associated with
the development of the novel: the novel with its endless appetite for
facts, for the most paltry details, and with its egalitarian resolves, its
awakened concern for simple ordinary people, and, very soon, for
their simply ordinary daily lives, their family histories, their love

affairs and marriages, their business successes, their parish politics, their bedroom wars, as well as their dismal domestic tranquillities.

So the sun fails to flash from the slowly turning leather toes of those who were hung like rustlers from the leaning poles. This allows us to infer that their shoes must have been unpolished, perhaps abraded, possibly suede. Still, Belgrade is gray by custom and habit: grimy skies and grimy gray walls, wet gray streets, faces worn as the stones, and so forth, hence an absence of flash; gutters gray with slow gray water, and the rain faint, almost not there, light as fog, and so forth, hence a glitterless atmosphere; gray caps and collars coming down the damp street, gray coats, damp too, soot becoming a moist gray paste, bomb dust still in the wet air, too wet to drift, soon a drizzle of dust, and so forth; this parade of gray is the novel capturing the world in words, as if that were enough, as if that were all there was to it.

Then the reader arrives, the note taker, the critic, reading because of an idiosyncratic interest, because it is all, somehow, auto-biographical—*Madame Bovary* or *Moby-Dick*—*c'est moi*—and matching what each reader knows of the text with what each knows of the world, and watching the two sets scratch, like cats, their facts out. But what the reader reads is fiction (or what Danilo Kiš says has been dreamed in his story), and what the reader knows of the world is most likely incoherent, ideologized, incomplete, self-serving bunk.

Perhaps the most impressive piece in this collection is a Borges-ian pseudo story, what Kiš calls a "faction"—a monster with an essay for a body and a fiction for a head (occasionally vice versa). Called "The Book of Kings and Fools" (not, I think, a happy title), it concerns the history of the notorious *Protocols of the Elders of Zion*, a document that purports to reveal the plans of the Jews for world domination. Under Kiš's skillful hands this text becomes a character in a tale of intrigue and triple-dealing not unlike the history of Boris Davidovich, with his many odd jobs, his aliases, his incessant shifts of venue; because a lie that so many desire to believe comes to exist like any deity or yeti or pernicious social myth, propped up as it is by passion, poor character, and a grinding poverty of mind—one might say like the promised utopian fruits of the Russian Revolution, fruits that already lay rotting on the ground before the tree was fully leafed and were later served up as if they were made of precious metal, to admire but not to eat.

It is not unimportant to notice that when one speaks of the traditional novel, it is so often by referring to the psychology of its characters, the pattern of its plot, the accuracy of its environments; but when one is speaking of a fiction by Borges, Calvino, or Kiš, ideas come to dominate the discussion. Often a single notion controls the course of events, determines the fate of their imaginary agents, settles on the form of the whole. It is the sole sun of its system. Such fictions become meditations, but not by a Hazlitt or an Emerson, who might write to display the nature of their sensibilities and their intelligence as tourists in the region of some topic; but by a concept that searches for itself through its own exemplifications, where it finds itself realized somewhat in this facet or that aspect, as though it were the light that could not glisten from the slowly turning toe; a light that found no reflection in the puddles of the streets either, so gloomy was the so-called day, where the souls of the strung-up could not cast a shadow; and thus, in this negative way, seeks to define itself, not by the absence of reflection, but by the presence of writing. We can imagine, however, that the light did find at last the mirror of a woman powdering her nose in a narrow entryway, and about to mount the narrow, dark stairs. She might be going to her lover; however, that is an implication interesting only to former times. We—postmodernist trained—know she opened her compact to receive and illustrate and sustain the almost lost light . . . author of the page.

Every one of the nine stories constituting *The Encyclopedia of the Dead* concerns the character, corruption, and consequent fate of texts and the resulting endangerment of mind, bewilderment of heart, and debasement of the State that stem from such corruptions, as well as the advantages that accrue to politicians and their police.

But ideas aren't literature, any more than remarks are, or plots, or people, or noble truths, or lively lies, or Belgrade's morose gray streets; and I would not recommend the reading of Danilo Kiš on their account, or the reading of Jane Austen either. In Kiš's case, where the concepts are inconsequentially derivative anyway, it is the consistent quality of the local prose that counts. It is how, sentence by sentence, the song is built and immeasurable meanings meant. It is the rich regalia of his rhetoric that leads us to acknowledge his authority. On his page, trappings are not trappings but sovereignty itself. Hence it is not the plan, devious of design as it is, but its nearly faultless execution that takes away the breath and produces admiration.

NIETZSCHE:
THE POLEMICAL
PHILOSOPHER

I n an early, autobiographical essay, written for school, Friedrich
Nietzsche recalled that he found Naumburg overly busy—dusty
and indifferent as well as bewilderingly various—after the close,
quiet, neighborly life of Röcken, the tiny country village where he
was born. Naumburg would shrink as his own mind woke and
widened, of course, but the boy could not immediately realize in
what sleepy surroundings he would endure his early dreams. Over
the years this decidedly Pietist community, peopled in large part by
pensioners with their defensive pretensions, had lost its economic
position to Leipzig, its cultural eminence to Dresden, its political
boldness to repeated disappointment (even the intellectual center
of the Pietist movement had shifted to Halle), and it was now so
reluctant to grow or change that its population of thirteen thousand seemed to increase significantly when the three Nietzsches
arrived.

Nietzsche's mother, having lost her husband, then their child,
and somewhat at a loss herself, accepted the life of a widowed Frau
Pastor with a readiness to run from any risk unusual in one still an
attractive twenty-three; although, outside her husband's household, which continued to include his mother and two sisters, she
had little chance to obtain a decent livelihood. Pastor Nietzsche,
who suffered from Socratic fits of abstraction and debilitating
glooms, was as devoted a royalist as he was a Lutheran, recognizing, according to doctrine, the descent of divinity from God to

kings. He was outraged and humiliated by the revolution of 1848, when his son's namesake, Friedrich Wilhelm IV, bowed to the demands of an upstart rabble and, as a sign of submission, put on their rebellion's cockade. The pastor's brain softened, as they described such things then, and he died blind, in madness and despair, the next year.

In death, Nietzsche's father became what he only might have been in life: the simple good man, loved by all who knew him, whose shoes his son's small feet would grow to fill, and whose virtuous path those feet would faithfully follow. At the age of four, Nietzsche's future with his father was complete, but his future with his father's eulogistic figure had just begun. In *Nietzsche, "The Last Antipolitical German,"* Peter Bergmann reports that in the alley behind his new home, Nietzsche more than once heard, as though in a play he had yet to read, his father's ghostly warning voice. Of what did it warn him? Of disobedience, no doubt, although it would be more romantic to imagine that it warned him of his fate. "You are the image of your father," his grandaunt wrote upon the occasion of his confirmation, willing the resemblance, for at sixteen he was already beginning to doubt his vocation and smudge the family likeness. Nevertheless, Nietzsche would return to Naumburg with his own madness forty years later, and there, nursed by his mother as his father had been, he would affright visitors with the hoarse howls of his increasingly ravenous and unkempt death.

So, safely keeping to her husband's orbit, and wearing his village pieties like a medal round her neck, Nietzsche's mother took her son and daughter, Elisabeth, to nearby Naumburg, where the survivors, rejoining the two spinster aunts, squeezed into the grandmother's gaunt back rooms, submitting to her regimen and rule as well, while inadvertently completing the circle of skirts which was later to account, in many minds, for the philosopher's misogyny, and soothe if not excuse its sting.

Like many of Nietzsche's aversions, this one would be misunderstood. In his day, women not only carried the venereal consequences which would later infect him (as historical suspicion has it); they also bore much of the culture onward the way they bore babies; and, as the philosopher would diagnose and define their case, they had a community of ailments to show for their service. Among them the passive emotions flourished; resentment drove the buggy in which religious solace rode; misdirected energy was relieved by flashes of torpidity; female intelligence and talent went into the management of the male and the making of coquettes, shrews, majordomo mothers, humorless saints and drones. It was common knowledge that their masters—those self-designated kings of creation—could be led by the nose, if not by the penis, to whatever place it was wished to put them, and into whatever project it was desired their powers should be employed. Nietzsche clearly preferred unconventional and emancipated women like Cosima Wagner, Malwida von Meysenburg, and Lou Salomé. "Go to women?" he wrote, "Then take the whip," but in that famous jokey photo of himself and Paul Rée, pulling a cart like a pair of oxen, it is Lou's hand that holds the knotted rope.

The ultimate issue is an ancient one, which Nietzsche's hyperbolic rhetoric inflates but whose enlargement reveals a fatal equivocation. We are carried in the womb like pooches on a cushion, but after that the encounters of our wishes with the world are often as painful and damaging as the collision of cars. Sometimes we find it simpler to alter the world, bend it to our will (in which case we aspire to be masters of it, and call our knowledge of it "power"); however, we may instead find it advisable to alter ourselves, to redefine, redirect, or set aside our desires (in which case we shall seem to submit like slaves). What is critical is how correctly (and courageously) we understand our powers, and whether we are willing to generalize our condition and make a habit of our responses. If we are Stoics, we shall feel we can command nothing of the world and at best but a bit of ourselves. Tamburlaines may, for a while at least, have larger visions, more confident and grander aims. Frequently, unable to take matters into our own hands, like subtle Figaros, we manipulate the hands where matters do rest, managing ordinary men by means of bribery, blackmail, seduction, denial, and nagging; kings and queens by flattery, scheming, treachery, and petition; and the gods through priests, sacrifices, and by prayer. Our characters congeal around our choices, and our moralities make the best of it. So some of us grow up small boys, arrogant and imperious, inclined to throw tantrums when our wills are thwarted; others of us feast on renunciation, fattening our spirits until they poke from our bodies as our bones do; still others go about kowtowing to circumstances, crying that "what will be, will be," like the reassuring chirp of birds; or we sing instead the song the sirens sang, make an art of our passivity, prepare our bodies to be as drawn on as banks, and open our legs there like a purse.

Any observant childhood will confirm the fact that there is scarcely a crime that does not wear some virtue's face, or a virtue that isn't inwardly villainous. Nor is there a familiar moral quality we haven't long found the cliché's contempt for. In Nietzsche's case, these were principally, and most immediately, obedience, piety, chastity, modesty, neatness, industry, sacrifice, and service. Later mercy, pity, and sympathy would be added. Bullied by benevolence, the young are routinely made victims of virtue, and it does not take them long to realize, as they are forced to internalize their obligations, what other interests these serve: that stinginess becomes frugality in straitened circumstances, that honesty is a kind of spiritual disarmament which traffics, at the same time, in the brutalities of frankness, that neatness is an enemy of history and change, or that a disdain for frivolity is a form of fear. The traits that gain the medal for goodness do not make their owners lively or attractive persons. It is wit and energy, quickness and sensitivity, responsiveness and enthusiasm, skill and daring, we warm to—signs of vitality, in short—not the dozens of "do nots," however wholesomely embodied, which the authorities have thought up for their profit.

We become Stoics (if that is where we end up) not because reality is good and relentlessly rational, but because we feel powerless to affect events and are willing to be put in our place like a knickknack on a shelf, to cover ourselves, like our eventual graves, with dust. If we have to accept what we get, why not imagine that it's just what we want? Our early sense of the injustice of justice will soon be driven off with kicks and curses, like a stray, to be replaced by a blindfolded figure holding scales. Another scenario has us advising one reddened cheek to offer the other, since such a gesture calms the smiting palm, decreasing the slaps of our masters; and we celebrate humility and obedience for the same wise reasons of weakness. Thus—and inevitably—the strong promote programs of exercise for themselves while recommending rest to everybody else; the cerebral study chess and pretend its bloodless board is one of battle; while wimps practice patience, servility, and patriotism. Nietzsche bit our values as if they were suspicious coins and left in each of them the indentation of his teeth, because, for him, only the hard, not the soft, was genuine.

At sixteen or seventeen, a passage like this one from *Human, All Too Human* will read like a truth table; or, perhaps one should say, it ought to:

What fetters the fastest? What bonds are all but unbreakable? In the case of men of a high and select kind they will be their duties: that reverence proper to truth, that reserve and delicacy before all that is honoured and revered from of old, that gratitude for the soil out of which they have grown, for the hand which led them, for the holy place where they learned to worship—their supreme moments themselves will fetter them the fastest, lay upon them the most enduring obligation. The great liberation comes for those who are thus fettered suddenly, like the shock of an earthquake: the youthful soul is all at once convulsed, torn loose, torn away—it itself does not know what is happening. A drive and impulse rules and masters it like a command; a will and desire awakens to go off, anywhere, at any cost; a vehement dangerous curiosity for an undiscovered world flames and flickers in all its

senses. "Better to die than to go on living *here*"—thus responds
the imperious voice and temptation: and this "here," this "at
home" is everything it had hitherto loved! A sudden terror and
suspicion of what it loved, a lightning-bolt of contempt for
what it called "duty," a rebellious, arbitrary, volcanically
erupting desire for travel, strange places, estrangements, cold-
ness, soberness, frost, a hatred of love, perhaps a desecrating
blow and glance *backwards* to where it formerly loved and
worshipped, perhaps a hot blush of shame at what it has just
done and at the same time an exultation *that* it has done it, a
drunken, inwardly exultant shudder which betrays that a victory has been won—a victory? over what? over whom? an
enigmatic, question-packed, questionable victory, but the *first*
victory nonetheless: such bad and painful things are part of
the history of the great liberation.

In Nietzsche's case, disillusionment (of which he became the
magician in chief) seems to have been a gradual, even a gentle
process, despite the "shock of recognition" just described. He is
sent to Schulpforta, a fine school, where he is a successful student;
his mother watches his progress with a wary but deferential eye,
and his sister dotes. Adolescent ambitions, inflated dreams, a not
unmerited conceit, continue into middle age. His ideas will un-
dergo a radical change, but the metamorphosis of his emotions
will be incomplete. Nietzsche offers his worship, his belief, with a
youthful—though, later, a suspicious—ease, only to withdraw his
injured soul as if his body has been burned. He will idolize anything
—a field of endeavor, a period of history, ideas and individuals—
and each with equal ardency, only to see them come up short
when measured, not only against his own over-the-rainbow expectations, but against the far more agreeable standards they set for
themselves and claim to meet.

Nietzsche is headed for the clergy, of course, but he applies the
critical methods of research, then popular at his school in the study
of the classics, to traditional Biblical texts (much as an early hero

of his, David Strauss, had done in his revisionist *Life of Jesus*), and with predictably catastrophic results, too, because secular techniques will secularize their object, just as the Cabalistic methods of the Deconstructionists allow their hermeneutical suspect to confess to any crime; but his disaster had its own thrill, like Samson bringing down the temple, because Nietzsche now had the inside dope, the lowdown on those high ideals, and could wear his intellectual superiority as a medal. It became difficult, in Nietzsche's eyes, for a social form or a system of ideas to escape its origins, however hard it struggled, and this allegedly scientific, etymological method gave God's Word a natural source, an all too human mouth.

Although every philosopher has a hometown, time of life, and troubles, and no one is so naive as to imagine these may not intrude upon, deflect, or aim his work, philosophical ideas and their development are traditionally not supposed to stand or fall upon the character of their source or the environment of their birth, even though a knowledge of both may help us understand the philosopher's point of view; nevertheless, Nietzsche (like Socrates) will not allow his work to be adopted like a stray dog looking for a home. Philosophical positions should not pop up like billboards along the highway (PLOTINUS IS THE ONE!) (PLATO HAS THE FORMS!), as if an ad had been sent from an agency on high, or the message were pretending to be a pronouncement of Reason itself. Nietzsche wishes to persuade us, certainly, but not to think what he has thought or write what he has written; rather, he wants us to *do* what he has *done* (an attitude shared, apparently, by the later Wittgenstein). He wants us to become an exceptional kind of *self*, so that our speech and writing may have an exceptional sort of *source*. It is a quintessentially romantic attitude.

Most of his arguments appear in the form of parables, and much of his evidence is obtained from his profound understanding of himself as a psychological subject. It is not characteristic of philosophers to be so personal or concrete. In the passage I just quoted, we have only to measure our own rough awakening with the one it

describes in order to accept or reject the account in general terms
—hardly a decisive method of demonstration, yet, after all, something. David Hume, that renowned empiricist, looked into himself,
by my count, only once, and failed to find an impression he could
call "David"; the remainder of his evidence derives, as is so often
the case, not from the sensations he esteems, but from the shortcomings of his forerunners—or forestumblers, as they always turn
out to be. Nietzsche is neither genially sloppy in the gentlemanly-
English and cultivated-amateur manner, nor ponderously solemn
and cloudy in the professorial-German style. Is he, in fact, a philosopher at all? Perhaps he is a kulturkritik.

Some of the sophists peeved Plato; there is no doubt about it.
Envy and malice and petty spite are not unknown among philosophers, who have aimed many a low blow at one another, made
snide remarks, and written splendidly caustic pages. F. H. Bradley
and George Santayana were two of our better mudslingers. But
their sense of disgust or superiority—Bradley's toward Mill, for
instance—is not a functional part of their philosophy. Having exposed the shallowness of Mill's mind by traditional philosophical
arguments (presumably), Bradley then paddles the puddle as if it
were an errant pupil's backside. Nietzsche, on the other hand, is
anger and outrage; he wants to hear idols break; he wants to cry
out, as Amos did, that "God spits upon your sacrifices!" People are
to wake up to the pain of their oppression, the shame of their
exploitation; they are to understand the campaigns of hypocrisy
being waged against them; they are to stop following false prophets,
and listen to Zarathustra. Passion, not thought alone, inks his
pages. Dismay, exasperation, anger, outrage, disgust, humiliation,
disappointment: they fuel his philosophy, and it is little without
them. Exhilaration, joy, exuberance, excess: they feed it too. How
he hates being duped, being lied to. Especially by himself. How he
loves life when his headaches will let him.

So to write about Nietzsche, as is naturally and normally done,
in a scholarly, sobersided manner, analytically, striving for cool
clarity and academic understanding, or unhistorically, as if ideas

were blossoms which never saw stems, is already to deny him his claims and fall foul of his criticisms. To write about him in the Germanized French fashion now popular, or to Heideggerize him, is to tarnish his gleam and cover his confusions with confusion. The very pomposities he punctured now surround him with an atmosphere of self-serving artifice.

Gilles Deleuze, for instance, in an essay anthologized by David Allison (*The New Nietzsche*), writes about Nietzsche in a style at once pretentious and barbaric:

> The Eternal Return is the being of becoming. But becoming is double: becoming-active and becoming-reactive, as well as the becoming-active of reactive forces and the becoming-reactive of active forces. Only becoming-active has any being; it would be contradictory for the being of becoming to be affirmed by a becoming-reactive—that is, by the becoming that is itself nihilistic.

"Big books are big sins," David Krell observes in his study *Postponements: Woman, Sensuality, and Death in Nietzsche*, "but big books about Nietzsche are a far more pernicious affair: they are breaches of good taste." On the other hand, to adopt his style, to mimic his manias—who would dare? how could that be done? and would it not mean an unhealthy (certainly un-Nietzschean) submission?

Although not a gifted linguist, Nietzsche made an exceptionally rapid advance across his chosen field, for he was offered a professorship even before he had received his degree—an unheard-of honor, and one that consoled his mother for the loss of the son she hoped would be a pastor. In short, the scholarly road was open, and Nietzsche could have been swallowed and digested by the system as easily as a raisin in bread pudding. But he had discovered Schopenhauer, and soon Wagner, the classical Greek world, was more real to him than the god of Bach, the god of his father. Nietzsche's musical compositions were rarely esteemed, but he hammered away at the piano impressively and could lose himself in a crowd of notes, becoming as noble and energetic and poetic as they were, sweeping forward like the force of the will itself through the pure space of the spirit.

Wagner's pagan use of the pagan gods, his nationalism and the notion that one is best fed through one's roots, his overwhelming oceanic style and totalitarian dream of an encompassing art, above all his depiction of even godlike life as a contest, sometimes between primitive forces, sometimes at the more sophisticated level of song itself: all these appealed mightily to Nietzsche, especially when they were as palpably embodied as they were in the composer, or so solidly set forth in the composer's roosterlike sense of himself, where no barnyard was big enough, no walk that wide. They appealed for reasons that never reached reason, really, but, as Nietzsche himself suspected, expressed the longing that ran the length of his character—the length of his life—and essentially shaped his philosophical disposition.

The single substance of which the world was made might have been Matter; it might have been Mind; it might have been Energy or Spirit or some biological drive to survive; but, for Schopenhauer, it was Will (believed to be Will, I think, in a reductive mood, because things were felt to be willful—whimsical, stubborn, oppressive); and when everything is Will, Will—to *be* Will—had to will its own enemy, an opposite with identical features, as if the right arm were to be pitted against the left. And each of us is nothing but a bit of that big Will willing its quarreling twin. Our wills build their own houses and call them bodies, just as the world's body, at level after level, is such an objectification. Life is not suffering, exactly, although suffering is an almost inescapable consequence. In a word, life is "struggle." In a Greek word, it was *agon*, the term Nietzsche would use to push aside Plato's *logos*, since words were at war too. Why not?

The most immediate of Nietzsche's antagonists was his own body, which must have seemed an open rebellion of bones and organs, a mean and rowdy mob of ailments, altering with mood and clime, diet and exercise, capriciously coming and going in ways he could never control or reach an understanding of, although there was always the fear that his father's madness was his mentor and his father's death his present enemy. In Schopenhauer's scheme, which Nietzsche for so long a time embraced, this vigorously weak self was a materialization of his own will, a self which constantly had to be overcome; but what sort of self, he had to wonder, would waylay itself like a bandit on the road?

Aristotle's ethics is an ethics of health, a program of biological fulfillment and perfection of function, which aims to end in a man with more soul than most—with, that is to say, more actuality, more form, more mind—the species at a particular peak. In Nietzsche's ethics (which in some ways resembles Aristotle's) the hunt for health is metaphorical, like the military figures that parade through his prose as though they were troops in review. The health his morality affirms has been previously despaired of, and the higher, super-, overman is not a peak but a cloud. Nietzsche's imagery of belligerence has been discounted by some philosophers as another unfortunate case of poetry, but its metaphorical function does not make his language any less warlike, any less meant. His figures populate a dream, a dream they wish were a reality. "Onward, Christian soldiers, marching *as to* war," the song says— just a figure of speech—but soon the cross that's going on before is going off like a gun or a cannon.

Of course, the superman doesn't sport blue underwear: he is an artist, a saint of the lonely soul, a poet of new possibilities, a godlike creator; but never suppose that Nietzsche didn't wish his idealized superior spirit wore jackboots and could kick in some teeth. Nietzsche's fury is the fury of a disappointed—indeed, rejected— lover of Man, not the shrug of one who has always known Man was no bargain and not worth a baseball player's spit; his fury is not confined to his sickroom by design; and when he compares his books to bombs, he wishes them neither to come apart harmlessly like a piñata or a handful of confetti, nor merely to alter, suddenly, the placid state of someone's mind. He bloody well wants boom!

How he envies Richard Wagner—the successful pariah.

Nietzsche is forced to relinquish his professorship in Basel for reasons of health, but he has other reasons. His book *The Birth of Tragedy* has not been happily received by the specialists in its field: his critics see that its scholarship is unsound; that its case is based on special pleading; and for them *that* is its dubious originality. His students have drifted away, and disillusion—that old shade—has darkened his view of the academic life. Indeed, pursued by a clamoring throng of symptoms, he moves from hotel and inn to lodger's little room one day, then to a gracious spa the next, as if his pain could be left behind like an overlooked sock. He suffers frequent chills and fevers, horrible headaches, cough, diarrhea, vomiting, faintness, cramp, catarrh, sleeplessness, the discomfort of hemorrhoids and shingles, anxieties that lodge themselves like sand in his eyes, so that his eyes burn and run from pain and shame and weariness until they swell shut. He is cupped and leeched and blistered. He is souped and tea'd and put on diets. He takes long walks in the company of his thoughts, and dictates to his alter ego. Occasionally a friend or woman hired for the purpose will write things down for him, but the method is awkward, and his amanuenses often have annoying habits. They jiggle their knees.

Nietzsche's so-called aphoristic style is partly due to the conditions of composition his manner of life forced upon him. His thought proceeds in disconnected snippets formed between distractions, or, when there is a blessed period of painless weather, in big bursts like a fragmentation grenade. Nietzsche is terse at length, and grandiosely gnomic; going on and on is natural to him, the way *Zarathustra* was compiled, or *Human, All Too Human*, by adding one more book to the book, and then another; but a volume of a thousand and one aphorisms is as odd as one of a thousand and one epiphanies. Actually, he characteristically composes in Biblical chapters, full of parables and fables, and in sentences which almost line themselves up to be numbered, as Wittgenstein's do in his *Tractatus*, though, I suppose, for quite contrary reasons.

As his heroes fail him, the way he felt Strauss and Wagner did, by selling out, and his profession seems imprisoned behind the walls of cautious, regimented scholarship; as his quarrels with his mother and his sister, because of their differing beliefs, grow more frequent and acrimonious; when his friends drift away, no longer able to bear the company of his misery, and his few enthusiastic readers, too, no longer approach him; then the habits of the solitary become even more pronounced: he writes out loud as one talks to oneself, filling the void with his voice (*Zarathustra* reads as if monologued to a crowd of imaginary millions). He decides to say yes, to reject Schopenhauer, at the point in his life when pessimism seems confirmed; to continue against the grain when it fills the whole field of existence. So he continues to compose, though he can't read, can't see his own hand. He writes when his head can scarcely hear his shouts, praising his isolation, using it to see as only an insider—outside—can see. Otherwise, he is in bed with a migraine or a troubled stomach, wearily riding a train, escaping skies which the clouds cross too rapidly, or ducking a persistent drizzle, an enveloping fog. He endures cold winters in stoveless corners, shrouded in sweaters, but he can barely survive enervating heat, dust, windlessness, or the glare of the sun on his sensitive eyes.

Hyperbole is his *de trope* (I succumb to the temptation to say), and Alexander Nehamas's book *Nietzsche: Life as Literature* demonstrates its excellence immediately with a shrewd discussion of Nietzsche's multiple styles and his joint use of aphorism and hyperbole. Not only does the latter call out like a barker at a carnival, and even promise to reveal enticing secrets to the unsuspecting (as the sideshow may); it provokes the opposition that Nietzsche needs, because his texts, like Schopenhauer's Will, are written *into their own teeth*. This expansive, inflating figure, used in conjunction with a constricting form like the aphorism, finds its scope defined and its boundaries drawn. An aphorism holds hyperbole like a balloon in its tiny fist. I would add that hyperbole, by pushing against all limits, is experimental, revealing unexpected attractions in ideas which nobody would ask to dance, uncovering hidden weaknesses in proposals which would seem to stand well enough if not pushed.

"Go to women? Then take the whip!" is an exchange suspicious of itself. Exaggeration undermines. The overblown bursts. It is the correct rhetoric, all right, for an outcry in a rented room, a shout through the heart.

Nietzsche's chronic illness, his quicksilver intellect, his scornful attitude, his *agon*, yield him a very privileged point of view: a perspective on perspectives. One of his most remarkable qualities is his ability to see others as he sees himself, and then to see himself, first, as one in a mine does the ore in the earth, and then as one who breathes the dust of the roads, and then as one asway in a lofty balloon. Nietzsche praises Dionysus because Nietzsche is Apollo. He says yes because all the ordinary evidence favors no. And from the immediate weakness of his own upbringing—narrow, dogmatic, handed down—he draws his strength: an outlook that is original, wide, and free. (Not so free as not to be tethered, but tied, now, to a new tree.) Having dumped the gods, the elemental oppositions that the early Greeks employed to understand the world become checkers in his daily game. We could arrange their names in a dozen ways: forgetfulness and memory, participation and detachment, action and reflection, solitude and society, harmony and discord, sickness and health, et cetera—man and beast. And game it is. His is the only philosophy that grins.

The concepts that engage most of Nietzsche's commentators— the will to power, for instance, eternal recurrence, and the superman—function almost like lids, because they stop up a tendency in his thought and keep it from fully expressing itself. The genie, having worked its magic, is lured back into the bottle. Nietzsche is not a philosopher of subjects and predicates; he is a philosopher of verbs. He is not a grammarian, looking for rules, but an innovator and revolutionary who suspects syntax of many serious metaphysical sins. As a philosopher of flow, he reduces objects to the sum of their effects, denies the distinction between agency and action, and sullies every Kantian purity with his doubts and disloyalties. Like a number of other philosophers, whom he is not often believed to resemble, such as Hegel and Dewey, he hates fine lines and sharp distinctions; he habitually confuses psychology and logic; he has a smeary mind.

Since nature has no destination, the random rules. Free will is an illusion, not because the threads of fate are spun and cut by nodding, dotty, or malicious gods, but because chance holds in its hands every absence of reins. Action, without a cause that can be counted as a reason and serve as an excuse, is as whimsically willy-nilly as any turn of the cards. Society invents both cause and agent in order to assign responsibility and indulge its vengeance.

The argument for eternal recurrence, probably borrowed from Heine, can wear, for a time at least, a reasonable face: if the universe is made up of a finite number of indestructible elements randomly combined during an infinite space of time, then every event, and every combination of events, will certainly recur like ticks and tocks, yet more often than any watch can count. However, since Nietzsche denies the existence of elements in the ordinary sense, this argument is not of much use to him, although he employs it anyway. It is not clear *what* returns so eternally—in what degree of generality or in what detail: things? thoughts? courses of events? debacles? theories? crowning glories? types or cycles? my life in my favorite brown shoes—my life, as well, with a pair that's blue?—and every other variation, including nuclear holocaust on the eighth day? or will a world arrive in which pain precedes injury, fire means smoke? one where birds will walk west in the winter? where Rome will fall first and then pick itself up to advance toward Greece? What *is* clear is that the river you can't step into twice will circulate its water, its fish and its flotsam; will use and reuse its bottom and its banks; so that what passed once, and was celebrated for that fact will be back, not just twice or thrice, but thrillions of times, like a tireless loop-the-loop. Since what goes round comes round for no reason, Nietzsche treats every state of life as a culmination, an end, as if all the points our wildest arrows struck were, precisely, the bull's-eyes aimed at. This is not easy, for he also knows that throughout all change, the world will remain full of dupes, dolts, and fools. His yes (which could have been a no to an endless wheel of meaningless suffering) has been called esthetic, since he is treating life the way one must treat—for instance—*Finnegans Wake* or *coitus uninterruptus*.

The privileged point of view of the superman, similarly, tames what threatened to be a relativism run wild; and the same Nietzsche who marks down systems of philosophy from realities to fictions, who treats truth as an invention of predatory organizations, and regards good and evil as advertising gimmicks, dismissing free will like a faithless servant, nevertheless hires the misleading phrase "will to power" for its rhetorical effect, follows and flaunts his own truth like a fanatic, invoking it constantly in both books and letters, as well as urging fortitude, optimism, energy, honesty, and the like on all we hapless victims of circumstance, while condemning hypocrisy, willful ignorance, and every sort of cultural self-serving with the severity of a hanging judge.

Eternal recurrence and the will to power are not the only conundrums in Nietzsche (I do think most of them are best answered with a pun), and Alexander Nehamas attacks them boldly, head on. He has a good philosopher's handicaps, however, because Nietzsche's ideas are principally literary and function fairly well at that level; but the ambiguities of his concepts, as we scoot across them, increase with the weight on the skate and the depth of the cut; so that, over and over again, we can see the commentator's argument move away from the meanings of Nietzsche's texts the way a chemical analysis of pigments must carry us past the painting they constitute. One need not always agree with the manner in which Nehamas unties Nietzsche's tangles, or with how he harmonizes what are apparently conflicting passages, or puts up tidy fences around patches of fog, to appreciate the relative clarity of his approach and the undoubted brilliance of his results.

Nehamas's level of analysis is more appropriate to Nietzsche than most, but even he could profit by being obedient to the passage from *The Gay Science* he quotes: "Oh, those Greeks! They knew how to live. What is required for this is to stop courageously at the surface, the fold, the skin, to adore appearance, to believe in forms, tones, words, in the whole Olympus of appearance. Those Greeks were superficial—*out of profundity!*" The Greeks can be praised for their Apollonian pursuits (an appreciation of surfaces), because they have previously taken the Dionysian path, thus executing (as if in anticipation) one of Nietzsche's characteristic U-turns.

What Nehamas has done is to advance a hypothesis concerning the controlling center of Nietzsche's thought, which, if accepted, would make marvelous sense of a great portion of what Nietzsche has written. Then Nehamas tries to show that his construction can be safely inhabited.

Nietzsche wants to warn others against dogmatism without taking a dogmatic stand himself. His unparalleled solution to this problem is to try consciously to fashion a literary character out of himself and a literary work out of his life. In what follows we shall examine his solution. We shall ask what is involved in the creation out of one's own self of a literary character whose views are exclusively philosophical; what philosophical views about the world and life make this project possible; and whether the effort of turning life into literature escapes the problem of dogmatism and the necessity of turning nature against something that is also nature. [*Nietzsche: Life as Literature*, Cambridge: Harvard University Press, 1985, p. 137.]

The belief that Nietzsche was willing to exchange life for language should be attractive for a number of reasons, not least of which is the habit writers have, so helpless before the big bad world, of generally doing just that. It is their version of Faust's pact. Caught as he was in an ailing body, a body increasingly confined to a chair or bed, with a dim-eyed view from a rented room, even the painful scrawls that Nietzsche was increasingly obliged to attempt must have seemed to him shows of strength, and those features of language he felt he could control, and was healthy, alive, and at home in, a remedy for his skeptical isolation, even as he shaped, in his final work, those desperate outcries claiming greatness for himself. *Ecce homo*. Look *in* on me—upon the triumphant madness of my mind!

Nietzsche, of course, is a classicist, and trained in linguistics. Words are the Orphic wind-eggs of his world. Then, just as the power of a line, a scene, a character, an image, or a symbol in a literary work (I am not speaking now of their psychological impact upon a reader) can be best measured by the extent to which each modifies remaining meanings (such a range and reaching out of influence being one definition of the will to power); and just as the significance of a sign depends upon its differentiating functions (according to Saussure); so does an agent disappear into the enactment of its actions, and all things, like the words which name them, find their definitions dissolving within a complex and sometimes far-reaching system of relations. Although Nietzsche is aware that "classics" are created by institutions interested in furthering their society's cultural aims, esthetic characteristics are the only ones that seem to survive Nietzsche's critique of conventional values. Wagner may disappoint, but music does not, nor do the plays of Sophocles and Shakespeare. Not every hero has fallen, clay-footed, from his pedestal by the time Nietzsche comes to write *Beyond Good and Evil*. Beethoven, Stendhal, Heine, Schopenhauer, Balzac, remain, with the sole figure of Napoleon left to represent the political, but only because Nietzsche deems him an artist, not a corporal (as if, alas! that *excused* this small man's enormities). Nehamas has written a number of good pages on this.

Indeed, during Nietzsche's lifetime, the bitter abandonment by the best of the bourgeois—their artists—of the very class that had brought them into being, and the subsequent flight of these artists from politics, morality, and religion (as conventionally understood) into the exclusivity of their crafts, was considerable, if not complete. If Nietzsche is the philosophical organ of modernism, then that organ functions in a body that grew up like a town around it. Finally (an element, I think, that Nehamas does not sufficiently stress), Nietzsche's quince-eyed look at the history of ideas resulted in the denial to philosophical explanations of the reality they claimed to describe, and returned them to the language they were made of. Upon that return they became fictions. In a sense, *The Birth of Tragedy* is the birth of Nietzsche too, because it contains his major metaphysical discovery: that of an existential disjunction within the material continuities of nature. It also displays the liberated skepticism of his mind and the traditional character of his emotions. Many of his present admirers hold Nietzsche's philosophical biology against him, yet without it, and his dreams about the Greeks, you do not have Nietzsche.

It is with rueful longing, sometimes, that the naturalist in us undertakes to describe the life our longing calls "the idyll of the animal." We ponder the spider as it spins, and end in admiration for its patience, its persistence, the instinctive geometries of its web, even its ruthless indifference—a callousness it cannot be blamed for; or we track the lion to and from its lair, or watch the tiger in the tense alertness of its stalk; and we envy how organized the insects and animals are, how—to us—they seem always to express the essential; they know nothing, we think, of distraction, guilt, excess, anxiety, delusion, pride, shame (Nietzsche's example is a herd of grazing cows, unmolested by memory or foreboding, the present passing from one ruminating stomach to another as if life, when processed, delivered only milk); and how fortunate these creatures are, we imagine in such moments, because each of them possesses the superior efficiencies of its species; they fit without their measure being taken; whereas we perceive a painful inexactitude in our forms and functions; the fit is the tantrum we throw when we fail to find our station; and so we say we have great gifts instead, really contriving an excuse, since we have these gifts because we need them, because basically we are a handful of opposed thumbs: we don't know how to live.

Our knowledge, as philosophers tell us, may be our glory, but our curse is a weakling's dependence on it, and a suspicion of it, as if, instead of the wheel, we had invented the crutch. Or, rather, it is as if the crutch had invented us.

We have a hunch that our liver is as full of silent life as a mollusk, that our heart and lungs close and open automatically the way an eye blinks; we are also aware that hunger is as recurrent as history, that the sexual urge comes round again like the wheel of a fast car; so that the instinctive creature is there somewhere inside us where we both love and fear it (we can only hang on to life, Nietzsche said, like someone clinging to the back of a tiger); but unlike the bedbug, which can bite with its first breath, we require a babyhood to bellow and whine and wheedle our way through, during which time we are handed by society the habits we hadn't the wit to bring with us into the world, and repeatedly told by the same unimpeachable source that such and such traits, this or that ambition (constituting the character of an emperor or housewife, for instance, the ideals of an officer or priest), are as inborn as our bosoms or the shapes of our noses (God-given, not man-made); that the manners we shall be asked to adopt will be as natural as dueling or monogamy; that our pilgrimage to Mecca is as required as the one that sends birds flying south; or that our kowtows are as tied to our species as the fawning of the spaniel: bits of behavior which may be initially hidden, but which only need, like a deb, to be brought out.

So the sundering we sense between nature and culture lies not like a canyon outside us, but splits our being at its most intimate depths the way mind breaks off from body. It is still another version of that bitter bifurcation long ago decreed—our expulsion from Eden—although it differs from the apparently similar Cartesian crease across things in the fact that the two halves of us once were one; that we did not always stand askance like molasses and madness, logically at odds, but grew apart over the years like husbands and wives draw themselves into distant corners of contemplation. "Even the observant animals are aware," Rilke wrote, "that we're not very happily at home, here, in this our interpreted world."

Dionysus, the god of the grape, stands for a kind of metaphysical conviviality. Under his influence, we lose our sense of separateness, because our consciousness and its objects merge. Experience is no longer a movie. We become lost in life, moving as the sea moves. Guilt gone, shame gone, we are free to do—and be—without reproach, as animals are. Knowledge, for the Dionysian, is based upon the principle that only like knows like (that you have to be one to know one), and it hires out none of the tasks of life, but performs each of them as someone rounded to the world would: jack of all trades, jill of every skill.

Apollo, on the other hand, floats on top of the flux, casts concepts over chaos like nets—such nets as magically create their own fish. Like many modern artists who felt that their consciousness had become corrupted by certain of society's "civilizing" lies, and who wanted, consequently, to resee the world, philosophers like Schopenhauer, Nietzsche, and Bergson attacked the tendency of the mind to divide the continuous into discrete parts, to capture change in classificatory pens like cattle in a stockyard, and to replace experience with the ideas that described it, responding to notions, not to things—or, rather, fabricating things right and left: first filling the mind with thoughts, and then the world with their objects, like the most industrious middle-class manufacturer, miraculously making ice cubes out of what might really be steam.

Only an Apollonian could have invented Dionysus, because the Dionysian is too deep in the wallow ever to wonder.

In his personal life, this division represents Nietzsche's natural longing for an active role, his unconsummated desire for community, his loathing of the lonely sick man's obsessive introspection. It hardens the commonplace and almost innocent observation that "everyone has his own point of view" into an inescapably vicious parochialism, as if the pie, once cut, could never be imagined to be whole. At the level of rhetoric, the Apollonian disposes schemes and tropes like a general, while the Dionysian regards every format as concealing unscrupulous interests and threatens to expose and defy them all, so that to be carried away into absurdity is almost an obligation. At the level of concept, the Apollonian will distinguish even in a fog the low-lying from the highly piled, pea soup from gruel, whereas the Dionysian will treat every cut as a wound which needs immediate suturing. As far as art is concerned, the modernist's tendency toward parody and self-reference, for instance, is Apollonian, while its revolutionary extremism and love of excess is Dionysian. Any attack on things (such as nonobjective painting is perceived to be) will meet with the grape god's approval, not because objects as such are deplorable, but because the very fact of their definition is. Finally, at the level of ordinary life, and biologically speaking, the duality describes a consciousness fatally turned against itself and continuously engaged in civil war.

Man makes himself, covering the creature within (if "within" is the right word) with culture's various costumes. He surrounds himself with himself, so that even the wilderness is soon a plant in his park-sized gardens, a specimen that requires tending to stay wild. By minding his manners, man reaches the level of the all too human, only to become, as he does in some cases, a Western European or a Mandarin, and finally squeezing himself—fat foot for a thin shoe—into some petite subspecies like the French.

Nietzsche's complaint about civilization is not Freud's, or, again, Rousseau's. It has another emphasis. Pent-up instinct does not threaten the peaceful orders of society like a boiler about to burst from the pressures of its libidinous steam, for there is little peaceful, and nothing rational, in these designs, only expressions of hypocritical dominance, coerced subservience, unmerited glorification, and a systematic corruption of consciousness. Civilization is not worth repairing. On the other hand, recovering the savage's natural nobility is impossible. The phrase "noble savage" is an oxymoron. Nobility is a concept of culture. The question is whether man might not advance himself beyond his present miserable condition of interior and exterior tyranny into one less founded on lies, one less illusory, more satisfying and fulfilling. There is no Aristotelian seed, no primal potency, no indwelling great-souled aristocrat in infant form like baby Hercules, struggling to emerge in him; but perhaps an implantation might be tried.

Nietzsche's thinking sometimes appears utopian; however, its only U is the aforementioned U-turn it delights in taking. One cannot expect societies to improve themselves. They are fatally caught in their own coils. Only the individual who frees himself from each and every one of them, who stands apart, as though —in Nietzsche's imagery—on the peak of a mountain, has the opportunity to become exemplary. Nor is the exemplary man a representative man in Emerson's usage. Hitler, Stalin, and Mussolini stand for Man more appropriately than Goethe or da Vinci. Unlike Moses, when Zarathustra descends from his heights, he brings no tablets of the Law, but only his shining self. In this sense, Nietzsche's attitude is anti-political, un-ideal, and anarchistic to a degree that calls Kant to mind: it recommends the rule of oneself by oneself, of the alone by the alone.

What does a person have to believe, then, to believe in this essentially beliefless and desystematized system? One must believe that around the world, and throughout time, a very large number of comprehensive outlooks (including their corresponding cultural practices, of course) have been held—honored, loved, obeyed—by collections of people from less to large. One has to regard many— if not all—of these cultures as opposing one another in practice and contradicting one another in principle, either entirely or at some significant point. One would have to conclude, consequently, that only a few such practices could be correct, only a few such principles true, while most—if not all, again—must be wrong or false. Although a logical law is being invoked here, and no philosophical names are being taken, it remains the case that nearly every value system and significant outlook on reality is not only threatened with falsehood, as it were abstractly, but is false on its face—is risibly absurd, painfully silly, woefully confused, criminally corrupting, ruthlessly exploitive.

Nevertheless, these numerous hilarities (and they need only be held up to view, as Bouvard and Pécuchet do in Flaubert's magnificent annihilation, to provoke the profoundest and saddest laughter) have not prevented great civilizations from espousing them; from, in fact, being shaped and helped to their heights by them, whether Greek or Persian, Hebrew or Roman, Aztec or Mayan, Chinese or Yankee. In short, reality, whatever it is beyond our representations, does not compel anyone to a particular form of existence, or a particular set of values, the way it forces ants into hills, bees into hives, or baboons into their colonies. There is certainly no natural morality, in that sense, no true way of life.

It does not follow from this relativist premise that all modes of existence are equally okay. Some are a whole lot better than others, but that judgment cannot rest on any factual foundation, but on concepts like "freedom," "fairness," "form," and "fulfillment."

The Greek sophists had already seen that if virtue alters, like the weather does, from Athens to Sparta, then the truly fortunate are those who control the currents and can make it rain in the mountains and snow on the plains as they prefer. Nor are constitutions, traditions, and legislative assemblies the only forces, or priests and politicians the sole controllers. Weak of body and of intermittent mind, Nietzsche is nursed first by his sister and then by his mother, each of whom enjoys the pleasures of such powers, and has her plans. Finally, Nietzsche will be buried beneath the misreadings of his texts, and his message made to mean whatever sister or the sophists say it means, because Nietzsche has a biography which grows longer even in the grave. And he knew that at least the vehemence of his opinions would lie there beside him, just as the syphilis-induced madness of his mind was symbolically suited to dismay his final days.

At one time, in Western Europe, when Church and State were still important rivals, the cultural life of the people (its aspirations, moral norms, even the functions of its arts) were in the keeping of the Church, and remained in the realm of the sacred. The State progressively secularized or politicized the cultural arena, and Nietzsche foresaw the terrible dangers inherent in this development and opposed it. But he stood on the side of the Church without a church to stand beside. In the United States (that forerunner of every future) the separation of the two powers (desirable as the divorce is) has permitted commercial interests to take over culture and determine values, successfully invading and subverting both politics and religion. That conquest is what capitalism has come to signify. Politics and religion (as well as art) are now simply business by other means.

Having rejected Christian dogma and seen the Church's dominance pass to an even more resolutely vulgar and military-minded nation-state; feeling helpless, certainly, before the dismaying cultural forces then at work; Nietzsche lets his shadow fall upon the only world where he is strong. He ultimately adopts a Stoic posture, despite his denunciation of similar strategies of "self-discipline," concealing his inwardly aimed adjustments to society beneath a helmet of hyperbole and metaphorically aggressive shield-slapping. The esthetic impulse emerges most genuinely from the medium of its expertise, so that when Nietzsche works out upon himself, the self he shapes is cast first, like a shade, upon a sheet. It is a beguiling form, but one his fingers fashion.

In an exceedingly interesting, and often touching, collection of memories about Nietzsche called *Conversations with Nietzsche*, edited by Sander Gilman, Ida Overbeck, the wife of one of his oldest friends, writes:

> I always believed that Nietzsche, despite all opposition to Christianity, was not an enemy of religion, however aloof from it he stood, and that he was himself even capable of producing religious effects. The superman as a substitute for God and the doctrine of return as substitute for immortality, however, seemed not to be very tenable idealistic fantasies.

Just as activities that seem quite different from one another (such as adding a bar bill or rolling the dice to see who will pay it) can turn out, on inspection, to have the same form (as do climbing a ladder, of course, and advancing through the company, or polishing the silver and going to confession), so may convictions that appear quite opposite and antagonistic result in indistinguishable attitudes. Predestination (the faith of his father) and chance (the floozie he courted) have an affinity for each other, as does the view (he also went with) that reality is made up of the meaningless movements of matter, caroms that occasionally throw off an inconsequential spray of sparks we call consciousness; because each renders agents impotent before affairs, so that we are, in effect, riding on the back of a tiger, a cork bobbing upon an indifferent swell, or a character captured in an already written book. The importance of these doctrines, as far as the individual is concerned, is that they protect, enhance, and justify an attitude; they express a philosophical disposition; they don't merely, in some circumstances, seem reasonable or appropriate, or momentarily work in one's favor, although they may certainly possess such advantages; rather, they reflect an indigenous state of character and mind: of melancholia, impulsiveness, helplessness, paranoia, megalomania, anality, and so on. For the masters in any society, profit and power are an ideal's principal payoff, whereas its value for the individual often rests in the comfort, consolation, and security it provides. Honesty in a philosopher means that he will deceive himself first. Despite their professed allegiance to rigor and clarity, philosophers have joyfully danced to jargon's tunes and religiously carried out the rituals of obfuscation. The truth holds nobody back.

The superman is not a replacement for God. The superman is one of the elect. Eternal recurrence is thought to justify the fall of the littlest sparrow; and every evil in the world, insofar as it is a part of a work of art, only adds to the interest of the drama, like the blood on Lady Macbeth's hands. In addition to the many sympathies between Nietzsche's ideas and his father's pastoral ones, there are formal affinities too—between the rhetoric of the prophet Zarathustra, for instance, and that of the prophets Amos, Isaiah, and Jeremiah. In *Nietzsche's Zarathustra*, Kathleen Marie Higgins has placed Nietzsche's work very firmly within a context of traditional dogma. In the Christian drama of redemption, for instance, the future is past before it reaches the present. This is no less true in Nietzsche.

The two Nietzsches—critic and castigator, affirmer and celebrant—usually have different admirers. During his sad last raving days, according to a report in Gilman's collection of reminiscences, he was given to brooding and was largely unreceptive to his surroundings—playing with dolls and other toys.

> When states of excitement come over him, his mother best knows how to calm him down. She caresses him, speaks to him in a friendly tone, and when he wants to scream she fills his mouth with small slices of apple or easily digestible delicacies, which he then chews and swallows while growling dully to himself.

I think I prefer my Nietzsche without the bits of apple in his mouth.

AT DEATH'S DOOR:
WITTGENSTEIN

The Wittgenstein home in Vienna, it was said with some exaggeration, held seven grand pianos, a condition that certainly stamped it as Viennese. It also housed five sons, the first three of whom were suicides: one by drowning, one from a gunshot, one through poison. The two sons who remained often considered taking their own lives, too, but, through some inadvertence, did not. The family's three daughters fared better in this regard because, although just as much was expected of them, it did not include measuring up to quite so many marks or reaching quite such stressful heights.

In those days, if music appeared to be the rosy flush of Vienna's fame, suicide seemed its fever. The newsworthy surface of society was regularly ruffled by someone's dramatically premature demise. There was Otto Weininger, whose crackpot book *Sex and Character* Wittgenstein, in his early years, admired; Ludwig Boltzmann, important for his work in statistical dynamics, and one with whom, equally early, Wittgenstein wished to study in Vienna; the poet Georg Trakl; notables like the architect of the Imperial Opera House, Eduard van der Null; aristocrats of a rank as elevated as the Baron Franz von Uchatius, including actual imperialities such as the Crown Prince Rudolf himself—each a distinguished suicide.

For the old, dying is dismal and takes the shine from death. One has grown accustomed to the succession of small disappointments that makes up most of life, so the failures that have followed one about like a smelly, undismissable mutt now resemble a faithful, if antic, companion. The young, however—still so near the time when they were not alive that not being alive again exerts a powerful fascination—cannot help but look at the threat of the years to come and expect them to be as marked by loneliness, remorse, and triviality as those that they have so far survived. Success turns down no soothing bed of rest either, since it can seem to supply but the starting place for yet another, more arduous, climb. Life, they have to wonder (since they once had such hopes for it), life comes to . . . is for . . . what? And if life is so precious, why is so much of it—everywhere around them—habitually, extravagantly, wasted? If life is a meaningless chore, it is well one's chores are concluded promptly, and the mess swept. Thus the suicide skips dying and goes to death as through a door—a door he may slam, if he likes, as he leaves.

In households like the Wittgensteins', what is remembered of the mother is often pale as an old print tacked to an out-of-the-way wall: its image gray, stiff, still, ornately ovaled. It is the father who is the moving Figure, the Presence, the Ghost of the Olden Days. It is his chains that will send their rattle through the rooms and bind the occupants to a presence that is past, yet a past that will not release its outlived days to die away in rings of weakening reverberation, but one whose hold grows greater by being gone.

Gone, or for the moment far away, the Presence is enlarged by the erasure of what seems irrelevant about its actual Being until it can be simply felt as moral authority, heard as stern commandment, seen as shining example. That the Presence picks his teeth, is forgetful, frequently falls asleep and is afraid of dreaming: these foibles are mislaid; every sign of weakness is turned to point the other way. Whatever is ordinary fades until only a giant is remembered, one that is cross and condemnatory, implacable, its sentences certain, its judgments final. One thinks of the anger, the terror, the cringing obedience, the need to please, that Kafka's father inspired, and how the father's frown became a crease across his son's face, and how loathsome the son's sense of servitude was to both of them. For such a son, too, a role was reserved, defined for him from the beginning, waiting for him like his plot in the cemetery: to husband a wife, father her children, to head a household, to emulate a feared figure, to overcome, to succeed . . . in short, to be what he hated and could not compel himself to be.

Karl, who would occupy the Presence in this case, had a vigorous intelligence with an energy to match, and set a brisk, if not impossible, pace. He was quick of both head and hands, decisive, charming, bold, brutal (he became a successful industrialist), good-looking, confident, arrogant, witty (more German than Jew, he was loyal to his culture, not to God), a despiser of failure in any form, and of every form of humbug. Like the dyspeptic Flaubert, who compiled a dictionary of thoughtless thoughts in common use, or more likely Karl Kraus, who publicly exposed them, he snipped outstanding imbecilities from periodicals and papers and, in later life, sent them to his son Ludwig, who took custody of the collection.

To Karl's beleaguered sons an early death must have seemed the inherited fate of the family. In any event, Ludwig faced a life, as we read of it, that was remarkably free, almost from its inception, of those pleasures that fasten, like lions, young teeth to their meat; that tempt them to pranks, into forbidden explorations, or lead them to enliven dull routine with frivolity and flamboyance. There was, along his road, but rare success and frequent failure: success that was usually deceitful and temporary, and failure he took so to heart it could scarcely beat beneath the burden.

Dutifully enough, Wittgenstein begins the study of mechanical engineering in Berlin, but shortly finds an excuse to enrich his education in Manchester and on the moors near Glossop, where he designs and flies his own kites during aeronautical and meteorological experiments. This is 1908, when he's nineteen, and the flying machine is more than a dream. Although he had the inventor's handyman mind, in addition to the abstract intelligence he would later display, his attention quickly turned from the kite to the motor that would drive it, and then, by stages that were by no means direct, to physics and the formulas that expressed its principles (from the craft to its engine, from the propeller to the propeller's torque and the algebras of air, from the movement of molecules finally to the behavior of numbers). Wittgenstein flew to the fundamental as naturally as his kites and balloons rose in the wind, so that even when he whistled Mozart, the dexterity of his tongue and lips was still in the service of the logical articulation of an idea. One of his more dazzling—and puzzling—notebook entries runs: "Musical themes are in a certain sense propositions. And so the recognition of the essence of logic will lead to the recognition of the essence of music." Schopenhauer, whom Wittgenstein had been reading, would have put it the other way around: "Propositions are in a certain sense like musical themes. And so the recognition of the essence of music will lead to the recognition of the essence of logic."

Taught by tutors, and with consequently little training in how to plod through a discipline from one bleak peak to another, it was easy for Wittgenstein to appear to drift toward whatever was prior and basic and presumably free of the clutter and tarnish of applications. Very soon his father's funds were financing a sojourn in Cambridge, where he took in Bertrand Russell's lectures the way some people might take in the Taj. In no time he was suffering from that fever for first principles we call philosophy; that heavy hunt for ultimates that only skepticism, or the petty grind and pretentious rites of graduate schools, can cool.

Initially an eccentric, "unknown German," Wittgenstein eventually made known to Russell, and then to Moore and Keynes, to Lytton Strachey and other members of the rather notorious Cambridge society called "The Apostles" who endeavored with mitigated success to recruit him, a presence that was a furious jostle of warring qualities—of emotional highs and succeeding lows, of course, ranging from intense excitement to despondency, yet an active, elbowing crowd of all kinds of other contraries as well. He was shy but quick to correct his superiors. He had a poor opinion of himself, but he repeatedly required special treatment, and he regularly expected, for himself, an ungrudging suspension of the rules, since as low as he often felt he'd sunk, most of mankind still lay beneath him. If others understood their true condition, they would feel terrible, too. His misery, however, wanted no competition.

Wittgenstein's manners were formally aristocratic and coolly correct, except when he was excoriating someone's errors, because his pursuit of truth was often an excuse to be rude. He would feel bad about his behavior and apologize, but not without reminding his victim of the nearly sufficient reason that had provoked him. He believed that menial tasks were humbling and generally good for you, except when menials did them, and then they became demeaning. His taste was for an elegantly simple life, with the simplest part of it, of course, an absence of the demands others might make of him. He approached people as warily as an animal from the wild, one whose recurrent and natural impulse is to run away. Although he seemed unusually self-absorbed, driven in upon himself as one in pain, he sought in his studies the solution to problems of apparently the most impersonal and objective sort. He prized solitude, especially for his work, and was instantly furious when any course of thought was interrupted, yet he dropped round to Russell's rooms nearly every midnight to bounce ideas off those patient walls, or to recount his weaknesses and consider suicide. As Russell writes in 1912:

> Wittgenstein is on the verge of a nervous breakdown, not far removed from suicide, feeling himself a miserable creature, full of sin. Whatever he says he apologizes for having said. He has fits of dizziness and can't work—the Dr. says that it is all nerves. He wanted to be treated morally, but I persisted in treating him physically—I told him to ride, to have biscuits by his bedside, to eat when he lies awake, to have better meals and so on. I suppose genius always goes with excitable nerves —it is a very uncomfortable possession. He makes me terribly anxious, and I hate seeing his misery—it is so real, and I know

it all so well. I can see it is almost beyond what any human being can be expected to bear. I don't know whether any outside misfortune has contributed to it or not.

Stubborn, arrogant, critical, demanding, prickly, solipsistic: was it only his intellect that saved him from being principally a pain in the ass? Russell initially found him "obstinate and perverse." Very soon, however, he was referring to Wittgenstein, with affection though understandable condescension, as "my German." "My German friend threatens to be an affliction." Was he only a crank or really a genius? "My German, who seems to be rather good, was very argumentative." "My German engineer, I think, is a fool."

Consulting my own brief memory of the man, I am inclined to think it was not Wittgenstein's brilliance by itself that impressed Moore, Russell, Keynes, and the others, but the fact that he did indeed burn with a bright, gemlike flame; that his commitment was not merely quirky but intensely real; that he brought to his investigations the desperate energy and concentration of one whose mind has drawn a noose around its body; because if his reasoning failed to reach the necessary degree of clarity and insight, if it showed itself to be more than momentarily incompetent, then Wittgenstein might not decide upon another day of life, but choose suicide instead—hanging his head in order to throttle some sinfully inadequate thought.

The Wittgenstein of the *Tractatus* might be characterized philosophically as a romantic rationalist. He is a "rationalist" because he believed in grounds and foundations; because he thought that these were to be found in the fundamental principles of logic; because these principles, in themselves, were easy enough to understand and could probably be grasped in a single mental intuition, so that what difficulties there were would have to be ascribed to the shortcomings of the thinker, not to an inherent darkness or complexity in the proper objects of his thought; because one could make the move from logic to the world without damaging or mislaying all the latter's furniture. He is a "romantic" because he be-

lieved that thinking clearly, correctly, sincerely, completely, was
the central human obligation and a moral struggle; that one made
oneself, consequently, into a soul that could see, and then saw—
then plumbed and discovered—just as Rilke, for example, felt he
had to become a poet first in order to write his poems, rather than
become talented, wise, or strong, by trial and error, effort and
exercise.

In the realm of morals and manners, Wittgenstein disdained
principles and programs, justifications and excuses. Talk was a
screen for who knew what weakness. He made most of his decisions
in secret, because (although he would pace up and down through
his miseries with Russell) most talk disguised motives and entangled
the mind; it led others to think that they had a say and some
authority over your soul; it encouraged "saws"; it proceeded from
partial truths to arrive at falsehoods like a late train. One's acts
ought to spring spontaneously from the sort of person one was:
calculation suggested subterfuge; obedience suggested servility.
Hence his frequently brutal frankness, his lack of social concealment, his mysterious reversals of course and changes of heart.

Character was something that simply showed itself in the way
one thought, in the way one lived. Style and idea were inseparable,
so he rarely troubled to hide the fact that what was most important
to him was the course and quality of his own mind. It was, after
all, his art. His impatience with what he took to be lackadaisical
reasoning, philosophical obfuscation, or any weakening of intellectual resolve was severe and immediate, and based upon the identification of knowledge with virtue, and of the right to exist with
the claim of creative accomplishment. It was always all or nothing
with him.

I do not believe that Bertrand Russell had wings, so he can't
have taken the young Austrian under one, but he did gradually
grow fonder of this intense intelligence. Russell's treatment of his
friend does him great credit, I think. A hint of jealousy (or perhaps
envy) shows up later, but this is only a speck on what is otherwise
an unblemished record of magnanimous behavior on the part of

the older, more established, and more esteemed philosopher. Russell was a man, furthermore, of quite different cut and character from Wittgenstein's: sensual, worldly, keenly observant, calculating but capable of real devotion, and able on occasion to achieve the impulsive life that Wittgenstein longed for and, paradoxically, planned, yet could never achieve because his personality was far from free and easy, because it was, instead, neurotically impacted and impaired.

Wittgenstein makes immense demands upon Russell's time, his patience, his energy, his ego. In the name of philosophical truth, the student is mercilessly, sometimes scornfully, critical of his teacher's labors. Russell takes the criticisms to heart, however, only to find the easy flow of his work slowed, its course altered, its publication consequently postponed. Although Russell sometimes allows himself an impatient rejoinder, his appreciation of Wittgenstein's genius never weakens, and he welcomes his surly friend's regained warmth and return to friendship whenever it occurs. Russell reports to Lady Ottoline Morrell:

> We were both cross from the heat—I showed him a crucial part of what I have been writing. He said it was all wrong, not realizing the difficulties—that he had tried my view and knew it wouldn't work. I couldn't understand his objection—in fact he was very inarticulate—but I feel in my bones that he must be right, and that he has seen something I have missed. If I could see it too I shouldn't mind, but as it is, it is worrying, and has rather destroyed the pleasure in my writing.

Russell became aware of Wittgenstein's mystical tendencies very early. Still, his ardent young pupil's love of logic can hardly have prepared the positively inclined Russell for Ludwig's later romance with informality, or his repeated religious temptations. He did not immediately realize that Wittgenstein, in removing reason from the realm of religion, was really protecting faith from certain destruction. An urgent need for salvation pursued Wittgenstein always, and it intensified immediately following the First World War (during the time the *Tractatus* was being translated, titled, prefaced, and published by his English friends) when—among his choices for the future—suicide, teaching school, and a somewhat monastic withdrawal from society were the favored alternatives.

Wittgenstein distinguished himself as a soldier; and despite the hardships of many campaigns, the crassness of the common soldier, the repeated bollixes of a decrepit bureaucracy, the cultural limbo of military life—conditions that he patiently endured—the war perversely supplied him with something he desperately needed: an objective hell that could replace his private one, and an equally dangerous outside enemy. In the army there were not only orders of several sorts, aims of various kinds, discipline and routines; there were hands other than his own hand raised against him; there was death as it might come to a comrade as well as to himself, a death unwilled, even unexpected. Thus Wittgenstein performed under fire with that coolness that comes when a world gone mad asks for sanity from the asylumed, and through hardship and valor he recovered the ordinariness in himself, felt as his fellows felt, and had his small sins swallowed by more substantial woes.

Wittgenstein tells us that when he was about twenty-one, at a performance in Vienna of a mediocre play, the necessary word was nevertheless said (as if a random note had completed a chord in his heart), so that the possibility of a religious life, stripped of the theology that had previously rendered it unacceptable, became suddenly attractive and real. The revelation, if that is what it was, lay in the assertion by one of the characters that he was, in effect, "beyond the fell clutch of circumstances," that nothing bad could happen to him. Wittgenstein gave this bit of bragging a semi-Stoical interpretation, and it reappears later as one of the consequences of the *Tractatus*. The world is an ensemble of facts. Nowhere among these facts are there any values to be found, nor are any values connected to them by whatever devious means a philosopher may imagine. To all the chief questions of culture "it" is totally deaf; it neither promotes nor prohibits; it neither disdains nor cares. It's it, and that's that.

No manner of prestidigitation can transform a value into a fact (although existentialists pretend this is possible), but I am certainly free to affirm the world, as Nietzsche exhorts us, or to deny it, as Schopenhauer inclines. However, if that liberty were as real as Stoics (for example) think, why would I be tempted to view existence despondently when joy, instead, were happily at hand? In a suicidal mood, Wittgenstein writes to his friend Englemann:

> In fact I am in a state of mind that is terrible to me. I have been through it several times before: it is the state of not being able to get over a particular fact. It is a pitiable state, I know. But there is only one remedy that I can see, and that is of course to come to terms with that fact.

I think it is reasonable to suppose that anyone concerned to give an account of Wittgenstein's life would be determinedly interested in what—precisely—that fact was: its nature, its etiology, its consequences. For decades following Wittgenstein's death his followers (and he was a philosopher with followers in more than the usual sense) kept silent about what I presume they knew: the master's homosexuality. Would it have embarrassed them, even with the precedent of Socrates to stand on? They were certainly embarrassed by the mysticism in Wittgenstein, as well as by his intense moral concerns. My teachers made him out to be the same sort of hard-boiled positivist they were. He was the spiritual center of the Vienna Circle. His name could be joined with Russell's, of course, and with Frege's too, but with few others, certainly not with Schopenhauer's or Spinoza's.

While the frequency of homosexuality among philosophers is probably no more than average, it should be borne in mind that philosophy is a bachelor's occupation. Most philosophers are unmarried males whose consequently less care-laden lives encourage longevity.

The first volume of Brian McGuinness's projected two-volume biography, *Wittgenstein: A Life*, continues the pretense. Reluctant as McGuinness's pages are even to turn, they nevertheless present us with the picture of a pathologically driven personality whose prickly petulance and swings of mood we are forced unpleasantly to place alongside his philosophical achievements; whose passionate presence we can only intermittently glimpse in the letters of others, or in some lines of his own, but rarely in the biographer's pale, pussyfooting prose, through which little that is powerful pushes, not even the harmless letter p like a daffodil or a daisy—a letter that might stand for the point of it all.

All that McGuinness says about Wittgenstein's homosexuality is contained in two footnotes, which, if they could have been pushed a bit farther away, would have found themselves entirely off the page. The first, which refers to the philosopher's sexual preferences for the first time, we must wait until page 196 to receive. Then we are slipped the information in an astonishing "by the way." "This is perhaps the place . . ." McGuinness blandly begins. The question that elicits this "revelation" is whether Russell disapproved of Wittgenstein's homosexuality, whether it played any part in the cooling of their relationship. Probably not, is McGuinness's reasonable conclusion. There were so many others besides Keynes and Strachey, in all walks, in every way, since homosexuality in Britain is as common as schoolboy caning. Then why, we have to wonder, were Russell's letters to Lady Ottoline Morrell on that subject not quoted when so many others were? Why wasn't the issue raised when it was central to the story being told, rather than long after the uneasy fact, as is done in Ray Monk's far franker and more adequate account? Why did we have to learn at this time that "intrigue" is the biographer's code word (borrowed from Keynes) for homosexual flirtation, since it might have helped us understand his earlier account of Wittgenstein's election to the Apostles? And why did we have to pass through two-thirds of the book under the impression that our subject had a lively soul but no body?

The second footnote occurs 100 pages later, near the end of this volume, and it concerns that one "particular fact" that Wittgenstein could not get over. To the suggestion, offered by another writer, that the philosopher was experiencing guilt about his homosexual encounters, McGuinness does everything for his subject but take the Fifth. "I have not paid much attention to this hypothesis," he says:

> It is above all an unnecessary one, as I hope I have shown, and it is in fact totally incompatible with the frank discussion of Wittgenstein's difficulties which I for one have had with close friends of his from that time.

It is, however, the only hypothesis that makes sense. Instead of the offending proposal, McGuinness would have us accept hopeless simplicities instead: that Wittgenstein was tempted to suicide by the example of his brothers; that he felt he was not perfect; that he was in despair over the human condition; and that he was principally kept from the deed by the offense he knew it would give to his faith—factors that may have been important, certainly, and even sufficient, if we knew what they meant. McGuinness may have had frank discussions with Wittgenstein's friends, but he has not had one with us. We have no other choice but to imagine a man driven along the edge of life by sexual shame and unspeakable guilt, half hoping for the excuse (that combination of cowardice and courage) that would take him over the edge—out of grief into expiation.

Some of McGuinness's shortcomings as a biographer can be attributed to inexperience and a lack of literary skill. He often cannot make up his mind what to include, what to leave out, what quietly to decide, what openly to debate. There are indications that he has postponed—for a second volume—divulging certain information that we may badly need now. Although the Russell material is wonderful, he can't do much more than hand it to us. In any case, he is unable to revivify a scene or create any kind of narrative sweep, nor does he weave thought-lines and life-lines together very well (it is admittedly difficult); and he seems happy to refuse every opportunity to conjecture. His discussion of the *Tractatus* (as well as a number of other technical points) is not nearly careful enough to interest a professional and will be wholly confusing to an interested layman.

Furthermore, McGuinness's coyness concerning the sexual life of his subject leaves the reader wondering whether he has given no account of such a life because Wittgenstein didn't have one, or because evidence is massively absent, or because the facts are being suppressed in order to protect the philosopher's "good name," as well as the good name of unnamed others. Since McGuinness gives us no help with these conjectures, except by his silence to encourage them, the reader loses confidence in his guide and, in addition, begins to suspect the sources he cites, since Wittgenstein's followers (as I've already suggested) have frequently been jealous about the ownership of ideas, and overly imitative and protective of their teacher, even to the point of aping his stammer, his gestures of intellectual effort, his expressions of despair, and pretending to his impatience, aspiring to his arrogance. It is not just one disciple who betrays the master. All of them do. And the master who encourages sycophants begins the sellout by betraying himself.

There are a few vocations (like the practice of poetry or the profession of philosophy) that are so uncalled for by the world, so unremunerative by any ordinary standards, so inherently difficult, so undefined, that to choose them suggests that more lies behind the choice than a little encouraging talent and a few romantic ideals. To persevere in such a severe and unrewarding course requires the mobilization of the entire personality—each weakness as well as every strength, each quirk as well as every normality. For any one of the reasons that a philosopher offers to support the principle he has taken in to feed and fatten, there will be in action alongside it, sometimes in the shade of the great notion itself, coarse and brutal causes in frequently stunning numbers, causes with a notable lack of altruism and nobility, causes with shameful aims and antecedents. This has to be understood and accepted. Valéry's belief that every philosophy is an important piece of its author's autobiography need not be rejected as reductive; for whatever the subliminal causes and their kind are like, the principle put forth must stand and defend itself like a tree against the wind; it must make its own way out into who knows what other fields of intelligence, to fall or flourish there.

The psychological space between a work of intellectual will like the *Tractatus Logico-philosophicus* and the energies and organs supporting it, between the fears and foolishness and childish avowals of the unsophisticated self and the forms of its sophistication: these are far from thoroughly explored or understood. It seemed to me there was a chance, in McGuinness's book, to shorten some of that distance. But the steps taken have been tentative, as if the full truth about the breath within the trumpet might sour the tones the trumpet told, as if against the force of Wittgenstein's uncompromising search for form there was still some strength for shame.

EZRA POUND

I t is too easy—the name game—in this case.

Christened "Pound, Ezra Loomis." If used as a verb, "pound" means to beat. If used as a noun, "pound" signifies a unit of weight, a measure of money, pressure of air, or physical force. From time to time, apropos poetry, Pound wondered which should be sovereign, the verb or the noun, and concluded, if his practice may be entered as evidence, that the verb was most noticed when knocked off the sentence like a phallus from a kouros—"Spiretop alevel the well curb"—and when effects were hammered back into their causes with naillike hyphens—"Seal sport in the spray-whited circles of cliff-wash"—hence into a compaction like a headache . . . splitting.

As location, a pound sequesters sick animals and strays. "Places of confinement for lawbreakers" is the definition that immediately precedes Pound's name in *The American Heritage Dictionary*, after which we encounter the listing for "pound of flesh" and read of "a debt harshly insisted upon." Certainly a pound is a large bite by any standard, yet it resembles, in being Shylock's payment, the *neschek* of the Jews: money for the rent of money; not a gnaw, but, in the way it feels coming due, not a nibble either. It is a tax on use, this thinning of the dime, as if money would otherwise be free of entropy; although to put the bite on someone has come to mean to beg for a loan, possibly as a return of favor, where the request is clearly not intended to invite the interest of the loan's own teeth.

So one meaning of "pound" has a relative called "blood money." It suggests racial forfeiture.

On the other hand, the pound of flesh we subtract from the flank of a steer may increase our girth and relieve many a primordial anxiety. We call it "putting our money to work." Wear and repair, profit or loss, depends upon your point of view, the angle of the bank and the direction of the bounce. Our poet depended without protest, for much of his life, upon funds supplied by the family of his wife.

Ezra Loomis Pound was born in a tidy white frame house in Hailey, Idaho. Hailey was like the little mining town of song and soapy story, salooned among mountain-sized stones; yet when Ezra's father moved back to Philadelphia, it was to work at the United States Mint, unintentionally obedient to the resonances of his name. Consequently, Pound was Amurrican right down to the potato, right down to the silver and gold in them thar hills, or, as we complained of it during the Depression, to the paper in them thar bills.

Pound had a Homer for a father, and, following his Pre-Raphaelite devotion to whatever was medieval, an almost German love for the Greeks. Appropriate to this passion was his grand-mother's maiden name, Loomis. Penelope wove and unwove and rewove on one to put off her suitors, but the return of her hero was also artfully, persistently postponed, since he was usually stranded somewhere, an exile—as the poet would say—enisled.

Then there was his allegedly Egyptian initial syllable, *Ez*, which he said meant "rising," so that it could be followed by *ra*, which, of course, stood for the sun. His parents pronounced that ending, wrongly, "ray," but got the part about getting up in the morning right. It was a version he preferred for a long time. Everybody else's "Ezra" was Hebrew, a prophet's name meaning "help" and designating a scribe of the Law of the Lord. The Biblical Ezra believed in racial purity too, and castigated the Israelites for spilling their holy seed among strangers—taking strange wives and adopt-ing their ways. Pound's alternative reading, "Rising Sun," aside from the pun on his aspirations, sounded Sioux or Cheyenne rather than Egyptian. In the end, he settled for a folkmarked "Ole Ez," a designation backwoodsy, cracker-barrel, and American, clean through from clown to crank, and admirably suited to the village explainer he had become. Suffering a village explainer, Gertrude Stein said, was all right if you were a village, but if not . . . not.

On the way to that comfortable "old shoe" locution, Pound enjoyed learning that the phonetic translation of his name into Japanese would yield a joke: "This picture of a phallus costs ten yen"; as well as the fact that James Joyce had instructed his children, because of Ezra's kind monetary assistance, to address him as "Signore Sterlina." He invented Aesopian names for T. S. Eliot and himself. He was Brer Rabbit while Eliot was Possum, both down-South aka's, and as quaint as a picture postcard of St. Louis. He spent some time as E.P.—a memo signer's initial—and concealed himself behind various noms de plume like someone playing peekaboo: he translated a French thriller while pretending to be Hiram Janus (a two-faced American hick, we must presume), and signed the art and music reviews he wrote for *New Age* with the names B. H. Dias and William Atheling; whereas he was simply T.J.V. when he covered drama for *Atheneum* and Marius David Adkins on the day he was fired from a similar post at *Outlook*. It was not for shame he hid himself, because he padded his slender study of George Antheil's nearly nonexistent theory of harmony with old performance notices. As Alfred Venison he wrote terrible parodies of Tennyson. Pound also recognized the cute connection of his name with Robert Browning's Rabbi Ben Ezra even before Conrad Aiken began calling him that. These nicks, dimins, and anons were but a few of his personae, since he sometimes summoned the spirits of Andreas Divus, Sextus Propertius, Bertrans de Born, Arnaut Daniel, François Villon, Guido Cavalcanti, and others, including the tortured soul of the poet Ri Haku (whom misconception created when Ole Ez read the Chinese ideograms for Li Po as if they were Japanese), in each case in order to seize them for his muse.

He also liked to press his name into words like "EZthority," "EZucation," and "EZuversity," as if they were slabs of fresh cement (and in a manner now associated with the fast-food chain— "eggs McMuffin"), just as he constantly jostled the language and upset its spelling, not quite concealing his resentments and animosities behind the jocular.

Pound realized that some people thought he resembled The Savior, an appearance he did not neglect to cultivate; nevertheless, he worried more than a little about his Semitic look and claimed, concerning his given name, that "the goddam yitts pinched it as they did everything else." Of course, it was the Quakers who pinched it (if pinching, here, is possible), and his father who attached it to a family name as plain and workmanlike and literal as Smith, Carpenter, or Wright.

What's in a name? Pound would distort the names of people he came, for whatever reason, to dislike—thus Lincoln Kirstein was dubbed "Stinkum Cherrystein," and the radio commentator H. V. Kaltenborn, called "Kaltenstein"; "-stein" was apparently his all-purpose Jewish suffix. Gertrude Stein felt that people grew to resemble the name they had been given, as if it contained an important element of their fate. In the case of Ezra Pound, whose self was so problematic, around his first name there remained an uneasy aura, while his last had a weight too relevant to his obsession.

Ezra, whose person was mostly putty and pretense and whose home address was next door to Nowhere, invented a rude and outrageous "poetic" self to perform its dance in public. Behind an American air of confidence and bumptious arrogance, he concealed uncertainties, shyness, innocence, naiveté—American as well, Yankee as all git. He also hid his massive ignorance of nearly everything, including literature, behind a few out-of-focus facts and generally impertinent judgments, becoming, in this way, a person of opinions: views he then watched at work as children watch an ant farm. He used his undoubted generosity to insinuate himself into other people's lives, appropriating, if not their efforts, at least their reputations, to himself. He behaved a lot like a manager of prizefighters who has a stable of stiffs, one of whom he might send out against the opposition at selected times, and whose failures he would excuse and defend as energetically as he would crow over their occasional success. He created movements, galloped to the sound of every trumpet, railed and hectored, bullied and petted, aided and pressured, handing out advice as if it were alms; and while in the business of doing the Lord's work and waging the good fight, actually did win some big ones, really did assist some important writers at critical times (most particularly Eliot and Joyce), and did improve the state of poetry (although, listening to the pipsqueaking that passes for poetry these days, his improvements were not to be prolonged).

Pound was a pirate, and plundered selected texts as if they were captured ships. He embraced principles he rarely if ever practiced (like the vague admonishments of "Imagism"), maneuvered both behind the scenes and in front of the lights, always in support of "modernism," a movement in his own case oddly made of pagan materials, medieval mannerisms, and Swinburnean swan song.

Between them,

Cave of Nerea,
    she like a great shell curved,
And the boat drawn without sound,
Without odour of ship-work,
Nor bird-cry, nor any noise of wave moving,
Nor splash of porpoise, nor any noise of wave moving,
Within her cave, Nerea,
        she like a great shell curved
In the suavity of the rock,
        cliff green-gray in the far,
In the near, the gate-cliffs of amber . . .

Eventually form went one way and content another, the meter was thumped on a tub, and the message pasted like a label to the snake oil he was selling. When his work was right, it was as pure as a line drawn by Matisse. It possessed the pleasure of a sweet, long-empty song—monotonous, incantatory, sybaritic—descriptive of what was not, or was no longer, or had been at one time written of, and sounding as if it had been overheard while being whispered through the pages of the past like an echo from Nerea's cave, as if it came from the touch of a bit of lonely beach to the lap of a spent wave.

> And the wave
> > green clear, and blue clear,
> And the cave salt-white, and glare purple,
> > cool, porphyry smooth,
> > > the rock sea-worn.
> No gull cry, no sound of porpoise,
> Sand as of malachite, and no cold there,
> > the light not of the sun.

In *A Serious Character: The Life of Ezra Pound*, Humphrey Carpenter has measured out Pound's long, problematic life at about eleven pages per year. "Measure" is, I think, the right word. Differently than in many massive biographies, where the data sogs like the morning porridge into groddy heaps through which the author's spoon can be seen to have faintly stirred, here the disposition that has been made of what is known about Pound is always orderly and clear, with a minimum of fatuous conjecture, especially of the psychological kind, untrammeled by idiosyncrasies of style or pushy charm of manner, and with an apt sense for the proper weight to be placed on each detail of the life so as to balance it against the others, including a fine understanding of the role of the work, its quality and meaning, as it bears upon that life or is a product of it.

The course and character of Humphrey Carpenter's narrative is so subtle yet unassuming that the reader only belatedly realizes with what calm and patient control the biographer has permitted the mud of his study to settle so that a figure may emerge, and how free for his own responses he has allowed the reader to feel, although Carpenter certainly makes, and makes known, his own estimates. This book's covers do not enclose a volume of evasions and excuses, nor do they open on a courtroom or lead us to the analyst's couch. The scholar's high tone, averted eye, and carefully washed hands are not in evidence here; neither is the accusatory rant of the reactionary (with whom Ezra Pound had so much in common, in literary matters as well as political), and it is this splendid judiciousness—fair, lucid, calm, unflinching, complete—that distinguishes the biography, and quite beautifully enables A Serious Character, in Pound's fine phrase about the proper aim of verse, "to cut a shape in time."

As I followed Carpenter's account of Pound's career, rereading the poetry at each point where the level of the Life reached it, my memories of all those initial meetings with the man in his letters, and the poet in his verse, accompanied me, just as I imagine similar recollections will flavor the pages of many readers of the biography. I remembered the stunning impression that the early poems made: their lyrical intensity, odd phrasing, original line breaks, exotic qualities, the unashamed "this is poetry" feel of it, the sudden intrusion of the colloquial—invariably electric—nevertheless a contemporary way of speaking, which was then bent into strange archaic shapes. We filled our mouths with his lines, heard the word with Ezra's matchless ear, and listened to a noble, raucous, wrathful music.

Damn it all! all this our South stinks peace.
You whoreson dog, Papiols, come! Let's to music!
I have no life save when the swords clash.
But ah! when I see the standards gold, vair, purple, opposing
And the broad fields beneath them turn crimson,
Then howl I my heart nigh mad with rejoicing.

And in the letters I found a man my heart could hold close: exuberant, playful, dedicated, generous, and full of rage over all the right things. How he hated the Philistines—oughtn't we all?— and hadn't he shaken the dust of provincial America from his feet to walk the romantic paths of the troubador poets? hadn't he shoveled the nineteenth century, that hated age with all its bourgeois ways, into the grave? and blown outmoded sentiments into smithereens, and commanded us, instead, to make it new? brash? fresh? right? true?

And hadn't Ezra Pound befriended the young and supported everything experimental? and gone out of his way to encourage quality, however various, in Frost, Eliot, Joyce, Ford, Lewis, Williams? And when T. S. Eliot had ceased to be an affront and become a façade, Ezra Pound was still rattling his chains—a ghost, perhaps, but with the power to affright. And when T. S. Eliot had thrown that simple and popular plainstyle about his shoulders like a shawl, and turned into a regular pundito—despicable in his respectability—Ezra had continued to be complex, dense, and disagreeable—an irregular bandito—doing what we were all supposed to be doing: distancing ourselves from the ruck, our hand against every hand that wasn't thumbing its nose. So if you were not a friend and fan and follower of Ezra Pound, you were at the very least a simp and a lazily inactive enemy of art, and hence of all real advancement in man. It meant you were still in love with "that old bitch gone in the teeth / that botched civilization" we all took such easy advantage of, enjoyed, and gleefully rejected.

So when, in 1949, the first Bollingen Prize for Poetry was awarded to *The Pisan Cantos* by a divided and distracted and courageous jury, how we all rushed to the freshly drawn front lines in order to spit ink at our enemies. If we had reservations (and I had a good many), we left them behind as though they were ploughs, while our weapons were seized like the throat of the foe. Pound shouldn't have gotten the prize because *The Pisan Cantos* were, on the whole and with the exception of the now famous "Pull down thy vanity" passage, a chaotic and self-indulgent mess, and certainly not superior as a work to William Carlos Williams's second *Paterson* volume, against which it chiefly contended. Yet Pound should have gotten the prize because that was the most powerful punch which could be thrown at the reactionary's nose.

However, he had given aid and comfort to the enemy . . . and what an enemy! But he was now most wrongly incarcerated, plopped into a loony bin, and unable to stand trial or further embarrass anybody, since we U.S.'ers had stooped to a ruse of the Reds and called him gone in the head. If our society was going to treat literature with an indifference both casual and profound, it had no business punishing any poet for what that poet said. Still, should we show sympathy for this traitor and anti-Semite whose vile hatreds rise from his verse like steam from fresh dung? Nevertheless, there are lines here and there, lines like feathers fallen from angels; there are heavenly tones, and places where the words pace as only Pound could pace them, back and forth, as someone in meditation; and surely there should be a prize for that.

It is difficult to admit to a flaw in Flaubert, any lapse in late Cézanne, or to say that Schoenberg had perhaps not found the right way, or that certain magisterial albeit monotonous and soporific works of our Modern Movement were a mistake, a mistake worse than dreadful—merely dreary. It is difficult because the enemy is still out there, growing stronger with every so-called advance in the media, in the scoop-up profit of its enterprise and the passivity of the experience it provides, growing more Philistine, more commercial, more hopelessly "pop" during every advertising break, through every sappy sitcom minute.

Humphrey Carpenter has sailed serenely between those who would now just as soon forget the Problem of Ezra Pound and those who, just as intently, would like to get the bastard. Carpenter has accomplished this not by being either mealymouthed or serpent-toothed, but by making certain that when he was confronted with an esthetic judgment, he made one, and when he was faced with a moral judgment, he made that; and by not harping or playing prosecuting attorney; and by not shoveling loads of unpleasantness under acts of generosity or rhymes of genius; by refusing every special plea; and, above all, by keeping calm. He sees through Ezra Pound without, on that account, failing to see him. It is a feat worthy of salute.

In the United States, it can at present be taken for granted that a serious writer in almost every genre will be at least liberal. The "Poets for Reagan" T-shirt was a humorless joke. However, the camps of the early modernists in most of the arts (not in theater or architecture) were full of fascists, fascist sympathizers, and other lovers of on-time trains; there were many anti-Semites, sexists, denigrators of other races, upper-class apes and royalist snobs. The list is dismayingly long, shamefully familiar, and I shall not write it down. Although they may have taken over the esthetic left, their revolutionary fervor did not spell past the *g* in lives typically "bourgeois." Writers had not yet gotten used to the fact that in contemporary society their presence, their opinions, their work and its quality, mattered not a whit. The state would not alter its course half a smidge whatever their ravings, and the writers deeply resented this indifference. Robert Frost was adored as much for his white hair and his aw-shucks country manners as he was for his cold-comfort country pomes. Inside Pound there was a fuming Ezra, inside Eliot a droning Elder Statesman, inside Faulkner a bag of South wind.

We can follow, in Pound's career, the classic course of the disease that arises from the continued sufferance of social disdain and unconcern: how it begins in this or that specific instance of rejection; how the poet starts to glory in the fact of it, to form his very self in terms of such an image; how he augments the facts by acting within that definition and earning further and confirming slights; and finally, how a theoretical raison d'être arrives, after the fact, indeed, but in time to justify one's hostility as a perfectly honorable and adequate response to the connivance, animosity, and stupidity of the world.

Ezra Pound called the Jews yitts. My father called them yids or kikes, and as much as I detested his thought and its hostile tone, and refused to listen to any more bitter jokes about President Rosenfeld, I grew used to it; it did not surprise or shock. (Pound referred to the president as "Jewsfeldt" and "Stinkie Roosenstein.") Anti-Semitism was fashionable, and came in many cuts. There was the anti-Semitism of the snob, who viewed Jews with the faint distaste reserved for every nouveau riche and social climber; there was the economic anti-Semite, who associated the Jews with money-lenders and shylocks of all sorts, from simple shopkeepers to muni-tions czars; there was the religious Jew-hater, who still thought of them as Christ-killers; there was the political Jew-baiter, who felt they infiltrated the system secretly, seized control of it, and, in effect, went about poisoning wells; and there was the racial purist, the blood-taint anti-Semite, who feared, more than anything, the fouling of family lines and the mixing of races and was especially apprehensive about customs and qualities even faintly from the East. It was natural for these antagonisms to join and run together for a while like wild dogs, but they could separate too, and even snap at one another sometimes. Henry James's anti-Semitism ap-pears to have been mainly social, as we might expect, and T. S. Eliot's was probably of the same kind; whereas Ezra Pound's was principally economic and political. He certainly couldn't care that they'd killed Christ.

It was felt that even the safely assimilated Jew was wont to wear black beneath his gay party gear; that he had that funny skullcap to cover his nefarious thoughts; and that behind his practiced worldly smile was concealed a cunning Talmudic look. Jews slunk through society, clannish and conniving, in league with anything you didn't like, secret emissaries of the East, supporters of Commu-nism and revolution, and possessed of a guile gained over centuries of gulling the Gentile to get rich. Even in Hailey, Idaho, where there weren't any, they knew that.

The mind's well-being was the well that was poisoned. One doesn't own a little anti-Semitism as if it were a puppy that isn't big enough yet to poop a lot. One yap from the pooch is already too much. Nor is saying "it was only social" a successful excuse. Only social, indeed . . . only a mild case. The mild climate renders shirt-sleeves acceptable, loosens ties and collars, allows extremes to seem means, makes nakedness normal, facilitates the growth of weeds. Since the true causes of anti-Semitism do not lie with the Jews themselves (for if they did, anti-Semitism might bear some semblance of reason), they must lie elsewhere—so, if not in the hated, then in the hater, in another mode of misery.

Rationalist philosophers, from the beginning, regarded ignorance and error as the central sources of evil, and the conditions of contemporary life have certainly given their view considerable support. We are as responsible for our beliefs as for our behavior. Indeed, they are usually linked. Our brains respond, as well as our bodies do, to exercise and a good diet. One can think of hundreds of beliefs—religious, political, social—which must be as bad for the head as fat is for the heart, and whose loss would lighten and enliven the spirit; but inherently silly ones, like transubstantiation, nowadays keep their consequences in control and relatively close to home. However, anti-Semitism does not; it is an unmitigated moral catastrophe. One can easily imagine how it might contaminate other areas of one's mental system. But is it the sickness or a symptom of a different disease? Humphrey Carpenter's levelheaded tone does not countenance Pound's corruption. It simply places the problem plainly before us, permitting us our anger and our pity.

Donald Hall's luminous memoir of his meetings with Pound in *Their Ancient Glittering Eyes* reports that Pound repented of his anti-Semitism, calling it a mistake and a "suburban prejudice"; but the tone of that repentance is all wrong, suggesting that Pound had made some error in arithmetic on his tax forms which turned out to have unpleasant consequences. Anti-Semitism is not a "mistake," or even a flaw, as if it left the rest of its victim okay and in good working order. Like racism, a little does more than go a long way; it goes all the way.

Karl Shapiro, who had opposed giving the Bollingen Prize to Pound, wrote then that, in his opinion, "the poet's political and moral philosophy ultimately vitiates his poetry and lowers its standards as literary work." I think, however, that, although the poetry has certainly been vitiated by something, the evidence of Carpenter's *Life* is not that Pound's anti-Semitism was responsible, but rather that a virulent strain of the mistrust of one's own mind (a fear of thinking, like a fear of heights) and a habit of emotional disassociation were the chief culprits. Pound had no moral philosophy because he was incapable of the consecutive steps of thought, of the painstaking definition or systematic and orderly development of any idea. Carpenter wonderfully extracts and puts before us the faltering steps of Pound's "argument" in his *ABC of Economics*, for instance, and they are the staggers of a drunk. He dismisses *Guide to Kulchur*, with good reason, as a disjunctive mélange of rant and bile. Disjunction is Pound's principal method of design. If he saw the world in fragments, it was because he needed fragments, and because his psyche hated wholes.

In a whole, the various parts might get in touch with one another. In a whole, the grounds for their meeting might be discovered and explored; but Pound preferred spontaneously combustible juxtapositions, ignitions that would take place without the need of connection, as if powder and flint would fire without a strike, or any spark.

Pound took care never to interrogate the fragments themselves (because he might inadvertently treat them as wholes). He asked neither how they were constituted nor where they had been, just as he kept the pieces of his family in fragments: his wife, Dorothy Shakespear, in one place; his son as soon as possible in another; his mistress, Olga Rudge, in a third; their daughter in yet a fourth; and so on. He would seek out remote and relatively exotic figures to write about and translate (where he would not be so easily exposed, and where his cavalier way with data would go relatively unobserved). He perfected the snip system of quotation, and the snipe system of assault, never keeping to the field but darting about from concealment to concealment like an Indian. He created collages out of pieces of his mind, his peeves, his helter-skelter reading; and he flitted from enthusiasm to enthusiasm like an angry bee, because his enthusiasms encouraged him to sip, to fly, to sting. He detested academics (many of whom he bamboozled just the same), and I suspect it was because they "dwelled." They hung over and on to things; they wrung them like wash sometimes, leaving them flat and dry; but they did probe and pick and piece together. Pound wanted to treat most of his opinions as beyond question or analysis, beyond explanation, as if everyone ought to know what they were, and how they were, and why (Carpenter demonstrates this repeatedly); thus he protected the emptiness of his ideas from being discovered by keeping the lights in their rooms lit but never going in.

The poet's irascibility, his bullying, his bluster, his adoption of moral outrage, his name-calling, his simplifications, his omissions —how long the list is—work to keep the wondering, thinking, quizzing world at bay. If you are confident that four and four make eight, you may be bored if asked to prove it, but hardly angry and outraged. Vilification protects the self-evident from any self for whom it won't be.

It is always dangerous to define yourself, as Pound increasingly did, in terms of your beliefs: I am Catholic; I am an anarchist; I am a fan of the flat earth. An attack on them is an attack on you, and leads to war. You can fight for a cause and make it come about, but you can never make an idea come true like a wish, for its truth is—thank heaven—out of all hands. What could Pound do, built of opinions like a shack, but hate every wind?

Pound's letter-writing style (and then his public prose and then his poetry) exhibits the same traits. Hokey spellings, jokey downhome ruralities, punny inventions, undercut the seriousness of whatever's said, even when it is cantankerous. Caps give weight to words which otherwise wouldn't receive it, and offer directions to the understanding which could not be got from the sentences themselves, because neither feeling nor conviction arise from within this prose. It is all punched in from outside. Sentences often fail to complete themselves. The rattle of ideas is regularly broken by conceptual silences that open suddenly like fissures (the hiatus is more frequent than the comma), by leaps of thought that do not include the notion of a landing. Pound's wartime broadcasts from Rome on the fascist radio (which were the basis for charges of treason later brought against him) were clad in such homespun that a few thought he had to be hoodwinking his sponsors.

No. Ezra was in earnest. This was one role he would play

through to the curtain. As Carpenter's account shows (and it is a genuinely moving one, even when it must move through this sort of material), Pound regretted his internment; he did indeed become a man on whom the sun has gone down (in a phrase from *The Cantos*); but he never really recanted; he never admitted he was wrong; he took courage from his fears to the end.

What Pound was afraid to face (I feel) was the fact that he was not, himself, a self, that he was a bundle of borrowed definitions, including that of the poet. Carpenter quotes Wyndham Lewis's accurate observation that Pound was "that curious thing, a person without a trace of originality of any sort" except the remarkable ability to wear a mask, adopt a tone. "When he can get into the skin of somebody else . . . he becomes a lion or a lynx on the spot." Leslie Fiedler has wondered whether Pound wasn't principally a parodist, so dependent was he upon texts other than his own.

I have to agree with Carpenter that the well-known "Portrait d'une Femme" is more nearly a picture of Pound himself than its ostensible model, Olivia Shakespear. The lady is seen as a still sea crossed by trading boats and awash with shipwreck and driftgifts. The poem concludes:

> For all this sea-hoard of deciduous things,
> Strange woods half sodden, and new brighter stuff:
> In the slow float of differing light and deep,
> No! there is nothing! In the whole and all,
> Nothing that's quite your own.
>   Yet this is you.

It is true (I think) that most of Pound's best poetry is based upon the work of someone else, and stems from his ability to release another language into English. It was what made him such an excellent editor. Time and time again, in *The Cantos*, amid a barren and chaotic landscape, poetry miraculously blazes up, and at the bottom of that fire a Chinese classic like *Li Ki*, for instance, will be found fueling it, or some other distant text. With so little spring left in his own legs, he could still rebound beautifully from someone else's words, because they—not love or landscape or the pleasures and problems of life—were his muse. Like lighter fluid's flame, these phrases (where, paradoxically, Pound was at last pure Pound) consume themselves without leaving a scorch, mar, or any other trace on the page. Lines like these—flames like these—"lick."

> This month are trees in full sap
> Rain has now drenched all the earth
> dead weeds enrich it, as if boil'd in a bouillon.

In his role as a Modernist, Ezra Pound is a great disappointment. He was a minor master of collage, certainly a fundamental Modernist technique, but he valued content over form, message over manner; a lot of his best language was artificial, and, as in the lines above, almost purely decorative, as if it had to be torn from time and place before it could flutter at all: a lyrical oasis amid hate's acrid heat. Pound championed many poets and novelists, but not for long, and not always with real understanding; he didn't like much modern art despite his enthusiasm for Gaudier-Brzeska; and although he had a hand in the Vivaldi revival, and was linked in love with a musician, and composed an opera with which he paralyzed all available ears, he disliked Beethoven, is said to have been tone deaf, and took no part in the serious musical movements of his time, as either a listener or an advocate. Consigned by society to the periphery, he began to take an interest in, and choose, the peripheral, and like many American writers he began to fade, concerning himself more and more, as the years went by, with the crank he was turning.

I suppose most of us want to make a difference. Pound wanted to make a real dent—not (I am afraid) because his dent would make a difference, but because it would make him. If poetry proved impotent, he would turn to prophecy, to politics, to dreams. If he could not act, he could at least assume the posture. So the dent he made was a stage dent, one which would do to advance the action of the play, but which was contained within the inconsequential frame of the stage. Poet/prophet: they were together in the old days, but they were two roles now, and neither paid.

Humphrey Carpenter concludes his exemplary biography with, appropriately, fragments: a few summary pronouncements, none of them about money. The last is a word in the margin of the *Nicomachean Ethics* at a point in the Introduction where the translator is summarizing the Philosopher's views. "The life of Action," Horace Rackham writes, "has no absolute value: it is not part of, but only a means to, the End, which is the life of Thought," and Pound's marginal word is "Nuts."

What a lovely word game we could conclude these remarks by playing. It is a very American response—"Nuts!" It is what our generals say when they are surrounded by Germans and asked to surrender. It is what adolescents say when they mean "balls." It is what people called Ezra, so they wouldn't have to call him something else. It also involves just the right textual bollix, because for Aristotle pure act and pure thought are one and the same.

AUTOBIOGRAPHY

We live in a time, we're told, of self-absorption. No longer is mankind the measure: me now metrics me. I envision a piece of blotting paper slowly blotting itself to oblivion. Certainly if tribes are more interesting than nations, sects more important than a common faith, and minorities major, then what could be more majorly minor than me: me, me, more me, as Joyce writes, me and mine and all that I have done. Yet self-regard has never been enough. We want the regard of others; they are to be looking as we look; we want them to be absorbed by the same self that absorbs us: see me see myself as you should see me; remember me when I'm a ghost; watch me turn myself into a book.

The power to see ourselves as others see us is granted only to such disengaged observers as arrive from France by slow sail. Even my mirror puts just that bit of me before my gaze which I permit to fall there. I cannot see all round myself: not anywhere I walk or perch or if I quickly whirl about to come upon my rear and take it by surprise. I might as well be asleep to such sides of me as disappear out of the corners of my eyes. Nor is the ugliness of my gnarled feet evident anywhere within my skin where I alone can feel what splendid shape they're in. I think I have a winning smile, but to those on whom my smile is so winsomely conferred, the slightly turned-down corners of its lips convey despair, disgust, disdain—I know not what uninvited attitude in addition—and invariably, if in tears, though I argue my happiness like William Jennings Bryan on behalf of God, the weeping will convict me of a lie, as far as mere onlookers are concerned; because we really believe in no other consciousness than our own, and must infer the contents of another's mind from the perceptions which arrive in ours: from an overheard voice, its screams and groans and heavy breathing; from a body, its weight and posture; from someone's gait, the swagger; and from the face, its signs. And to the groan don't we affix our own ache, to another's risen flesh our yearning, to the sly wink our own conspiratorial designs?

It is safer by far, some say, to rely on behavior by itself to speak. History is something we catch in the act, and only acts have public consequences. Internal states are not even evidence, for pains can be imagined or misplaced, their groaning faked; better to see where the bone is broken or tooth decayed (John Dewey once argued that an aching tooth was not sufficient evidence of something anywhere amiss), and if I promise to give another all my love, it would be wise of the lucky recipient to wait and weigh what the offered love improves, and count what its solicitude will cost.

Feelings are not a dime a dozen, but the price of eggs is eighty cents. Which, do you think then, really hatches chicks in the yard?

Yes, as Aristotle insisted, the Good is what the Good Man does. Does the geologist need to infer an interior to his rock to read its past? Does the botanist really interrogate her plants? Does the zoologist attribute suffering to his frogs as he runs his scalpel round their gizzards? Why, we could weep a world of pain into a thimble and have hollow enough left over for a finger, since consciousness never struts and frets upon the stage, or occupies a locker in the dressing room.

Biography, the writing of a life, is a branch of history. It requires quite a lot of labor, and therefore, when such a work is undertaken, one would expect the subject to be of some significance to history as a whole. Yet, except for the *Encyclopedia of the Dead*, as Danilo Kiš imagined it, where everybody's obit is presently complete or in meticulous construction, the majority of mankind rest, as George

Eliot wrote, in unvisited tombs, and have left behind them nothing of their former presence but perhaps a hackneyed scratch upon a stone. Futility is the presiding spirit at every funeral.

Caesar's assassins did not stab him with their souls. In Hades, their shades are not stained by the murdered man's blood. That blood caked, that blood colored, only the blades.

Biography, the writing of a life, is a branch of history, but a broken branch, snapped perhaps heartlessly from the trunk, at the moment when Montesquieu directed the historian's eye to larger themes, and toward those general social aspects from which the individual's traits, he believed, had more specifically sprung.

Yet if my tooth aches, it is after all my ache, though you may be better informed than I of the swelling; if my heart is sore, that soreness is unique, though its heaviness does not even tremble the balance bar; if I am afraid, do not complacently say you share my fear and understand my state, for how can you know how I feel? isn't that our unpleasant complaint? isn't that how we reject so much sympathy—stale candy on a staler plate? since, to accomplish our death there are a thousand similar and similarly scientific ways, but inside that shutting down of the senses, there is a dread belonging to no one else even in the same sad medical shape; there is a large dread like an encountered rat, huge, as if fat as an idol, bearded like some ancient northern warrior, yet as indistinct in its corner, and as ineffectual as lint. We can't make history out of that.

Knowing has two poles, and they are always poles apart: carnal knowing, the laying on of hands, the hanging of the fact by head or heels, the measurement of mass and motion, the calibration of brutal blows, the counting of supplies; and spiritual knowing, invisibly felt by the inside self, who is but a fought-over field of distraction, a stage where we recite the monotonous monologue that is our life, a knowing governed by internal tides, by intimations, motives, resolutions, by temptations, secrecy, shame, and pride.

Autobiography is a life writing its life. As if over? or as it proceeds? Biographies are sometimes written with the aid of the biographee, and these few are therefore open-ended too, centrally incomplete, for death normally does the summing up, the bell tolls for the tale beneath whose telling the deceased shall be buried, with the faith that he or she shall rise again on publication day, all ancient acts only pages then, every trait an apt description, every quality of character an anecdote, the mind squeezed within a quip, and the hero's, or heroine's, history headed, not for heaven, but the shelf.

If we leap rapidly enough from one side of this insistence to its denial, from the belief that only I can know how I am to the view that only another can see me really, we can quickly persuade ourselves that neither self-knowledge nor any other kind is possible, and, so persuaded, sink dizzily to the floor. Of course, we might, by letting the two positions stretch out alongside each other and observing how these two kinds of information are of equal value and complementary, conclude that for a full account both the "in" and the "out" are needed. That was Spinoza's solution. It is usually wise to do whatever Spinoza suggests.

How does autobiography begin? With memory. And the consequent division of the self into the-one-who-was and the-one-who-is. The-one-who-is has the advantage of having been the-one-who-was. Once. The-one-who-was is furthermore at the present self's mercy, for it may not wish to remember that past, or it may wish the-one-who-was was other than the one it was, and consequently alter its description, since the-one-who-is is writing this history and has the upper hand. Every moment a bit of the self slides away toward its station in the past, where it will be remembered partially, if at all; with distortions, if at all; and then rendered even more incompletely, with graver omissions and twists to the plot by the play of the pen, so that its text will no doubt be subsequently and inaccurately read, systematically misinterpreted and put to use in yet another version, possibly by a biographer bent on revising the customary view of you, and surrounding his selected subject with himself, as Sartre surrounded Genet, as a suburb surrounds a town and slowly sucks its center out.

The autobiographer thinks he knows his subject, and doesn't need to create a calendar of the kind the biographer feels obliged to compile, so she may boast she knows what her subject did on every day of his life beyond kindergarten and his first fistfight. He is likely to treat records with less respect than he should, and he will certainly not investigate himself as if he had committed a crime and ought to be caught and convicted; rather, he'll be pleased he's got his defense uttered early, because he understands that the biographer's subjects all end in the pen. No, he will think of himself as having led a life so important it needs celebration, and as sufficiently skilled at rendering as to render it rightly. Certainly, he will not begin his task believing he has led a botched life and will now botch the botch. Unless, of course, there's money in it, and people will pay to peer at his mistakes as they pay to enter the hermaphrodite's tent at the fair—ladies to the left, please, then gents, thank you, there to the right, between the chaste screen of canvas. An honest autobiography is as amazing a miracle as a doubled sex, and every bit as big a freak of nature.

The autobiographer tends to do partials, to skip the dull parts and circle the pits of embarrassment. Autobiographers flush before examining their stools. Are there any motives for the enterprise that aren't tainted with conceit or a desire for revenge or a wish for justification? to halo a sinner's head? to puff an ego already inflated past safety? Who is smug enough to find amusement or an important human lesson in former follies? Or aspire to be an emblem for some benighted youngster to follow like the foolish follow the standard borne forward in a fight? To have written an autobiography is already to have made yourself a monster. Some, like Rousseau and Saint Augustine, capitalize on this fact and endeavor to hide deceit behind confession. Of course, as Freud has told us, they always confess to what their soul is convinced is the lesser crime.

How often, in one's second childhood, does one turn back to the first. Nostalgia and grief, self-pity and old scores, then compete to set the stage and energize each scene. Why is it so exciting to say,

now that everyone knows it anyway, "I was born . . . I was born
. . . I was born?" "I pooped in my pants, I was betrayed, I made
straight A's." The chroniclers of childhood are most always desperate determinists. Here their characters were formed; because of
this wound or that blow, some present weakness can be explained.
And how often does that modestly self-serving volume wear its
author out, or he becomes bored with his own past and forswears
his later years. Sometimes, too, Fate cuts the cord, and the autobiographer dies in his bed of love, still high in the saddle of the self.

Since it is considered unwise to wait to write your life till you're
entombed and beginning to show your bones, you may choose to
do it ahead of time, as Joyce Maynard did, writing her chronicle of
growing up in the sixties, *Looking Back*, at age eighteen. Why not?
our criminals are mostly kids; kids constitute the largest chunk of
our silliest, most easily swayed customers; and much of our culture
is created for, controlled, and consumed by thirteen-year-olds. Wil-
lie Morris, having reached at thirty-two what the jacket flap calls
"mid-passage," paints, in *North Toward Home*, his cannot-be-
called-precocious picture of the South.

Many lives are so empty of interest that their subjects must first
perform some feat like sailing alone around the world or climbing
a hazardous peak in order to elevate themselves above mere existence, and then, having created a life, to write about it. As if Satan
were to recall his defiance of God, his ejection from Heaven, his
yearlong fall through the ether, and even his hot landing in a lake
of fire for our edification. Still, he didn't do it just to make the
News. Some choose to write of themselves merely as cavers or
baseball players or actors or mountaineers, or create the biography
of a business. Lives of crime are plentiful, as well as those of
daring-dodaddies from the Old West. Others linger, like Boswells,
at the edge of events, so that later they can say: "I was there, and
there I saw King Lear go mad; I can tell you of a king who cursed,
who cried, who called for his fool, who sat slowly down and sadly
sighed. . . ." Nevertheless, by accident sometimes you will find
yourself in an important midst, Saigon falling around your person

like a tower of blocks, or, as fortune smiles, find that you have undertaken for the state some tasks that turned out more wellish than sickly; then an account of them, of how it felt to have grappled with Grendel, or smelled the Augean stables before Hercules swept them, or had the blood of an assassinated president sprayed over your shirt as you rode in his cavalcade; yes, then an account might be of value to future travelers who might not wish to go that way.

We have well before us the apparently noble example of Bernal Díaz, who was a foot soldier in Cortés's army. Annoyed by the incompetence of earlier authors, who spoke the truth "neither in the beginning, nor the middle, nor the end," he wrote his own *True History of the Conquest of New Spain*, and prefaced his honestly unpretentious work with this simple statement:

> That which I myself saw and met with during the fighting I will write down, with the help of God, like a good eyewitness, very plainly, without twisting events one way or another. I am an old man of eighty-four and have lost my sight and hearing. It is my fortune to have no other wealth to leave my children and descendants except this, my true story, and they will see what a wonderful one it is.

We believe him because what he writes "rings true," but also because, like Cephalus in Plato's *Republic*, he is now nearly free of the world and its ambitions, of the body and its desires. Almost equally wonderful is the account by Apsley Cherry-Garrard of Scott's last Antarctic expedition in *The Worst Journey in the World*, or James Hamilton-Paterson's luminous description of life on a deserted Philippine island, *Playing with Water*.

Nonetheless, these aren't autobiographies yet, for they're not full; and no one wants to wade through your parents just to get to the South Face, or read about your marriage in order to enjoy your jungle escapades; furthermore, many of these memories are so completely about a few things seen or endured or somehow accomplished that they are little different from the excited jabber of the journalist who has stumbled on a camp of murderous thugs (you've seen the film) or stood in the square where the martyrs were made, and whose account consequently cannot be called by that uncle-sounding name of Auto, for where is the "I," old "I," sweet "I," the "I"? Though the so-called new journalism, which Capote and Mailer practiced for a while, made even reporters into pronouns, disgracing the profession.

Of course, there are a few minds whose every move is momentous, and a few whose character is so complex, complete, and elevated, that we wish to know how? and why? and a few whose talent is so extraordinary, their sensibilities so widely and warmly and richly developed, that we think (naively, oh so naively) that they must have bounced out of bed like a tumbler, cooked morning eggs as if hatted like a chef, and leaped to their work with the grace of a dancer. We think them gods, or Wittgensteins. Just because their off-rhymes did not smell like something spoiled.

But he has a lifeful of private knowledge, our autobiographer. He knows of acts, small and large, that only he witnessed, only he remembers; she recalls a taste from an ancient swallow, or a scent that her lover loved but only she remembers, or a feeling on seeing her first egg cracked or baby beaten; yes, surely Lincoln recollects the rain on the roof when he signed the Proclamation; and don't you remember when you were a burgeoning boy whacking off in the barn before the boredom of the sheep—how the straw stuck to your sweater, and a mysterious damp darkened the bowl of your knees? Yet of just what use are these sensations to a real biographer, whose interest is in the way you lived solely because of its possible bearing on what you did? And whose interest in what you did exists principally because of the perplexities to which it led?

Between ego and object we teeter-totter. When the autobiographer says, "I saw," he intends the report of his perception to modify his ego, not merely occupy his eye; he is the prophet who is proud he has talked to God, not the witness who is eager to describe God's garb and what leaves moved when the bush spoke.

But now for a little history of the corruption of a form. Once upon a time history concerned itself only with what it considered important, along with the agents of these actions, the contrivers of significant events, and the forces that such happenings enlisted or expressed. Historians had difficulty deciding whether history was the result of the remarkable actions of remarkable men or the significant results of powerful forces, of climate, custom, and economic consequence, or of social structures, diet, geography, and the secret entelechies of Being, but whatever was the boss, the boss was big, massive, all-powerful, and hogged the center of the stage; however, as machines began to replicate objects, and little people began to multiply faster than wars or famines could reduce their numbers, and democracy arrived to flatter the multitude and tell them they ruled, and commerce flourished, sales grew, and money became the really risen god, then numbers replaced significant individuals, the trivial assumed the throne (which was a camp chair on a movie set), and history looked about for gossip, not for laws, preferring lies about secret lives to the intentions of Fate.

As these changes take place, especially in the seventeenth century, the novel arrives to amuse mainly ladies of the middle class and provide them a sense of importance: their manners, their concerns, their daily rounds, their aspirations, their dreams of romance. The novel feasted on the unimportant and mimicked reality like the cruelest clown. Moll Flanders and Clarissa Harlowe replace Medea and Antigone. Instead of actual adventures, made-up ones are fashionable; instead of perilous voyages, Crusoe carries us through his days; instead of biographies of ministers and lords, we get bundles of fake letters recounting seductions and betrayals. Welcome to the extraordinary drama of lied-about ordinary life.

Historians soon had at hand, then, all the devices of exploitation. Amusing anecdote, salacious gossip, would now fill their pages, too. History was human, personal, full of concrete detail, and had all the suspense of a magazine serial. History and fiction began their vulgar copulation, or, if you prefer, their diabolical dance. The techniques of fiction infected history; the materials of history were fed the novelist's greed. It is now difficult, sometimes, to tell one from the other. It is now difficult to find anyone who wants to bother.

Nowhere would one find the blend better blended than in autobiography. The novel sprang from the letter, the diary, the report of a journey; it felt itself alive in the form of every record of private life. Subjectivity was soon everybody's subject.

I do not think it should be assumed that history, which had always focused its attention upon wars and revolution, politics and money, strife of every sort (while neglecting most everything that mattered in the evolution of human consciousness, such as the discovery of the syllogism, the creation of the diatonic scale with its inventive notation, or three-legged perspective, to be for centuries the painter's stool), had found its final relevance with the inward turn of its narrative, for it now celebrated the most commonplace and cliché-ridden awareness and handled the irrelevant with commercial hands and a pious tongue, as if it were selling silk.

Our present stage is divinely dialectical, for we are witnessing now the return of the significant self. Prince—not a reigning prince, of course—Madonna, not a saintly mother, to be sure—stars of stadium, gym, arena, and screen, constellate our consciousness as history becomes a comic book, and autobiography the confessions of celluloid whores and boorish noisemakers whose tabloid lives are presented for our titillation by ghosts still undeservedly alive.

If we think about composing our autobiography in any case, where do we turn but to our journals and diaries, our appointment books, our social calendars? We certainly ask for the return of our letters and review all our interviews to see if we said what we said, if we said it when they say we said it, and whose tape we may have soiled with our indiscretions.

But what are these things that serve as the sources for so much autobiography? There are differences between diaries, journals, and notebooks, just as there are differences between chronicles and memoirs and travelogues and testimonies, between half-a-life and slice-of-life and whole-loaf lives, and these differences should be observed, not in order to be docile to genres, to limit types, or to anally oppose any mixing of forms (which will take place in any case), but in order that the mind may keep itself clean of confusion, since, to enjoy a redolently blended stew, we are not required to forget the dissimilarity between carrots and onions, or, when composing our apologia, the differences between diaries and letters and notes to the maid.

The diary demands to be entered day by day, and it is improper to put down for Tuesday a date who closed your dreary eyes on Saturday. Its pages are as circumscribed as the hours are, and its spaces should be filled with facts, with jots, with jogs to the memory. Diary style is staccato, wirelesslike. "No call from Jill in three days. My god! have I lost her?" "Saw Parker again. He's still the same. Glad we're divorced." "Finished Proust finally. Champagne." And you are already disobedient to the demands of the form if you guiltily fill in skipped days as if you hadn't skipped them.

The journal still follows the march of the calendar, but its sweep is broader, more circumspect and meditative. Facts diminish in importance and are replaced by emotions, musings, thoughts. If your journal is full of data, it means you have no inner life. And it asks for sentences, although they need not be polished. "I was annoyed with myself today for hanging about the phone, hoping for a call from Jill, who hasn't rung up in three days. She said she would call me, but was she being truthful? Dare I call her, though she expressly forbade it? I don't want to lose a customer who spends money the way she does." "Parker came into the shop, what gall! and ordered a dozen roses! I couldn't believe it! I know he wants me to think he's got another woman. God, he looked gaunt as a fallen soufflé. I think I'm happy we're no longer together. He never bought roses for me. What a bastard!" "Today was a big day, a memorable day, because today I closed the cover on Proust, I really read the last line, and 'time' had the final word, no surprise there. I feel now a great emptiness, some sort of symbolic let-down, as if a soufflé had fallen." You may revise what you have already written in your journal, but if you revise a passage prior to its entry, you are already beginning to fabricate.

Virginia Woolf's *Diaries* are therefore misnamed. We can see, in her case, as in that of Gide's, the tyranny of the journal, when, like a diary, it wants to have its day-to-day say, and we are led to imagine its keeper asking from life only something worth writing about, living through the light for the sake of a few evening words, and worrying whether her senses will be sensitive, her thoughts worthwhile, and a few fine phrases turned during yet another entry.

With the notebook we break out of chronology. Entries do not require dates. I can put anything in I like, even other people's thoughts. The notebook is a workshop, a tabletop, a file. In one of mine you will find titles for essays I hope one day to write: "The Soufflé as a Symbol of Fragile Expectation." Rilke's *The Notebooks of Malte Laurids Brigge* are misnamed, for the language is far too polished, the episodes are too artfully arranged, the perceptions are too poetically profound, and there is not nearly enough mess; however, if his fictive *Notebooks* really resemble journals, Henry James's *Notebooks* are the real thing: a place to plot novels, to ponder problems, to consider strategies and plan attacks.

All three—diary, journal, notebook,—are predicated on privacy. They are not meant to be read by anyone else, for here one is emotionally naked and in formal disarray. Unlike the letter, they have no addressee; they do not expect publication; and therefore, presumably, they are more truthful. However, if I already have my eye on history; if I know, when I'm gone, my jottings will be looked over, wondered at, commented on; I may begin to plant redemptive items, rearrange pages, slant stories, plot small revenges, revise, lie, and look good. Then, like Shakespearean soliloquies, they are spoken to the world.

None of these three—diary, journal, notebook—is an autobiography, although the character of each one is *autobiographical*. A memoir is usually the recollection of another place or personality, and its primary focus is outward bound: on the sudden appearance of Ludwig Wittgenstein in Ithaca, New York, for instance, or how Caesar said, "You too?" before he fell, or what it was like to go to bed with Gabriele D'Annunzio. Even when the main attention of the memoir is focused inward, the scope of the memory tends to be limited (how I felt at the first fainting of the queen) and not wide enough to take in a life. Lewis Thomas takes the seventy-year life with which he assumes autobiography concerns itself, and first removes the twenty-five in which he was asleep, and then subtracts from the waking hours all the empty and idle ones, to reach a remainder of four thousand days. By discounting blurred memories, self-serving reconstitutions, and other fudges, his count comes down a good deal more. The indelible moments left will most likely be found to occupy thirty-minute bursts. Such bits, he says, are the proper subject of the memoir.

What gets left out? that I read the papers. What gets left out? that I ate potatoes. What gets left out? that I saved my snot for several years. What gets left out? my second attempt to circumcise myself. What gets left out? the shops in which I purchased shoes, my fear of the red eyes of rabbits. What gets left out? what demeans me; what does not distinguish me from anyone else: bowel movements, movie favorites, bottles of scotch. What is saved? what makes me unique; no, what makes me universal; what serves my reputation; what does not embarrass the scrutinizing, the recollecting, self.

And if we make a collection of such memories, they will remain like unstrung beads, because an autobiography has to rely on what cannot be and is not remembered, as well as on what is: I was born; I had whooping cough before I was three; my parents came to Sunnydale from Syracuse in an old Ford sedan. Edward Hoagland's piece "Learning to Eat Soup" captures this feature perfectly, composed as it is of paragraphs made mostly of memories: balloons into which the past has been breathed:

My first overtly sexual memory is of me on my knees in the hallway outside our fifth-grade classroom cleaning the floor, and Lucie Smith in a white blouse and black skirt standing above me, watching me.

My first memory is of being on a train which derailed in a

rainstorm in Dakota one night when I was two—and of hearing, as we rode in a hay wagon toward the distant weak lights
of a little station, that a boy my age had just choked to death
from breathing mud. But maybe my first real memory
emerged when my father was dying. I was thirty-five and I
dreamed so incredibly vividly of being dandled and rocked and
hugged by him, being only a few months old, giggling helplessly and happily.

A good deal of what we remember is remembered from paintings
and plays and books, and sometimes, as above, these are themselves memories, and sometimes they are memories of books or
plays or paintings . . . whose subject is the self.

Testimonies, too, have powerful impersonal intentions. They do
not simply wish to say: I was there, I saw enormities, now let me
entertain you with my anguished account of them: of how I suffered, how I survived, remembered, yet went on; no—no—for
they, those witnesses, were there for all of us, were we, standing in
that slow-moving naked line, holding our dead baby across our
chest to hide the breasts, never staring at others in the row, mum-
bling a prayer in a vacant way—yes—this is our numb mind, mankind's misery, no single soul should bear it, not even Jesus, though
it's said he tried.

The Holocaust ate lives like a fat boy on holiday.

It is healthy, even desirable, to mix genres in order to escape the
confinements of outworn conventions, or to break molds in order
to create new shapes; but to introduce fiction into history on purpose (as opposed to being inadvertently mistaken) can only be to
circumvent its aim, the truth, either because one wants to lie, or
now thinks lying doesn't matter and carelessness is a new virtue, or
because one scorns scrupulosity as a wasted effort, a futile concern,
since everything is inherently corrupt, or because an enlivened life
will sell better than a straightforward one, so let's have a little
decoration, or because "What is truth?" is only a sardonic rhetorical question which regularly precedes the ritual washing of hands.

I know of nothing more difficult than knowing who you are and then having the courage to share the reasons for the catastrophe of your character with the world. Anyone honestly happy with himself is a fool. (It is not a good idea to be terminally miserable about yourself either.) But an autobiography does not become a fiction just because fabrications will inevitably creep in, or because motives are never pure, or because memory will genuinely fade. It does not become a fiction simply because events or attitudes are deliberately omitted, or maliciously slanted, or blatantly fabricated, because fiction is always honest and does not intend to deceive. It announces itself: I am a fiction; do not rely on my accuracy, not because I am untrustworthy, but because I am engaged not in replication but in construction. There will be those who will try to glamorize their shoddy products by pretending they are true, and then, when they fail to pass even the briefest inspection, like the movies *JFK* and *Malcolm X*, dodge that responsibility by lamely speaking of "art." Fiction and history are different disciplines, and neither grants licenses to incompetents, opportunists, or mountebanks.

Next, in our travel across this map, we encounter the autobiography disguised as a fiction, presumably to prevent libel suits; for if the disguise cannot be seen through, what is the point of it as autobiography? and if it can, what is the purpose of the disguise? Conrad Aiken, possibly for the sake of objectivity, probably to injure only those who knew the code, put *Ushant* in the third person. Whether confessed to or not, many novels are autobiographies in disguise—so it is often asserted—and the chief advantage of this strategy, apart from the fact that the novelist need only remember what springs most readily to mind and can avoid all the sufferings of scholarship, the burdens of fairness, the goal of truth, is that the narrator of a novel can whine and grumble and play the fool without automatically tarnishing his author's own character, which would otherwise be revealed to be spiteful, small-town, banal, and cheap.

In his *Memoirs*, Juan Goytisolo occasionally shifts into the second person, the almost accusatory "you," in order that he may be more lyrical, more deeply involved, while at the same time escaping the cell of himself to peer into the local hells, the personal nightmares, of others. (The italics in this excerpt are Goytisolo's.)

You can now evoke the time at the beginning of the sixties, when you interviewed for L'Express *one of the political prisoners freed by Franco thanks to the international campaign for amnesty. Twenty and a bit years in the Burgos jail, with no horizon beyond the distant square of sky and the close, too close walls of his cell. After getting out, problems of adapting his vision to intervening spaces: dizziness, sickness, headaches behind the eyes. An even worse lack of adaptation to the new reality not assimilated in his subconscious. During the first months in prison, he had dreamt regularly of open spaces: his house, the village, people and places he knew as a free man. Then, surreptitiously, this ozone layer had rarefied until it disappeared: he stopped recalling the world outside the prison when he slept. If he dreamt about his mother, his mother was in prison. If he imagined his village, it was a village behind bars. The prison had penetrated his inner being and allowed him no escape whatsoever. The girls he had known in his youth, heroines of his nocturnal libido, always performed in a prison setting. The military tribunal's punishment thus won after many years an absolute victory: not only a prison for the body, but likewise for mind, imagination, and fantasy.*

The destructive power of reality over his dreams still haunted him retrospectively after sixteen months of free movement. The new girlfriends he went to bed with were invariably prisoners in the murky, elusive world of his nightmares. The prisons where he had rotted—bars, walls, courtyards, warders—maintained a cruel force. A hermetic, unassailable camp with no possibility of escape, his inner world remained anchored in prison. [*Forbidden Territory: The Memoirs of Juan Goytisolo, 1931–1956*, translated by Peter Bush, San Francisco: North Point Press, 1989; pp. 69–70.]

I quote this bit at length not only to show how one person's biography becomes a part of another's; but in order to exemplify the autobiographical situation as some see it. Denmark's a prison if the world is one, and each of us, as Beckett has repeatedly suggested, lives in the cell of the self, which merely widens to include our friends, our family, our ideas, our pets. The self is a crocodile named Midas, and whatever it touches is instantly eaten; whatever it does is as much itself as its leathery skin; whatever it dreams is crocodilian.

Nevertheless, we should not mistake the adjective for the noun. A fiction does not become an autobiography simply because some of its elements are autobiographical; an autobiography is not a form of fiction merely because a few passages are mistaken, or misleading, or metaphorical. Just as anything properly called philosophy may be assumed to be philosophical without need of remark, so to describe a text as autobiographical is to imply it is not a biography of the self by the self but is employing somewhat similar data or attitudes or techniques. And normally we would not study the autobiographical in order to decide what autobiography ought to be. That would be putting the quality before the noun. And the quality hasn't the weight of the horse or the bulk of the cargo in the cart.

Perhaps the gravest misuse of the adjective concerns the unconsciously epiphanal text. Any word, any gesture, any act, may reveal some bit of the inner nature of its agent, and if we seek concealment, achieving it may seem easiest inside clichés, behind conformities, by means of immobility or any of those responses that are so entirely required by circumstance as to prohibit individuality: running from the bull; answering "hi" to "hi" and "fine" to "howyadoin'?"; dying when shot through the heart. But if Kafka puts a period on a piece of paper, we are shortly trying to lift it to look on the other side. "Yes, he ran from the bull but in a feminine way." "His 'fine' was flat as yesterday's soda." "Did you notice? he wouldn't say 'hi' till I said 'hi'; otherwise, he wouldn't have recognized me at all but would have skated by."

Freud preferred to examine the little tics that accompany more intentional behavior—our slips, mistakes, our silly errors—on the ground that these were free to be determined more entirely by the inner self. So a painting that is wholly abstract might be more revealing of the painter's nature than a realistically rendered city street, because on the city street the lamp would have to go here, the pub's sign there, the leaded glass beneath, and the narrow sidewalk would have to accompany the stretch of cobbles.

However, autobiography is about a different business: it is an intentional revelation that may in addition, and by its openness, conceal; but it is not a fundamental mode of concealment, which then habitually slips up. And the finer the artist, the less likely epiphanies will be plentiful, because the requirements of form are far more demanding than most determining historical causes, and create their own outlines, their own noses, their own internal relations.

In an autobiography, the self divides, not severally into a recording self, an applauding self, a guilty self, a daydreaming self, but into a shaping self: it is the consciousness of oneself as a consciousness among all these other minds, an awareness born much later than the self it studies, and a self whose existence was fitful, intermittent, for a long time before it was able to throw a full beam upon the life already lived and see there a pattern, as a ploughed field seen from a plane reveals the geometry of the tractor's path.

When we remember a life, we must remember to remember the life lived, not the life remembered. For first there is the stunned child, the oblivious child, the happy child, playing in war-torn streets, stealing rings from lifeless fingers, pissing down basement steps, bragging to his friends of the horrors he has seen; and then there is the old man he will become, looking back, horrified by the horrors the child was a party to, outraged by the awfulness of it all; or, conversely, pooh-poohing those few tears once shed over a broken balloon—unimportant to the wise old observer writing down the words "broken balloon"—which, when those few tears occurred, stood for total disconsolation and the child's first sense of how fragile the world and its pleasures are. Upon the child the autobiographer must not rest her knowledge of Greek, her memories of deportation, of her father's fascism, of the many untrustworthy men she has had to turn away; yet she cannot look back as if blind to the person she now is, as if unable to think or write as she now can, just because she is recalling the death of her father, and how he sat for several hours in his favorite chair before the fire, growing cold beneath the warmth of his familiar and friendly flames.

So shall we undertake, first, to describe the nature of this historian who picks now at the scab of his history? And to do that, won't we have to split ourselves once more, as M. Teste imagines, becoming the observer of our present self, the so-called autobiographer, the self whose life has been no longer than . . . six hours? since it was then we decided to write an account of our life . . . ten days? since it was then our spouse left the family house forever . . . or, eight weeks? since it was then our finances were found to have been fraudulently obtained . . . or, twenty years? is it that long since we've changed? if we ever have; if we haven't been Sir Walter Scott, the author of *Waverley*, from the day we were born, when the nurse came to our papa and said: You have a bouncing baby boy, sir, the author of *Waverley*, who has arrived at fully half a stone; as if our books were in our genes as well as in our definite descriptions.

That's not an entirely silly suggestion. When, in former philosophies, the existence of a soul or self was argued for, it was always pointed out that our birth name named us as a subject, not as a predicate; that the subject was that enduring and unchanging substance to which life's changes occurred, and if there were none such, and the self altered as a cloud, there'd be no nucleus around which our characteristics might circle like wagons, no title to the text of our doings and days. Autobiography (the noun) was the search for and definition of that central self (which might indeed be genetic), whereas the autobiographical (the adjective) took up the cause of the predicates and was concerned solely with the accidents of time and place, the vicissitudes of the instincts.

Reading, haven't we often encountered a passage which perfectly captured a moment in our own lives? in language both apt and beyond our contriving? Mightn't we then collect these in a kind of commonplace book, arranging them chronologically in order to demonstrate, not the differences between lives, but their sameness, their commonness, their comforting banality? Three or four or five such compilations might suffice to serve for all personal histories.

And if—as we might imagine—it was the substantive central self which watched us while our outside self shaved (not the mirror); and if it was that same resourceful eye which saw through our daily life's evasions; and if it were timeless, always the same, through defloration, divorce, remarriage; then there is a very good chance it is also the author of any true autobiography; it is the ageless ego which compiles the history of its aging Other, pitiless as it should be, remote, immune to praise; and if so, might not it be the case that we are jointly human (instead of merely animals of the same species), because that sleepless watcher, like an eye in the sky, like God was once flattered to be, is, in each of us, pretty much One, unchanging and unchanged, even in Mozart or Mantovani, the saintly Spinoza or the beast of Belsen?

IV

THE VICISSITUDES
OF THE AVANT-GARDE

The term "avant-garde" has had a strange and ironic history. From the main body of an army in medieval times, two smaller units were detached: one protected the rear during retreats, or from surprise attack, and sent back stragglers and deserters; the other was composed of a line of scouts who went ahead to seek out, test, and estimate the enemy. By the sixteenth century, when the term was first applied to a literary movement associated with Pierre de Ronsard and Joachim du Bellay, the avant-garde had become seditious, because its enemy turned out to be the very military unit it was supposed to serve. Thus the spacial image of a marching army was modified to describe a course of rebellious events that had a temporal shape instead: initial spark, fanned flames, full conflagration, final burnout, concluding ash, and consummatory cinders.

Certainly Ronsard's great odes broke every established rule. They employed shocking and bizarre language, including some peasant idioms and coinages of Ronsard's own devising. They introduced a new orthography and abandoned traditional French verse forms for classical ones. Above all, against the conception of the poet as a clever craftsman, Ronsard chose not to notice the irony in Plato's *Ion* in order to claim for the poet the inspiration of the gods.

Ronsard and his work were young when they were given this belligerent description. Certainly the image of an avant-garde made up of rambunctiously inspired graybeards is essentially comic. Repeatedly, in many fields, the young find their way blocked by middle age and settled success, so they try to outflank their adversaries; they call for change when often they merely want to occupy the comfortable chairs of their elders. Not only do time and repeated employment relax the rigid posture of their pens; so does the passage of centuries smooth the once revolutionary roughness of what they wrote. Thirty years after the appearance of his *Odes*, Ronsard is striking notes most poets have sounded since the art began. Dust has closed Helen's eyes. Brightness has fallen from the air. Alas, poor Yorick, where are the snows of yesteryear? At the gravesite of a grandparent, you contemplate death differently than you do when you have one foot in your own.

> We owe death a debt: our bodies and the body of our work;
> We die to begin with, and then the waves of many ages
> Roll up to wash away our words;
> This is the fixed intent of Fate and Nature.
> God alone lasts; of man's poor parts
> There remains in the end neither heart nor husk.
> What's worse, man feels, man thinks, no more—
> A fleshless roomer in a tomb of dust.

The delightful irony is that God is now dead, whereas Ronsard's words are still being read. Deep down, where they lie, most poets must relish this result. Why else would their skulls grin?

During the nineteenth century, the avant-garde adopted a tone that was essentially negative and oppositional, and its chief enemies were members of the expanding middle class, the so-called bourgeoisie. This increasingly influential segment of society still embraced a kind of religious patriotism that many intellectuals felt had been thoroughly discredited. The bourgeoisie also practiced an unprincipled utilitarianism, a greedy love of money and its powers that left them open to charges of hypocrisy.

Avant-gardes are fragile affairs. The moment they become established, they cease to be—success as well as failure finishes them off. Their unity depends upon a common "no," not on some "yes" that is jointly loved. And insofar as the movement moves at all, it requires the shoulders of many others at its wheels, support which most of the artists suspect is actually their exploitation. Poems must be written, paintings must be painted, but mere coffeehouse talk is not irrelevant to the success of the cause, nor are letters, broadsides, feuilletons, essays, reviews, catalogue copy, the quarrels of the cafés and the slanders of the salons; nor are tumults in the stalls, outrages of public decency, arrests, or other excursions and alarms.

Every effort to prolong an avant-garde beyond a certain point becomes of doubtful value, because an avant-garde can have but a mayfly's life: the artists have only their negations to chorus; both their attitudes and their art will alter as they age; society's methods of co-optation and disarmament will, in general, be effective; their anger will be softened by success and their aims divided, their attention distracted; the institutions set up by most Establishments, even if assaulted, will take longer dying than most avant-gardes can expect to live; while the strength of the support groups, so necessary to the energy of any movement, are even more fragile and momentary, depending, as they do, on the loyalty of a publisher, the generosity of a patron, the length of a love life, the cuisine of a café.

Artists who do not grow old gracefully, but rage and change through the whole of life, find themselves, at the end, alone with their innovations and not part of a refurbished movement. In that sense, the later works of Goya, Verdi, Monet, or Yeats constitute a solitary interior development whose deepest effects, like those of Turner's final oils or Beethoven's last quartets, are sometimes delayed for generations.

Ronsard wearies of the world. He retires from court, cultivates only essentials: his art. But he lives long enough to see the need for a new avant-garde, because the traditional enemies of poetry have returned; Ronsard's reforms have been betrayed or abandoned. Nothing has changed (including the rust on old saws). Ronsard

writes some verses concerning the declining times to his old friend
Simon Nicolar, which begin:

> All is lost, Nick, the bad grows worse;
> The empire of France is empty as a beggar's curse.
> Vice is king and virtue's fled,
> The nobles have taken novel whores to bed:
> Sly courtiers, clowns, a vile race,
> Do park their asses in the muses' place,
> Gamblers, crooks, and chatterboxes,
> Lickspittles, fops, and bobbysoxers. . . .

This ferocious Pope-like poem suggests—when we put it alongside
all the others, in different times and places, which express the same
sentiments—that when the avant-garde turns against the army it is
scouting for, it does so because it believes that army has betrayed
the policies it had pledged itself to support, and that this betrayal,
as well as the rebellion which is a response to it, is chronic and
recurrent, if not perpetual.

There appear to be at least three kinds of avant-garde. One, such
as the architectural modernism of the Bauhaus, of Gropius, Le
Corbusier, and Neutra, aims to improve man and his life; it naturally allies itself with other forward-looking agents of change (the
machine, for instance), and it preaches progress with the sort of
rosy-cheeked optimism characteristic of metaphysical Rotarians. It
tends to be impatient with the past, maintaining that little can be
learned from history but its errors, and fearing nostalgia above all
other passive emotions. Although the members of this avant-garde
are largely arty intellectuals, there is a sense of common cause with
the impoverished and downtrodden—a shared powerlessness. This
is what I call the liberal avant-garde. Its influence is strongest
among the arts that have a public posture (architecture, theater,
cinema). When the liberal avant-garde wants to become doctrinaire, it embraces the fascism of the Left. Picasso, Le Corbusier,
and Brecht are characteristic types.

The avant-garde of Gautier, Degas, and Flaubert, however, has nothing but scorn for these pimps of progress. The talismanic word here is "original," and the focus of the group tends to be on individual and artistic freedom, on disengagement and withdrawal. Artists in this second group are ready to take from tradition and often oppose the present by looking to the past. They have a natural affinity with the aristocracy, and in general their movements are marked by an extreme dislike of the masses. Their image of the artist is the individual in his isolation. This is the conservative avant-garde, the avant-garde of Rimbaud, Lawrence, Eliot, Pound, Yeats, and Céline, and it is most prevalent among the poets. When it wants to become doctrinaire, it embraces the fascism of the Right, and often shows, alas, a racist face.

Both of these avant-gardes occupied important places in the movement called Modernism. Both were wholly opposed to the state of affairs in which they found themselves; both felt oppressed by the Establishment; both sought to produce something "new" and something thought to be revolutionary. Whether formalistic or expressionist, they shared a dislike of what was central to bourgeois taste (i.e., philistinism): representation and edification. However, history was still linear for the liberal wing; for them not every utopia was totally tarnished; society of some sort was still worth saving; and art could, as in the old days, do the job. The conservatives regarded such avant-gardes as fatally contaminated by bourgeois values; for them, society was not worth rescuing, only art was. Again, however—despite the purity and freedom they advocated— their works were scurrilously critical and contemptuous, and hence revisionary with respect to values. There was no hope to be found anywhere that would lighten their point of view or soften their animosities.

The conservative avant-garde poisoned itself. Its dislike of society could not be confined to the page, score, or canvas but seeped into the souls of its artists. As in Flaubert's case, retching became a continuous condition. The liberal avant-garde failed when its social program failed; when the Left took over; when Modernism became, for it, the new rule of reason and the real source of righ-

teousness. The urban reforms urged by many architects were ruthless, arrogant, and authoritarian. Yet when the political thrust of
this avant-garde was blunted (as it largely was when it migrated to
America), its radical works remained, ready for a reinterpretation
that might return Brecht's plays and Miesian buildings to their
origin in art.

One interesting chapter in the history of co-option might concern itself with the eagerness and ease with which corporations all
over the world made Modernism their business image, the sky-
scraper the cathedral of credit, and the steel cage a manifestation
of commercial hubris, while the domestic work of those same architects was largely rejected. Avant-garde apartment complexes,
on the whole, did not prosper, and tract housing went ranch as
readily as souring cream. Of course, architects tend to begin their
careers with less extensive projects and scheme their way from
factories and shops to banks and office towers; nevertheless, the
percentage of domestic architecture in the corpus of Mies, Aalto,
Saarinen, Le Corbusier, and Gropius (for example) remains shock-
ingly small. The Weissenhof project in Stuttgart (which commissioned Le Corbusier, Oud, Mies, and others to design apartments,
villas, and row houses) is unique in Europe, and suffered for a
while from indifference and neglect. Wright, almost alone, worked
as a domestic, yet even his houses, eventually admired and criti-
cally influential, did not make it in the market. No Levittowns were
built of his low-cost and brilliantly designed Usonian houses.

It was also natural for painters to take on the coloration of their
patrons, and for artists in general to exploit the system that exploited them, becoming personalities for the press and pets of the
powerful. Many remained unsure of themselves for some time,
unable to decide to whom to sell their souls, while others—poets
and composers, mainly, who would have prostituted themselves
for a shiny penny—looked on with envy while fame and fortune
went to flamboyant virtuosi, tyrannical maestros, over-the-register
opera singers, and abject scribblers of rape and romance. Initially
confused by the liberal image that critics had reflected for them,

John Dos Passos and Norman Mailer eventually righted themselves.

The existence of a third avant-garde is more problematic. The activities of any such "group," whether artistically oriented or socially focused, are so determined by the times that to call one sort permanent seems to court contradiction. Yet I believe there are works to which habit won't have a chance to get us comfortably accustomed; works that will continue to resist the soothing praises of the critics, and that will rise from their tombs of received opinion to surprise us again and again. These works may pay a dreadful price for the role they have chosen to play, but if they are going to be a permanent part of "the" avant-garde (that avant-garde common to all kinds), they must remain wild and never neglect an opportunity to attack their trainers; above all, it is the hand that feeds them which must be repeatedly bitten. They have to continue to do what the avant-garde is supposed to do: shatter stereotypes, shake things up, and keep things moving; offer fresh possibilities to a jaded understanding; encourage a new consciousness; revitalize the creative spirit of the medium; and, above all, challenge the skills and ambitions of every practitioner. Such a pure avant-garde must not only emphasize the formal elements of its art (recognizing that these elements *are* its art); its outside interests must be in very long-term—if not permanent—problems. It may have to say no to Cash, to Flag, to Man, to God, to Being itself. It cannot be satisfied merely to complain of the frivolities of a king's court or to count the crimes of capitalism or to castigate the middle class for its persistent vulgarity. The avant-garde's ultimate purpose is to return the art to itself, not as if the art could be cordoned off from the world and kept uncontaminated, but in order to remind it of its nature (a creator of forms in the profoundest sense)—a nature that should not be allowed to dissolve into what are, after all, measly moments of society.

In order to define the permanent avant-garde, or even suggest its possibility, I must turn in particular to such works as Bach's Six Sonatas and Partitas for Unaccompanied Violin, Beethoven's Opus

111, Liszt's Transcendental Études, Bartók's 1926 Piano Sonata, Schoenberg's Suite for Piano Opus 25, Henry James's *The Golden Bowl*, Rilke's *The Notebooks of Malte Laurids Brigge*, Kafka's story "A Country Doctor," Joyce's *Finnegans Wake*, Stein's *The Making of Americans* as well as *Tender Buttons*, Beckett's trilogy, late Turner and Rothko, some Duchamp, Hölderlin's late piece "In lovely blue . . . ," the poetry of Mallarmé and Paul Celan, Malcolm Lowry's *Under the Volcano*, Italo Calvino's *Invisible Cities*, that most beautiful and disturbing of diaries, Fernando Pessoa's *The Book of Disquiet*.

The critical theories accompanying these three avant-gardes—to defend, explain, and ballyhoo them—have, in addition to such customary functions, another one that is just as important, although less advertised. That function is to disguise, both to itself and to others, how backward-looking this forward-looking group of revolutionaries is. The avant-garde looks over its shoulder at the main body, of course, and by making that look adversarial, turns against itself as well; for it was once part of the main body; it was born in that body; and while it will reject resemblance, while it will wish to forget its parents and desire to shake the dust of its cultural village forever from its feet, it cannot escape its genetic links, its childhood history, and all its early loyalties.

In retrospect, neither Impressionism nor Post-Impressionism were as avant-garde as they were once made out to be. (The only true cuckoo in their increasingly comfortable nest was Cézanne.) Because the plastic artists made merchandise, commercialism came to them first, and asked, among other things, for the continuous production of the newsworthy and the interestingly odd; and there were plenty of journalists ready to supply the necessary subterfuges, welcoming each new wave of the future with artificial wonder and bought applause, earning their daily bread with a daily puff. In addition, commerce found it desirable if the work of art could offer the public "a handle" or two in order to facilitate the item's sale and co-optation, if not in the form of sweet scenes and innocuous material (Utrillo's Paris, for instance, as opposed to an

Olympia who stares intently out of the canvas to discomfit the stare we are giving her), then in the shape of personal scandal and comic cutups (such as self-mutilation and madness—always excellent; syphilis acquired from native girls—good; drunkenness and drugs —okay, but routine; tough talk on TV), or the really regressive literary reading Surrealist paintings asked for, or the smile-inducing puzzles contained in Magritte's visual puns. Such handles can magically appear without much help from anybody. If Proust is now one of history's social pages, *Finnegans Wake* is a carcass on which doctoral candidates feed.

So even the most secure members of the avant-garde were not untouched by this tension between the old and the new, success and starvation. Between Joyce's many interleavings, we can hear a sentimental Irish tenor with a wine-dark voice, while Leopold Bloom's Dublin is built of the Realist's heavy bricks. Nor should we ignore the fact that decorating the present with the glitz of an imagined future (a habit of Japanese architects) is every bit as reactionary as the cosmetic activities of post-mods who doll up their façades with familiar and colorful fragments from gone-by times. Art, the honest article, lives (with other realities) only in an active present.

If there were, beneath the eternally changing seas of sameness, a submerged and unrelenting avant-garde, like reefs upon which pleasure vessels might occasionally come to grief, then there would also have to be—since the avant-garde defines itself through opposition—a permanent class of philistines . . . a proposition quite easy to believe. In the fifties, such writers as Nathalie Sarraute and Alain Robbe-Grillet tried to dismiss bourgeois concepts about fiction by describing them (character, atmosphere, story, message, content, and so on) as "obsolete notions," yet these obsolete notions have remained as lively in their obsolescence as they were in their heyday: performing a minuet with mummies, if not a dance of death. Even Marx is not immune. Consider the characters who cross the stage in that drama of his: commerce, capital, industrialization, technology, the clash of classes, social uplift, glib scientism, a tantalizing determinism with its promised happy ending. The ranks of the political avant-garde are filled with philistines. Who else would want to enlist? As Robbe-Grillet remarks, "One thing must trouble the partisans of socialist realism, and that is the precise resemblance of their arguments, their vocabulary, their values to those of the most hardened critics." Both Right and Left want their art to be mimetic, and both share a naive faith in the explanatory power of narrative.

In the history of modern Europe, three great sources of cultural dominance have established themselves, and therefore, since avant-gardes say no, there have been, for them, three opponents: Church, State, and Commerce (although now we would say Corporations). That is: religion, politics, and business. Although Modernism was made of many avant-gardes (some, like Symbolism or Cubism, profound; others, like Imagism and Futurism, shallow), they were all united in their opposition to the middle class, to the rule of monetary values and an unprincipled pragmatism. At that time, the "modern" still had the power to shame: the painters shocked their clients; the composers created a frightful din to dismay their listeners; the novelists tore their readers limb from limb. But by dint of the dollar, nothing now abashes these consumers, for culture has gone Pop, and where Pop goes, goes the weasel.

In this sense, the avant-gardes of Modernism—liberal and conservative alike—opposed the elevation of the bottom line, and in so doing, acted more like rear guards. Even in Schoenberg's day, the paradox was painfully evident. In 1918 Schoenberg founded the Society for Private Musical Performances. Alban Berg wrote the prospectus. The intention of the Society was to withdraw both music and its performance from the reigning system, already compromised by commerce, so that those who came would have to come in ignorance of the program. There were to be no reviewers. The works performed were to be adequately rehearsed, and the performers were to be the servants of the score. It was not long before an evening of Strauss waltzes had to be given in order to raise money to sustain the society. The names of the arrangers of the evening's waltzes (Schoenberg, Berg, and Webern) may have dignified a string trio; nevertheless, somebody else's music was all these great composers had to sell.

The marketplace has always been important (you went there to buy vegetables and goats); so has the begging letter been, the charming smile, the grant application, the flattering dedication, the buttering up of influential critics and patrons, the wheedling of favors, and so forth, since these sometimes put money in the purse you wished to open at the market; but bins of potatoes, sacks of flour, tubs of fish, bolts of cloth, the bank, the bourse, investments in oil or heavy water, Cos. and Corps.—what these businesses and commodities stand for—have not always been the decisive determiners of cultural worth.

The religious tradition may have been based on fraud and hypocrisy, but at least it claimed to serve transcendental values. The State may have been another liberator that became a tyrant, yet it, too, pointed its gun at the sky where the flag flew. Furthermore, in each case, there were doctrines to be adhered to, ideals to be followed, practices that promised an improvement to the spirit. Now it's all Vic Tanny. And ideals last as long as their symbols can continue to be sold for profit. We have at last reached the democracy of the five-and-dime. The cross that hangs around the neck and the T-shirt that displays a product's logo deal, as we know, with illusions; but now illusions are all equal, and my bumper sticker is worth every bit as much as your rosary.

Alas, no one assails the artist anymore, only their funding agencies. The railings of a utopian socialist such as P.-J. Proudhon belong, sadly, to another century, when a word like "form" could fill a shopkeeper's soul with a surge of anger.

Art for art's sake, as it has been called, not having its legitimacy within itself, being based on nothing, is nothing. It is debauchery of the heart and dissolution of the mind. Separated from right and duty, cultivated and pursued as the highest thought of the soul and the supreme manifestation of humanity, art or the ideal, stripped of the greater part of itself, reduced to nothing more than an excitement of fantasy and the senses, is the source of sin, the origin of all servitude, the poisoned spring from which, according to the Bible, flow all the fornications and abominations of the earth. . . . Art for art's sake, I say, verse for verse's sake, style for style's sake, form for form's sake, fantasy for fantasy's sake, all the diseases, which like a plague of lice are gnawing away at our epoch, are vice in all its refinements, the quintessence of evil.

Oh, to be lice like that (if ever we were), gnawing (if ever we did) at the scalp and follicles of civilization! To be sure, artists wanted to reject Mammon and have their Mammon too, but it was once romantically supposed by both audience and author that the poet's or the painter's motives were ultimately out of the ordinary—dedicated, pure—and the avant-garde artist's aims more admirably elevated than anybody else's.

Theology invented a besouled self so the soul could be damned, saved, and fought over; and the State did the same with the taxpaying soldier-citizen, who was English or German before he was conceived, and a kindergarten patriot before he was confirmed. Now Capitalism and Communism have given us the economic self: either the worker who is defined by what he produces, or the buyer who is defined by the goods he consumes. We may not have a classless society, nor be aiming for one, but we are all equally crass; high culture rests on the same penny-ante base as low; preference is power; and pushpin, as Bentham said, is as good as poetry.

In the act of attacking their enemies, the avant-garde declared those enemies to be their equals—the main body. Can we nowadays imagine any self-respecting artistic movement turning upon the comic book, the blood flick, the gooey erotic romance, minimal moonshine or similar musics, painted photographs as large as small buildings, sideshow sensationalism and other vocal groups, TV's endless inanities, as if these had betrayed some noble cause, or had lured us off the high road of art and onto the low road of love and other lyrics? Any avant-garde that believes itself up to the mo should have the High Moderns as its foe, but these artists are, in fact, among the avant-garde's few friends, and its only equal; although there is at present some doubt about even that, because the avant-garde itself—in name, if not in substance—is now a trademark for the trendy. Avant-garde condoms should do well, like those unrepressed avant-garde underpants. Even if a genuine note were to be sounded, it could not be heard, for commerce has filled the whole of cultural space with rock bands, celebrity trials, and other little cultural commotions.

In a large and diversified market, if the numismatics magazine can make a profit, any heresy can too. Against such a Medusa-headed enemy there is no point in calling yourself an avant-garde. Rebel against the Establishment, bugger all or any, and your check will be in the mail. Against such an enemy, there is nowhere to aim your anger; there is no real object for your scorn because business, they will tell you, is in the business of giving its substance away: to museums to put on "the Greatest van Gogh on Earth," to orchestras to replay the classics, to public television to emasculate the masters, to writing-program writers to succeed with the superficial where other superficialists have failed. And from the makers of merchandise themselves, well . . . what will not be richly forthcoming: commissions for bank lobbies and boardrooms, investment acquisitions by conglomerates, arty trophies bought by the intrepid bankroll whose cultural greed will one day be honored with a gallery enshrining its purchases.

When there is no windmill to tilt at—tilt not. At the present time one can only practice silence, exile, and cunning, except that "silence, exile, and cunning" is a cheer for the basketball team representing the Sisters of the Poor. Why be silent? Because if you open your mouth, your saliva will be sold as a prescription for something. Why speak of exile when you live very comfortably as a gargoyle facing a quiet quad? And your cunning cannot compete with those who smell new money the way—as the old joke had it —Napoleon smelled de-feet.

Many and various are the vicissitudes of the avant-garde, and it is true that now there is nothing that a group of this kind can do that such a group once honestly did; nevertheless, there is one sort of something—one theme, one theory—that throughout all common connivances cannot hang its head, although the old romantic myths of the artist have been remaindered and each of his motives questioned. "To live is to defend a form," Hölderlin said. It might be defended still, if painters refused to show, composers and poets to publish, and every dance were designed to be danced in the dark. *Non serviam.* That would be a worthy no.

But it will never be uttered.

Where shall we find breath enough to say such a long, long word?

EXILE

et us begin where we began—in darkness: a darkness in which there was yet no color to the skin, no distinction between thine and mine, no tangle of tongues, no falsely alluring ideas, no worries which might spread like an oil slick over our amniotic ocean; hence no hither-and-thithering either, no mean emotions, treacheries, promises, prohibitions, no lifelong letdowns. We began in a place where darkness really did cover the face of things, and not because the shades were drawn and the lights were out, but because darkness was our ether, and let us sleep. It was a world where *¿Qué pasa?* could be honestly answered: *Nada.*

What colored this darkness with calamity? We soon grew too big for our boots, our britches, and our own good. So the walls of our world moved against us, squeezing us out as though we were a stool: what a relief for the old walls, loose at last, lax as a popped balloon; but what confusion for us, now overcome by sensation, seared by the light. Some still call it a trauma—birth—and the earliest Greek poets bewailed the day just as the babies bewailed it, explaining that we cried out at the cruelty of being cast into the harsh bright air where perceptions and pain were one, where screaming was breathing.

Before, we had been in nurture and in nature's care, and although poisons may have seeped into us, or our genetic codes been badly garbled, all our exchanges had been innocent and automatic and as regular as our pulse. Now, suddenly, we were in the hands of Man; that is, in the hands of Mom and Dad, proud in their new possession, proud because they have fulfilled their function, happy because they are supposed to be happy, cooing their first coos, which will be our first words—*coup de coude, coup de bec, coup de tête, coup de main, coup de maître, coup d'état, coup de grâce*—while we wonder why we are wet and where the next suck is coming from, or why there is so much noise when we bawl, why we are slapped and shaken, why we are expected to run on empty and not scream when stuck or cry when chafed, not shit so much, and not want what we want when we want it.

Life is itself exile, and its inevitability does not lessen our grief or alter the fact. It is a blow—*un coup de destin*—from which only death will recover us, and when we are told, as we lie dying, that we are going home, we may even be ready to welcome the familiar darkness, the slumberous emptiness of the grand old days when days were nothing but nights. For the carved crusader merely sleeps in the stone above his stone, the lady rests her alabaster hands upon her alabaster breasts, the sword, her gown, the cross upon the shield, her smile, her diadem: they sleep too, until the Day of Redemption Dawns. Perhaps that is the last lie we shall be told, however, for the advancing darkness is a darkness we shall never even dream in. It will not be the sincere zero of a release after long suffering—a quilt-covered quiet, the past recaptured, a womb reoccupied—but the zero with the zero in it. It will not be the Nothing from which nothing comes, but the Nothing that is nothing but its no—and a no, in addition, that is nothing but the pure, brief round of its wholly hollow o.

When Adam and Eve were expelled from Paradise, according to the Christian story, death, pain, and labor followed them to serve as punishments for their transgression—for falling for the first apple that fell in their lap. With an orchard of pears, plums, and cherries to choose from—the Tree of High Times, the Vine of Accomplishment, the Hedge of Military Hardware, and the dense Bush of Indecision—what must they do but pick a piece of fruit a worm has recommended. For the Greeks, far wiser in my opinion, life was a sentence, the Denmark that made our world a prison, and the body was the coffin of the soul. That attitude became a poetic tradition, so that centuries after the Greek poets had grumbled that the worst thing that could happen to a man was to be born, while the best was to get to the end as quickly as possible, Guillaume du Bartas was writing:

> You little think that all our life and Age
> Is but an *Exile* and a Pilgrimage.

That things were better for us once upon a time—before the revolt of the Angels (all those puissant legions, Milton wrote, whose exile hath emptied Heaven to fill Hell), before the Fall, back in the Golden Age, prior to the Flood, the destruction of the Tower of Babel, when giants walked the earth, when there were real heroes, honest kings, and actual dragons, in any case before we were brought, through birth, into this brutality—is a belief that constantly accompanies us and somehow gives us comfort. The comfort, of course, is in the note of grace it lets us sound: that wretched things will one day be put right, and the wrongs of our distant forefathers finally paid for in full, and death will release us from present pain, and we can go home again to Paradise.

We continue to mimic these mythological banishments with ones of our own. The Greeks punished people by driving them out of their cities, by sending them into exile the way unwed former maidens were sent away from the door of their family home—with babe and blanket and much weeping—into the cold and falling snow. Even Hades was considered just another foreign country, a lot like Persia, where the barbarians bowed down to their superiors, sniffing the dust of their lordlings' feet.

As we invariably exclaim: how things have changed! A vast reversal of value has taken place. Children want to leave home and hometown, the sooner the better. Down-on-the-farm has been replaced by up-on-the-town. High on the hog is not where we choose to feed, but on the shrimp and the sole and the slaw in our low-cal life, a life through which—in lieu of jig—we jog. Money is our country now. We go where it goes—we followers of the cash flow. There is nothing more seductive than the bottom line. Money makes the world go around, the song says, but the world keeps the wheel of fortune spinning, and that's as warming as the Gulf Stream to us all.

Money. The Japanese make it. Hong Kong smuggles it. Singapore launders it. The Swiss hoard it for everybody. The Italians style it. The French flavor it. The Germans mark it. Americans lose it. The English pout. The Russians long. The Chinese make change.

Increasingly, to be exiled means to be sent to a place where you can't conduct any business.

In our brave new world, there isn't a single exciting word that won't fit upon a billboard. Pictures contain our immediate information. We go blank when the screen does. Our previous definition of the human—that we reason; that we reflect upon ourselves; that we make tools, we speak—is in the shop for microchip repairs. We are really, when you count performance and tabulate behavior, not supercomputers but a lot like locusts, little chafing dishes maybe, small woks, modest ovens, simple furnaces, barbecue pits and picnic grills: we consume. A universe is burning—a forest for our flame.

We number ourselves now in billions, a profusion so dangerous that were we, all told, to fart in unison, we would flatulate and methane the world; and were one to strike a match at such a moment . . . boom would not be the half of it.

We also live in an age of migration and displacement. Driven by war, disease, or famine, out of fear of genocide or starvation, millions are on the move, by boat, mostly, as it has always been. Not every foot of ocean is under someone's boot. But boot people don't let boat people land. And, as if to balance those who have been thrust out of their country like a dog to do its business, there are an equal number who have been shut up inside it; who would leave, if they could, in search of freedom, a better living, compatible ideals.

So we have learned to punish people by keeping them home as well as by kicking them out. Yes. Stay home at the range, with Mom and Dad and their ideas; stay home by the monitored telephone, out of sight of the shops and markets, behind the bamboo, lace, or iron curtain; stay home, where home rules rule and the roost has already got its rooster.

Then, when the walls come tumbling down (as, eventually, they always do), the confined will run away in search of freedom, unaware that they have been sent into exile by circumstances.

We should always allow the Greeks to instruct us. You may remember how the soothsayers came with their worry to the king when Oedipus was barely born and scarcely asleep in his cradle. They foretold what every father fears: your son will succeed you, and enjoy all you now enjoy, and possess the love of your wife in her role as a mother; her breasts will be no longer yours, nor her caresses, nor her looks of love; your son's youthful vigor shall shade you and stunt your growth; and he shall slowly edge you into your grave with the negligent side of his sandal. In heed of these warnings, the babe was taken to the mountains during the night, his ankles pinned the way a skinned lamb is trussed for the spit, and there he was abandoned in the belief that the cold wind would freeze his heart, and his lungs would expel his soul with their last outcry of breath; hence no human hand could be blamed by the gods for the child's demise.

Of course the infant is rescued and raised by a shepherd who finds him in among the rocks or under a bush, or by an animal who takes him to her den (the stories vary), and he grows up in increasing puzzlement about his nature, because he doesn't resemble a wolf or a bear, or the parents who adopted him. Twice an exile—first into life, as we all are exiled, then into another country—and now an alien among his so-called kin. Why wasn't he drowned in a butt of malmsy, a method favored by the English kings? Or simply swallowed, as Cronos swallowed his children, or the whale did Jonah, or Mount Etna vain Empedocles?

This becomes an important theme. The dead have relatives, sons have mothers, few expungements are really complete. Six million erasures were realized, yet there remained still more Jewish names. The mother arms the swallowed son with a dagger, and there in the darkness of his father's belly, center of his father's powers, he slits his way out while the Titan is asleep, or (the stories vary) the Titan is given an emetic and vomits the gastrically scalded boy, or a stone is substituted for the baby's body (stories vary) and a gluttonous Saturn swallows that. In any case, the saved child seizes a sickle and cuts his father's cock, his father's balls, off and heaves them out an embrasure, over a parapet, across a cliff's edge, into the sea. It is an instructive story. More morals than an evangelist's pitch. The Greeks were great educators. Aphrodite, the goddess of love, rose from the ocean in the splash and, blood-borne, rode to shore on a shell formed from the foam of what had fallen. We could go on—it is tempting—but the tale would take us toward another lesson, rather than the one we are intent on now.

Let us move, for a moment, from myth to history. You recall how the friends of Socrates had arranged his escape. Athens had no desire to make a martyr of a man who had practically pushed them into voting his execution. His enemies would be well satisfied if the troublesome sage would go into exile like his protégé, Alcibiades, and encourage the decay of some other city. Let the gadfly bite another rump. Here was one horse, at least, who was weary of being kept awake. But Socrates declined, nettlesome to the last, claiming, among other things, to be a son of the State and unable to renounce his parentage. His arguments are interesting, although their reasons are hidden, and one of them can tell us something of what exile is. He claims, of course, to have gotten fair treatment at his trial. All he, or you or I, can correctly ask of the judicial system is that it give us our due, and Socrates felt that he had received it. If the umpire's call goes against him, he can't then take himself out of the game in a snit, a game whose rules he has accepted and whose advantages he has enjoyed. Above all, exile is amputation, a mutilation of the self, because the society Socrates lives in is an essential part of his nature, a nature he cannot now divide.

In short, Socrates invokes three principles, none precisely put, but each profound: he affirms the importance of due process (which means he places a sound method above any result, however right it might chance to be, if it remains unsubstantiated), he believes in the co-relativity of rights and duties (which means that none is inalienable, but that each right is earned through the discharge of a corresponding and defining obligation), and he takes for granted a kind of anatomical connection between individuals and their society (which means that our community is to each of us like a shared arm, and is thus a vital increase of the local self).

We are generally related to other things and persons in one of three ways: instrumentally, as Locke saw us connected, in terms of our interests, so that the State, for example, is seen as a means to the individual happiness of each of its citizens; collectively, as Hegel saw us constituted, in which we are all functional elements contributing to the health of the whole; and, as I shall call it, Socratically, where the community is an essential organ of the self but not the sum of that self.

Families, societies, governments, are properly dissolved, on the instrumental view, when they fail to serve the interests of their members, just as we would replace a broken drill bit with another, or an incompetent business associate with a go-getter, or a losing football coach with one who will win. Let us suppose I am a bachelor troubled by nerves, acne, and anorexia. Life seems pointless, i.e., without sexual direction. My doctor advises me to marry. "Marriage will clear your complexion, calm your nerves, fatten you up." So I decide to say "I do" and await the benevolent consequences. After several years, however, my zits return, my nerves refrazz; once again I can't keep my pasta down. Clearly, divorce is indicated.

Under the concept of the collective, on the other hand, individuals can be substituted for others when they fail to perform their function, the way a pitcher is replaced on the mound, because it is the team that will continue (doesn't our alma mater?) even though the coach and those who played for him have passed into history. The bachelor who happened to have bad skin was admitted to the

Family in order to perform his function there, as husband and father, even grandfather eventually. If, however, his performance is poor, then he may be removed for a better breadwinner, or for one whose social standing is on steadier stilts. Families, in this ruthless fashion, sometimes survive centuries of misfortune and calamity. We have seen teams limp through losing season after losing season, with coaching staffs dismissed and players continually shuffled.

This example allows us to observe that, although the team itself may be collectively constituted, the owner's relation to it may be completely instrumental. If the club not only loses games but also loses money, he may sell it and establish, instead, a line of ladies' ready-to-wear. Money, of course, is the pure and perfect emblem of instrumentality, and that is why, though so universally desired, it has always been, by the better sort, despised. The true fan naturally thinks of the team as a kind of artificial totem, through which the community enjoys and suffers together the team's varied fortunes, maintaining a common temperature, as if every citizen shared the same heart.

A common blood is a common bond in the case where the community is defined as the shared self, like a public park or a library, belonging to all but owned by none. If my arm is injured, I feel sorry for that part of me; I worry about that part of me; I tend that part and try to heal it; and even if it has offended the rest of me, I do not amputate my limb. Only when the whole self is threatened would that remedy be recommended. The loss would be mourned, and considered irrevocable. So if our young man's skin breaks out again, or if the family's fortunes decline because of him, he is not to be turned out of doors. Rather, the reasons for his earlier happiness must be discovered, the healthy state of affairs restored, and the family's welfare, in that way, sustained.

Exile, as I am trying to define it, is not a condition that can arise for the instrumentalist. I can, of course, be separated from my rod and reel, my hamburger franchise, my seventh wife, and that separation might be costly, especially if the fish are biting, or my wife is wealthy or especially litigious; but "exile" would always be far too strong a word for what really would be an inconvenience and a disappointment, even if these were severe.

Under the collective conception, exile is an unmitigated catastrophe for the person expelled, since the entire self would depend upon the definition given to it by the State. On the other hand, the State which has cast that person out need suffer nothing, nor the other citizens sense a loss, so long as the job that was once done continues to be done obediently and well.

Athens may wish him out of the way, but Socrates will be missed, because his contribution, and the contribution of every citizen to the State, has to be regarded as unique, so long as we are speaking of society as a shared self. Only here does each man's death truly diminish me, in Donne's famous phrase, because only here is each individual, without any sacrifice of self or its sovereignty, a part of the whole.

City-states were small, both in population and in territory, so that when the city felt it had a dangerous element in its midst—a cell which was becoming cancerous—expulsion was the reasonable recourse. But a body beset by enemies may not only attack and kill them, or send them away with a violent sneeze; it may seal them off inside itself, forming a sort of Siberian cyst. Countries with colonies can penalize one of them by shipping it idealists, convicts, and religious zealots. Individual malcontents, if simple disappearance isn't feasible, can be tossed overboard, marooned, or left to the mercies of the wilderness, as Oedipus was. For its victim, exile has two halves, like a loaf cut by a knife. Heart, home, and hearth fill one side—the land the exile loses; while foreignness, strangeness, the condition of the alien, occupy the other—the strand on which the castaway is washed.

Despite the grim character which the Greeks gave it, the term "exile" nowadays has many honorific, romantic, even poetical applications. Paris is clearly the most favored modern island of exile, but it is difficult to take seriously the punishment that sends you there. American writers who took extended vacations along

St-Germain because Paris was Paris and because of the favorable
rate of exchange liked to think of themselves as exiles, although
they readily went home when their money gave out, or to further
their careers.

Henry James and T. S. Eliot became expatriates out of sympathy
and convenience, and from a vague distaste for their place of birth.
In a way, they had been English all along, and the move merely
confirmed their identity. Only Ezra Pound was ever a real exile,
and that didn't occur until his incarceration at St. Elizabeth's. Shut
away in an asylum for the insane (a common resort), he achieved,
after those many years in Europe, exile's dubious status among the
discomforts of home. These days there are a lot of things you can
become besides an exile: you can be an immigrant, an undesirable
alien, a displaced or stateless person, a dissident, an expatriate,
a deportee, a wetback, a criminal, a colonist, a tourist, a Flying
Dutchman or other boat person, a Robinson Crusoe, a Rushdie, a
Wandering Jew.

To be exiled is to be flung not out of any door but out of your
own door; it is to lose your home where home suggests close emotional belonging and the gnarled roots of one's identity. I cannot
be exiled from café society because I never had a home there. I
can be blackballed from my club or cashiered from the army, expelled from school or ejected from the game, but I cannot be exiled
from any of them. However, those black people who were enslaved
and carried out of Africa: they were being exiled from the human
race, and reduced to instrumentalities, to livestock, to machines,
to money. Black people have not yet been let into America. They
are the dark artery that is denied.

I can be forced from my homeland by a usurper, or by a con-
quering army, but so long as I cannot feel I have been excluded by
the country itself, I am not really an exile. Exile involves rejection
by a loved one, as if the face in your mirror grimaced when it
looked out and saw you looking in. Exile is a narcissistic wound.

Our species cannot regenerate a limb. Only in rare cases, and
immediately, can any severed member be reattached, sewn back

like the finger of a glove. Perhaps one can pretend to be a tourist for thirty years, as Gertrude Stein did, and never be an exile, just a Yank on an extended trip abroad. Perhaps one can write in Trieste, Zurich, and Paris while becoming more Irish than ever, a Dubliner of dreams. Perhaps.

A friend has told me how it felt to flee East Germany as a child of ten, and to leave behind the real companions of her heart. She had a number of dolls, which she cared for in a most motherly way, and she reported to them everything that happened to her, and shared with them what she read, and explained to them how she felt and what she thought. Above all, she invented stories for each one, since each was an individual and had personal preferences. It was natural that the stories would begin to intertwine, creating a single enriched narrative, one part of which she would then relate to the doll most deserving of it, while another part she would tell to the doll desiring that. So she had a special listener for each part of her life, a listener who listened with the same sort of attentive ear, and sympathized, and supported, and forgave, perhaps more perfectly than her own heart could, whatever needed forgiveness, hugs, reassurance, tears. She was told that when she left she could take only one doll. The family's exit would be illegal, and they would travel light. But to choose? And to leave one thread intact and snap the others as if you were your own malignant fate? She never played with dolls again, and never invented another story. She says that for a time she closed down her soul like a shopfront's steel shade.

She could return now to "her native haunts," of course. But her doll days are over. When you are exiled from a space, you are also exiled from a time—in my friend's case, a childhood. The hurt heart heals, but the healed heart still hurts.

What exactly is the crime for which exile seems such an appropriate punishment? There are scoundrels aplenty in our midst: murderers, muggers, robbers, rapists, vandals, addicts, pushers, extortionists, kidnappers, car thieves, counterfeiters, safe crackers, seducers, embezzlers, arsonists, pickpockets, pornographers, purse

snatchers, con men, molesters, skimmers, usurers (so many scoundrels we may really be in *their* midst); those who make obscene
phone calls, beat babies, steal from the poor box, drink or gamble
away somebody else's savings, adulterate and poison, forge and
deceive, censor and otherwise practice intimidation, or are guilty
of cheating, harassment, libel, misrepresentation, plagiarism,
peeping, high crimes and misdemeanors, including terrorism and
treason; and all of these, and all those I haven't listed who nevertheless belong there, like those whose dogs foul the walkways, who
litter our alleys and deface our walls, who chop down old trees and
tear down old buildings, who poison the air and offend the eye
and din their dins in our ears—they are simply put in the pokey
and kept securely penned for varying periods of unpleasant time;
but none of them, including those who threaten the welfare of the
State by running from the enemy, selling secrets, disobeying their
superiors, or abusing their high office, are sent into exile.

Rulers frequently suffer this demeaning fate, often as a simple
consequence of usurpation; but we must remember that in any
game of king-of-the-hill, it is the hill which must send you spinning
if you are to taste true exile, not a knock on the head by some kid
who wants your job. And if a kid anyway, then only by your own
son (the classic configuration, although nowadays a daughter will
also do), who has to have the people behind him, as well as an
army and a couple of international cartels. Then it will be the hill,
indeed, that gives you the heave and the humiliation. At other
times, the rulers we lose are simply scoundrels who would have a
place or two reserved for them on my list of the common kind if
they didn't happen to be playing Big Daddy behind some polished
desk and, like Ferdinand Marcos, probably ought to be jailed for
bad taste, murder, and theft but for many reasons, most of them
morally obnoxious, escape this result through exile.

Who else? People of the wrong race sometimes. Yes. However,
the ghetto is not a place of exile, or even a sealed-off area of infec-
tion. It is a convenient circle of moral and religious confinement,
which has the further advantage for the State of being economi-

cally useful. As in the slums in which black people are put, the occupants of the ghetto are encouraged to go out to do the Turk's work, the Mexican's, the Yugoslav's labor, to dig holes and touch caps, to fare forth upon a bus to ma'am the ma'ams and wipe cracks.

Who else? Artists. And among artists, it is only occasionally painters, sculptors, architects, who may have their shows closed, their buildings reviled, their casts smashed. They are rarely banished for the reason of their work. Nor are musicians—who may have performances disrupted, who may find that the concert halls are closed to them, who will receive excoriating reviews and then an ornately orchestrated silence—ordinarily ushered out of the country on account of a run of seditious notes.

The case of Socrates continues to be instructive. It was Socrates who felt, and taught, that the soul was the only true mover of the body, and that therefore it behooved us to learn its makeup, and something of the way it went about its business. Like plants, we had appetites, and these impelled us; in league with the animals, we had feelings and perceptions as well, and these sent us in search of satisfactions; but, in addition, and unlike any other creature, we could direct ourselves by means of reason to responsible ends. Speech was the principal organ of influence. Through speech we made our thoughts known to others, and through speech each aspect of ourselves endeavored to persuade our differing desires, by reasoning, flattery, or shouts, to fall silent. More often than not, the exiled are novelists and poets, journalists and playwrights, or any others, whatever their occupation, who speak out or up. Put generally, though I think centrally, what is exiled is nearly always someone's word.

And when a musician is sent away in disgrace, it is what his music is said to say that is the cause; and when the painter is put out like a wildfire, mostly it is because of what his paintings are supposed to mean; it is the words which can be pulled from them, the ideas they then can be alleged to support, for which they are excluded. Socrates did not corrupt the youth by laying his lustful hands on them; he did not corrupt them by omitting to pay ritual homage to the gods; he corrupted them by teaching them intelligent talk; he taught them to quiz the wizards of the marketplace and the heavies of the politburo and the swifties of the courts, and to confront them in their places of power, where their walk would be most swaggery and their talk most confident; and there, in that advantageous atmosphere, were their words to be examined, weighed in a just debate with other words.

The pimps and prostitutes, cardsharps, bid riggers, and legal liars on my list: why should we suffer the expense of their long stays in our iron-bar hotels, and the pay of the guards who must guard them, and the cost of the high walls which hedge them in? why should death row be crowded with criminals who have grown old on appeals and three square meals a day? why not wrap up our undesirables and ship them to Cuba? goons and contract killers and burglars by the boatload.

Couldn't we pay some country to be our penal colony? As with radioactive waste, nobody wants wife beaters, bad-check artists, and confidence men. And so I wonder: why are writers always able to find a welcome under another flag when other kinds of bad guys are turned away at the border? Well, why are miserable and misunderstood wives so valued by the husbands of their neighbors? Over and over again, one nation's persecuted artists have become another's national treasure. The word which sounded foul in one ear may ring sweetly in someone else's. It was brave of Solzhenitsyn to tell the truth we wanted to hear about the U.S.S.R., and we were glad to give him a mountaintop from which to broadcast, so long as he set off his charges in the right direction.

Rarely is an exile lucky enough to be kicked out of New Jersey only to fall on his feet in Devon. Normally he is taken from his family and friends, deprived of his livelihood, his habits, his haunts; his ordinary avenues of expression are closed, his countryside is altered utterly, snow begins to fall in a world which had heretofore worn a Hawaiian shirt, the birds no longer sing the right songs, the flowers sport the wrong colors, nor are the car horns happy; the winds blow from unexpected corners, the cities smell of fish or beer or paper, clothing is uncomfortably odd, and the words which once came to your tongue like your own soul freely, unashamed, naked to a wife or husband, now have to hide in your head, for there is no one to speak to, no one to read what you've written, no one to know about and protest your case, or understand the displays of virtue which were called your crime.

You are no longer you when even your present daily life is as remote as a memory. You are no longer you if—especially—you were defined by your way of life, the things you loved, the ideals you esteemed, your language.

Contrary to this sour situation, celebrity exiles have often reported improved conditions: they got better jobs, were lionized, greatly overrated, given opportunities to express themselves—in dance, in painting, in design—in directions they could scarcely have foreseen. They were put on TV, asked their opinion, smiled at by strangers in the street, by the CIA debriefed. And there was tea on the terrace following the replay of their defection. Universities paid them to speak and offered them even more to teach. They had assumed, in effect, the mantle of a new profession: Herr Doktor Dissident, Professor of Exilese. And ease it is for some, and easy for some to shift tongues, to pick up this word and that and grammarize themselves, to adapt to a new, far richer life than they, earlier, could have dreamed.

They might have remarried, adopted a team (the Washington Redskins, most likely), discoed around a lot, acquired a taste for scotch, begun to forget the wretched whom they once resembled and who lay in prison still or slid still in fear down gray streets or slept lightly as the cat sleeps when in the pound. It became equally easy to discount or forget their fellow exiles who hadn't landed in swimming pools with surrounding lawns, but who found themselves taken down every peg possible, driving a taxi through streets they couldn't recognize or pronounce, selling bruised fruit, cleaning houses when before they had owned one—patronized or ignored, handed a visored cap or a broom, and cast adrift where there was neither water nor a boat.

To enjoy such success, cold wars need to be kept on the flame.

To enjoy such success, other exiles are unwanted competition: for limelight, available sympathies, access to the goodies of the new good life. Back in the old country, they had often cultivated a fine hatred for one another, so why should they change this comforting relation just because both were in a new place? Besides, only they, of this country or that, region or that, race or that, language or that, were true victims of this or that kind of cruel repression, grim persecution, special pain and particular rage; only they, that is, were exiles really, exiles in extremis, with an island in their name, exiles in essence. Others were carbons, copies, no-accounts, unable to muster up the misery, the enmity, the enemies, that might give them an honest exile's status and an entry into the aristocracy of the properly deposed.

In order to exaggerate their plight, exiles customarily inflate their former reputation. Where are those honors they once enjoyed? where are their precious perks? they must drive their own car, shop for themselves, suffer fools who pretend to know their language, their literature, their history. For the sake of complaint, forgotten are the chains, the long lines, the mistrust, the fear, the cramped flat, the fat spouse. Remembered are their small sales, loss of all influence, the successes of undeserving others, the still fat spouse, lost land, food smells, songs.

Who are those who make this transition most easily? those for whom exile almost turns out not to be? The lucky ones scarcely cared about their native soil, were into making it by hook if not by crook, were cosmopolitan in their dress and tones and taste and bones, and had early on freed themselves from clan and family, from countryside and climate—perhaps as children they had spent time abroad, become fluent in the right language—perhaps they lived in an apartment complex on a city block amid a lot of similarly anonymous buildings, saw only the sky through a sooty window, and wrote on mimeograph paper. Coca-Cola and corn dogs comfort them now; their microwave knows how much better off they are—with clean sheets and a car, some good dope and their own towel. The region they had always cared about remained a region of the mind, and the mind was mainly a midden made of texts, of pages of reportage and consignment, and drama, of course, sentiment, sob stuff, high-minded alignments of rhymes recited in a Racinean hurry before being shot or having a head cut off; and they understood geography as a text, history as a text, texts as texts, and were able then to transfer themselves as on library loan from one book depository to another, suffering only the ordinary wear and tear of careless usage.

Most musicians, many dancers, quite a few architects, importers too, were already practicing arts as international as pizza. But among writers, those who did well in their adoptive country were those who learned the new language quickly (if they hadn't learned it in school); who stepped smartly into the idioms and lingo of the times; and who wrote in their new home as they had written in the old one: rapidly, breezily, glibly, satirically. For them, the forced switch from one language to another put both the new one and the old one in a revelatory light. They saw their mother tongue no longer as a daughter might see her mother, but as mother's seducer might, or the baker whom she owed for last week's rolls. And they saw their adopted tongue as an entirely new, wholly free, wonderfully energized way of thinking, because nothing of their rejected history clung to it, the lint of a past life didn't remain; it was as clean of guilt and memory and old emotion as algebra is (one reason why algebra has always been a haven for the haunted).

There was guilt enough. The old days had gathered it like cloud. That was one more factor in favor of another language, another country; because every difference was desirable, and every distance; because no matter what wrong your Motherland had done you, or how clearly mistaken in you it had been, or how unjustly you had been treated, how severely you had suffered, how long you had been made to play Job; you were nevertheless still haunted by your Father Figures, your idols of the Family; you were bitten by your conscience regardless; you called yourself an ungrateful whelp, disgraceful offspring, rotten kid—all the regular stuff—while knowing that your voice, at such times, was only the flavored echo of your enemies, that it was your own arm they were using to bring the gavel down, and *your* mouth which dolefully pronounced *their* sentence. That was another unfairness. Perhaps the final one.

Well, it is certainly sensible, under such circumstances, to make yourself over in the image of another culture, if you can, because you are going to want to call cabs and order croissants, and you may want to blow the whistle on the bastards who drove you from your homeland—a vigorous article in the local language might do that—or cash in on your new celebrity. It may be, however, as I've suggested, that you used your first language as superficially as you will use every other, just to request cold toast and tea, or to kiss off an unwanted lover, get a good lie going; and it may also be that you know no other way to use any language but badly, as if it were a laundry basket you could carelessly empty or a paper cup you could crush and throw away after use.

The scientist, for example, is presumed to be working at a level of concept which escapes the parochial, so that, although the summaries of his experiments are in German or French, his actual researches are not in French and German but in techniques of investigation, perception records, and logarithms.

Suppose our words spilled from our mouths as palpably as spit; suppose some were encased in soft pink clouds like cotton candy or encircled like comic-strip balloons, or came out in Gothic; suppose they filled up small rooms, and we waded through them to reach the phone or the door, and little language ladies spent the night collecting them in nets, hosing them into vats, and at earliest dawn trucks laden with the *logoi* slunk through the streets to great dictionary-shaped dumps. I suppose it only to indicate how well rid of our words we are. No sooner spoken than absorbed by the wide, though increasingly worried, sea of air around us. As for the similarly useless written word . . . well, we may die of our records; bad writing is more contagious than a cold; and if it isn't pieces of plastic and those wormy twist-ties that get us, it will be vast memo slides, a plague of computer print-outs, best-seller buildups, or stock-certificate subsidence.

But if your language is intended to be the medium of an art; if you, its user, are an artist and not a reporter, a persuader, a raconteur; if you aren't writing principally to get praise or pay, but wish to avoid the busy avenues of entertainment, to traffic in the tragic maybe, dig down to the deeply serious; then (although there are a few exceptional and contrary cases) you will understand right away how blessed you are by the language you were born with, the language you began to master in the moment you also started to learn about life, to read the lines on faces, the light in the window which meant milk, the door which deprived you of mother, the half-songs sung by that someone who loaned you the breast you suckled—the breast you claimed as more than kin.

Only if you spring fully grown from the brow of Zeus can you escape being born, and learning a language before you get big, and losing that language along with growing old. It is like living under a certain sort of sun, except that the word begins as merely the wind and weather of the spirit, because what occurs in the outside world initially as a kind of din is slowly made sense of and assimilated. Gradually, too, is a style formed, like the hardening of your bones and physiognomy, by degrees, the way your character comes into being—assertive and tough, mild and weak. That you will learn a language, then, is likely; that you will learn it well is unlikely; that you will live well is unlikely; that you will have a shape is certain; that your soul—that old ghost—will be the source of your speech and the words you write is a Socratic conjecture I support; the word is all the soul is, ever was, or wants to be.

So what is sent away when we are forced out of our homeland? Words. It is to get rid of our words that we are gotten rid of, since speech is not a piece of property that can be confiscated, bought or sold, and therefore left behind on the lot like a car you have traded, but is the center of the self itself. The excruciation of exile lies in this: that although the body is being sent into the world as Adam and Eve were sent by the Angel, the soul is being cast into a cell of the self, where it may mark the days with scratches on the wall called writing, but where it will lose all companions, and survive alone.

This claim of mine concerning the centrality of the spoken word is, of course, disputed, widely rejected, believed to be passé. In our picture-perfect time, who should accept it? Okay. So on your next date, draw a picture of your passion. Thus explain your needs. How far into real feeling will it take you? Will it not inadvertently possess a certain lavatory style? When next you are alone, and pondering some problem (should you call him? will she or won't she? does he like the amplified guitar better than the cradled bass? in what will she prefer that I express myself, chalk or crayon?), try posing your questions in terms of the flickering image so many say they love and see as the future's salutatory wave. Think through anything. Start small. Continue simple. But comic-strip the solution into being.

If we can read, it is expected that we also ought to be able to write, or, anyway, type. How many of us, in our camera-crafted age, can take a really good photograph, or copy a pictured face, or form an interesting image in any medium, or read a blueprint, understand a map or set of architectural plans, or even follow the right arrows when trying to catch a suburban train? If this is a visual age, why is our visual competence next to nil? We can't even doodle with any skill.

We could say, of Cronos swallowing his children, that he had sent them to hell inside himself. For quite a few of its sufferers, exile is a spiritual condition, not merely a geographical one. This is what many of our American writers of the teens and twenties meant when they described themselves as exiles, and when they weren't just putting on airs. Gertrude Stein said that when American expansion had reached the Pacific, there was nowhere else to go but "west in the head." And into the head we went. Then sent our luggage east of us to Paris. Where we spent our exile wasn't the real issue. James Baldwin wasn't sent into exile in France. His exile began before he was born, when the darkness of all our beginnings darkened his skin.

The expression "spiritual exile" is a metaphor, of course, but a significant one, since there is a large number for whom exile is only a pro forma punishment: they are doing well and have found a happy home in their adoptive country. "Alienation" pretty well describes the condition of heart and mind which constitutes the inner content of actual, of effective, exile. While alienation can be mutual, as it often is with married pairs, it is often as solitary as masturbation. Citizens can become alienated from their government without the nation noticing. That failure to notice is often part of the condition. Still, being indifferent to someone or something does not imply that you once upon a time felt otherwise, or that you must continue to mourn your separation.

"Alienation" as a philosophical term is no longer in vogue, so perhaps it is safe to pick it up again, if only for a moment. What is more familiar than your own face—the one there in the mirror, the face you are shaving? But what is that behind the head? It is a wall you've never seen, a wall the mirror has invented, and the head, too, wobbles on its neck now, as if it were under water. Remember how it felt to return after many years to the high school of your youth: how small the halls were; how tattered the blinds; how grim the lockers—a greasy green, and dented without design. Reality and memory were out of tune then, and now they are again.

The movement of the razor over the face, the scrape of the blade, the cream being pushed here and there like suds across a floor, have all leaped over oddity and reached the surreal. The operation of doorknobs is inexplicable. Doorknobs ought to be easy. We only expect bidets to be mysterious. But as alienation settles over our souls like a fog, features, operations, relations, without actually altering, offer us different points of reference, their aims shift, their essences dissolve. An inner weariness wells up; everything is an obstacle, asking us questions we do not understand. We issue the same old orders to our body, but despite that our limbs flair awkwardly; walking cautiously straight ahead, we still back into things as though blind; we forget how to sneeze.

At the same time, of course, how vividly, how accurately, how freshly, we see, for everything we had known well, we had long since ceased to know: the flag was noble; the flag always waved; priests, presidents, and poets were worthy of respect. And now the bathroom wall surprises us; so does the tone in our wife's voice when she says no once again—a sound which suddenly seems the same as the scrape of our razor. We really hear, perhaps for the first time, the gurgle of water down the drain—down the drain like the departure of all hope. In the blink of an eye, we've placed a Duchamp here, another there, until we have a world full of the familiar made strange.

We have spent a lifetime making things a part of ourselves, constructing, as they say, a second nature: learning to walk, to speak, to ride a bike, pick a lock, spoil a party, dance the fandango, wash dishes, shovel snow, swim, do our job, turn on, turn off, go to the bathroom, stoop to conquer. We had felt at home in our yard, with its swimming pool, until someone threw an open can of paint in it, until adolescents made a habit of swimming nude there in the middle of hot nights, until a squirrel drowned. We had felt at home in our home, freshly done in chintz and lacquer, until the kids brought their noisy punk friends in the den, the dog began pooping in a corner, robbers ripped us off, and the wife stopped making the bed. We had felt at home in our flesh until our flesh grew old, grew flabby, went fat and blue-veined, and then there was that stranger in the mirror with his red-rimmed eyes, and the stubble, every morning, like an early field gray with frost.

Then strangers invaded our private hunk of public space with their hands out and each of their unblinking eyes staring and staring. Then strangers came too close to us in the subway, and sat down beside us with empty seats on every hand. So now we come warily up to the ports of our eyes, and go about, even when alone, hidden deep within like a pip in a pumpkin, and protected from the actuality of everything, especially every touch, as we always did at rush hour, so as not to feel felt when packed in the train like a tin.

Alienation is the exile of the emotions—of hope, of trust—sent away somehow so they won't betray us.

The exile that I have personally experienced is one far less grue-
some than the fate that befell Cronos's children; it is not at all
dramatic like the epic of Oedipus; not a bit lyric, either, like a
ballad bemoaning the old days from the lute of a Slavic poet. It
does not even concern the exile of a person whose speech was
found to be offensive, and who was sent away where his message
could be heard no more. I am talking about the loss of the use of a
language (a use that, in my opinion, is its fundamental employment—the poetic in the broadest sense), and how that limb of our
language has been cut off and callously discarded.

This has been, of course, my subject all along. And someone
may ask, so complete has been its disappearance, what is this special use of language, and what makes it so special? Alas, to answer
would require another essay and an honesty absent from most
hearts. It is, first of all, a use of language which refuses to be a use.
Mere use is abuse. That should be the motto of every decent life.
So it treats every word as a wonder, and a world in itself. And it
walks along and upon them, even over dizzy heights, as confidently
as a worker on beams of steel. And it does not care to get on, but it
dwells; it makes itself, as Rilke wrote, into a thing, mute as the
statue of an orator. It reaches back into the general darkness we—
crying—came from, retouches the terrors and comforts of childhood, but returns with a magician's skills to make the walls of the
world dance.

Paul Valéry divided buildings thus: into those that were dumb,
and therefore would be, on my account, soulless, dead; those that
spoke, and would be, on my account, solid citizens and a worthy
norm, provided their speech was clear and honest and unaffected;
and those that sang, for these found in themselves their own true
end, and rose like Shelley's lark, through the heaviest atmosphere.

We have grown accustomed to silence from this sort of singing.
We make other noises. Yet it is an old rule of history that exiles
return, that they return wrathfully, whether a banished people, a
forbidden idea, or a barricaded way, to reclaim what should have
been their heritage. They return wrathfully, not only because they

remember and mourn the life they were taken from, but because the past can never be recovered, not even by a Proust, not if you wish to take up residence in it again. To listen to our stories, other selves have been invented to replace the dolls, who, if any remain, are alive somewhere in other arms. But of course poetry, if it returns, will never make us pay. No. It will not put us to death or in prison or send us, as it was sent, so sadly away. It will simply put us to shame.

THE STORY OF THE
STATE OF NATURE

1. THE DAWN OF THINGS, OR FIRST LIGHT

Imagine that, at a point in an otherwise empty space, an event the precise size of such a point takes place. We do not require the Big Bang. A flick of the Bic will do, the simplest spark of life, perhaps God's guilty shout like the king's in *Hamlet:* Give me some light!

According to the most popular conception of causality, largely derived from Aristotle, this brief alleviation of the general darkness will be followed by an effect occupying every immediately adjoining area. The preferred image is that of a single pebble striking the smooth surface of a still pond. Our initial disturbance, having done its deed, is indeed done, and passes out of the present into what will later be dignified as "history."

If Act I has the duration of an instant (so small as scarcely to exist), Act II is a membrane, an onionlike skin that is infinitely thin and the shape of a hollow sphere. Since every effect is required (by this theory) to change itself immediately into another cause, the little bubble of consequence which encompassed our originating point will find an additional film forming about it, as if the surface of the globe were constantly growing a further surface just above itself—like layers of atmosphere, like countries of cloud.

However, it is important for us to remember (what will be important later mainly because we shall have forgotten it now) that the vacancy created by the obligatory disappearance of the First

Cause into the sphere of its following Effect will be filled by one of
the consequences of that Effect, because every event which suc-
ceeds the first will be like a ball with an equal emptiness on both its
concave and convex slopes; so that creation will continue in two
directions: explosively outward in the direction of infinity, and im-
plosively inward in the direction of the dawn of creation, its first
light. The energy of any event will therefore be divided, inasmuch
as each will bear twins, one concave and expansive, one convex
and contractive—inspired and expired breaths.

When a particular contraction reaches such a degree of concentration that inwardly there is no place left to go, it will radiate
outward once more, although in a greatly weakened condition. To
complicate our image perhaps to a point of incomprehensibility,
we have to keep in mind the fact that every returning system will
have two sides just as the venturing systems do, so that twinning
will be incessant in both types. In short order, expanding rings will
encounter contracting ones, causing incalculable consternations,
collisions we may expect to become causes themselves, and so on,
and so in, and so on, and so in, ad infinitum.

If we return to the image of a growing globe for a moment, it is
easy to see how we might understand one bit of surface as causing
the character of the region most contiguous to it the way sweat
stains a blouse or a shirt. Such attention would be like running a
needle through our onion and following only the tunnel it tore. It
opens the path for a narrative.

With such a focus, the unitary nature of the rings is lost; they
become segmented, as if a circle of dancers were skipping away
from one another. But when I watch widening rings of water, am I
right to imagine each small piece of the wave causing only the
ripple "in front of it," or is the movement of energy through the
medium itself a continuous and unbroken whole?

Our story begins, abstract as it must be (its characters without
qualities, so brutal and distant), when we set up alongside this
continuum of activity a metronome to mark the stages—indeed, to
make them, since the notion of rings, spheres, layers, levels, de-

grees, thin skins, and lucent orbits is an invention of this clock, which insists, to accompany its monotonous ticks, on an appropriately parallel row of monotonous tocks.

The metronome's beats will encourage us to think of this three-dimensional circus we call creation as a single, regularly segmented line of time. It will furthermore fasten an arrow's head to the right, or expanding, end, so that the line will seem to intend its direction, and may even mean to strike something when it arrives—perhaps, like Cupid, a critical point in the cosmic heart.

Narration relies on the notions of event, cause, sequence, aim, and outcome. None of these can be assumed to be an essential part of the nature of things. We find them only in accounts of a certain kind.

2. THE DESCENT OF MAN

Men sprang, some say, from the dragon's teeth. Others argue that men are the terrible teeth themselves; teeth which rend one another like meat and close like a grate upon whatever life gets lodged between them. However, the fuller story only ends with men of that kind: carnivores who may eat up all creation. It begins, instead, with the favored creatures of the Age of Gold, the children of Cronos. It begins at a period when this god is in an unusually benevolent mood, for during that dawn of dawns men eat only acorns, fruit, and honey; they drink only the milk of goats, and are wholly unaware of worry, death, disease, or any labor.

Their silver-sided offspring seemed solely mother-made, so close to their mother's realm did they remain, living in the fields and on its bread the way, later, mice would occupy a farm. Men of the Silver Age were as ignorant as children, playful, careless, quarrelsome, like children easily distracted from their angers, also like children, incompetent at organization, and therefore incapable of war.

Then men of bronze, their torsos hard as the metal of their

spears, fell from the ash trees—broken off like branches, shaken free like leaves, such were the tempests of that time. They ate both bread and flesh, one slab upon another, and went to war as eagerly as to a parade, because they were as simple and pitiless as their ax blades and the cruel gaze of their eyes.

These creatures—gold, silver, bronze—each had the gods for parents: whether one alone begot them, forced them from a breast or brow, or whether they were a consequence of the noisy coupling of two Titans like the cars of a train, and given in secret to some natural resource—wave, plant, cave—to bring forth. In any case, they were pure descendants of the divine, however mean their spirits may have been, and bore the emblems of the sun, or moon, or earth, upon their banners; but the fourth race of men, also brazen, with chests as solid as shields, came from the wombs of mortal mothers, somewhat as Jesus did, and, like him, established themselves as heroes: the warriors, for instance, who besieged Thebes, who journeyed with Jason in search of the gleaming fleece, or those who waged the Trojan War and went to their reward in the Elysian Fields.

From godlike men of several sorts to those of heroic mold and then to men who were merely human: that was the descent. Last in line was the iron race, lacking even a lick of divinity, degenerate throughout, as Robert Graves describes them: "cruel, unjust, malicious, libidinous, unfilial, treacherous," and, above all, in every want, insatiable as the squirrel or the weasel—hungry though sated, after orgasm still bloodily engorged.

While this narrative deals with a specific species and not some anonymous point of plosion, and its stages are more discrete, bulky almost, it nevertheless has the same shape: a temporally calibrated, entropic departure from a privileged starting place. What it adds is evaluation: the early ages are better than the later ones—and not simply because they are prior or more powerful. Furthermore, loss of value in the effect is directly due to a weakening, a lowering of value, in the cause. In narratives, good and evil pass through stories like halls through a house where the occupants either sigh with relief and say the breeze feels good, or suffer a chill and complain of the draft.

3. ME ADAM, YOU EVE

The Greek version of the descent of man, which I chose to cite, did not attempt to personify its personnel; nor did it particularly care to designate a location, for presumably the entire world was every Age's oyster. It did add a few lively touches concerning diet and character, but its principal interest was genealogical. It is a tribal theory. The lines it draws are lines of blood. The familiar Christian account I turn to now, although confused almost to the point of incomprehensibility, creates a theater and a company of players, then puts them down in a most dramatic and attractive setting: a walled and gated garden with a river to water it, fruiting trees, creatures of various kinds to occupy its earth and air, a militant angel, God, and of course, enjoying a breeze, the devil in the costume of a serpent, as well as Adam and Eve in their eventual leaves. There are scenes and conversations; there is buck-passing; there are temper tantrums, dramatic confrontations, and all sorts of other advances in the art of fictional excitement.

The most important events are these: after God created the heavens and the earth (the latter a desert from whose depths water occasionally rose like a flooding Nile to moisten and soften its surface), he made man from the sand and the dust which was everywhere, and blew into him a little left-over yet divine breath as though he were a lung, so that man began to stir himself and endeavor to live. Then God designed the aforementioned garden and sequestered man inside it, denying him only the fruit of the tree which bore knowledge of good and evil, and warning him that the fruit was deadly, either because some part of it—skin, pulp, juice, seed—was poisonous, or because an awareness of sin would do Adam in.

God fashioned birds and beasts next, rather incompetently,

though they were formed from the same dust, because he wanted them to resemble man as man did his creator; yet, although they were alive like man, and ate and slept like man, they were otherwise far from family; so finally, with man etherized like a patient on a table, God cut one rib from Adam's side, and replicated it, and ran the replications through as many variations as a theme until he heard a full tune and had a title: she, Eve.

Eve does not become the mother of us until later, when, after listening to the serpent and having her pride piqued, she eats of the forbidden tree so as to become like one of the gods, and offers the fruit to Adam as well, which he devours, as docile as a dog. Neither dies on the spot or even falls ill.

The serpent was right about this. Rather, the fatal blow comes from God, who, in his anger at being disobeyed, promises to return them, after a painful passage through life, to the dust they came from, although Eve ought properly to fold up like a pocketknife into a rib again and disappear into the body of her spouse, though he be a corpse coming apart in the earth then like a dry biscuit. Lest either eat of the tree of life and live forever, Adam and Eve are forced out of paradise, its precincts closed, and I suppose, left in a state of permanent neglect, with neither he, Adam, nor she, Eve, nor it, Eden, in harmony or in happiness.

Our initial myth, that of a bubble-blown universe, was designed to exhibit the form which creation took, once it had begun and continues to occur. Its single-minded concentration upon structure leads us to call it "scientific." The stress, in the Greek story, is rather upon "what." It is vague about the mechanics and, of course, feels no need to rationalize. From time to time, Zeus simply calls for a new deal. However, the Hebrew tale does not simply describe the sorry state of human affairs; it seeks to justify that sorrow, so that our satisfaction with the story will be complete, since we shall now know not only how the world was formed and man was made (the way a potter makes a vessel out of clay), or what kind of paradise he was placed in, but why we must maintain our life by the sweat of our bodies, why women owe fealty to their men, why there is guilt and shame concerning many of our most powerful urges, why we reproduce in pain and with groaning when mother lions drop their cubs like overlooked gloves and fruit seems the easy outcome of every flower.

Narratives not only explain the events they describe; they anoint the explanation—they justify. In Plato's *Symposium*, when Aristophanes overcomes his hiccups sufficiently to make his speech, he does something none of the others, in their praise of the god of love, have done: he tells a story. This story not only speaks of us as once round, but suggests that we thought we were accordingly perfect, equal to the best, and describes how we wheeled ourselves up the slopes of Mount Olympus with the intention of displacing the gods. It is for this presumption (improper pride was Eve's error also) that we were sliced in two like a breakfast bun and left to hop about looking for our better half, bereft of our accustomed capacities like a clap which has been accorded but one hand for its accomplishment. So was the serpent doomed to slither along the ground, stinging human heels, suffering his skull to be crushed in retaliation; since all it has become, as a consequence of its sly advice, is a fatal fang, hidden in its head like a thorn in a bush.

Alleging that this original round race possessed three genders —symmetrically male, symmetrically female, and asymmetrically hermaphrodite—makes our search for the half we once had seem both right and reasonable, since most sexual preferences, on this view, are equally legitimate; although Aristophanes cleverly makes it difficult to see how the restored whole which heterosexuals pursue is something better than the sideshow endowment of a freak.

Stories of our innocent origins are not innocent. Genesis stamps its okay on the subservient state of women; victims of natural disasters like floods and volcanic eruptions seem to deserve their fate; and the so-called curse of Canaan, recounted in the same book, can be read as supporting slavery. The normal shape of a narrative (like an hourglass, it is so corseted by Time) and its customary content (its agents, actions, and their accomplishments) are both designed to disclose a comforting pattern in events, discover a true direction to existence, and give an honest meaning to life. It is essential that each pattern, purpose, and significance be inherent in the natural course of things, and not simply be the functional properties of some descriptive history like the concealed seams of a glitzy dress.

4. NOW YOU SEE ME, NOW YOU DON'T

Shepherds work alone on lonely slopes, and if they tell a fanciful tale, their sheep won't correct them. Gyges was such a shepherd, but it is Plato who offers us his history. Philosophers, as we know, work in even remoter regions with nothing but their own rectitude to rein them in. It seems there was a storm of such violence it opened the earth where the sheep of Gyges were grazing. Curiosity drew him into the gorge. Descending, he saw many strange things indeed, most particularly a bronze horse with doors in its side. As innocent as Alice, he opened one to find the corpse of a very large man wearing nothing but a gold ring on one of his fingers. Gyges removed the ring and returned to his sheep.

Some unspecified time later, at a meeting with other shepherds who were preparing their usual monthly report to the king on the condition of his flocks, Gyges discovered that by positioning the bezel of his stolen ring a certain way while he was wearing it, he became invisible. A simple turn restored him to the visible world; another twist and he was gone again like a coin in a magician's fist. With an ease and swiftness only anecdotes of this kind can accommodate, Gyges gets himself transferred from the mountains to the court, where he swiftly seduces the king's queen (not while invisible, one assumes, or was the invisibility the attraction?), and with her help murders her husband in order to become the ruler himself. We are not told what happens to him after that, although we know (otherwise than through Plato) that he will be the grandfather of Croesus, and that the ring makes him and his offspring very rich.

In *The Republic*, following Thrasymachus's intemperate outburst, Plato has Glaucon relate this story. If he had allowed Socrates to present it, doubtless other details would have been chosen, another point sharpened. Certainly my own summary (as with all of these specimen accounts) is just that: a description of a story rather than the tale itself, fully retold or performed. Mine is only a reminiscence, a little reminder of something we have all read. Oddly, none of these differences (among the tale, its various tellings, our memories, or its summary description) really matters. What matters here is its rhetorical employment by a very energetically held idea which is searching for a way to create for itself a sympathetic state of mind, as the story of Aladdin's wonderful lamp does in order to dramatize human greed. What would you, or anyone, do if you had robbed the grave instead of Gyges and found yourself with the ability to vanish from sight at will? Into whose bedroom would you be tempted to steal unobserved? what blows might be struck if every back were turned? what a lot of gossip could be collected for sale to the tabloids, what gross jokes played, friends amazed?

Narrative is indifferent to details and dislikes its swift flow impeded. It hastens from stolen ring to usurped kingdom with nary a care for complications. When Gyges first notices his own disappearance, it's because other shepherds begin to speak of him as if he were no longer at their meeting. Do his clothes vanish too? whatever he touches? if not, aren't his companions surprised by his sheepskin's sudden loss of occupant? Will the floor still squeak when he walks over it, and will the coins he has filched seem to float through the air though borne by his hidden palm? How did the adulterous queen feel, feeling Gyges and his lipless kisses? Is Gyges invisible to Gyges, and what is it like becoming disembodied as a ghost? Spooky, I'll bet, and disorienting to be never in the picture but always where the camera would be. Put *basta!* to scruples and complications. The narrative is already ten miles past the station. You cannot even hear the distant whisper of its whistle. In any case, its cars were always empty of such answers.

Narratives like the story of Gyges and his ring imperceptibly seduce their listeners, because they always solicit our participation: not for a naive or complacent identification with the protagonists necessarily (where each of us is Gyges, Eve or Adam, maybe God), or even with the rich raciness of their roles (where each of us takes the queen's place in bed, or the serpent's in the tree), but by an implication that extends to the idea of man in general; so even if I say to myself: "I wouldn't go down in that gorge—no way—or sneak that ring from that dead man's finger—not me—and I'm too good a guy, basically, to be bought by a little loose change, free flesh, or a position of power," nevertheless (and this is Glaucon's expectation), I can believe everybody else would; so when Glaucon suggests we place one such ring on the finger of a plainly unjust man, who has already flouted society's conventions without its aid, and then another on the finger of a man who has always behaved like a good worker bee, a diligent drone, my mind moves easily along the track which has been greased for it to the right rhetorical conclusion: beneath clothes, cosmetics, and conventions, where we confront the naked soul, there is no difference to be discerned between the sinner and the saint, both souls are so stained and opaque, except that the saint, in addition to his other vices, is a successful hypocrite.

The story of that state of nature, like narratives in general, prefers to take us from our present place and time to another, earlier, indeed original, condition, and it plays continually upon the differences. In a way, we always stand at the story's end. It moves toward us as Adam's does, explaining our life as it recounts his, justifying our miseries with his mistakes. Gyges is the dishonest heart in Everyman. Beneath his simple shepherd's garb and sunburned grizzle is a monster, pitiless and greedy, which only the shine of the public's gaze, the weight of their opinions, the force of their arms, keeps immobile, cold as the corpse that got hid in the horse that was buried in a chasm which had stayed a secret even to the earth.

5. THE WAR OF ALL AGAINST ALL

The most eloquent description of the state of nature, as well as the most plausible, I think, is that of Thomas Hobbes. His, however, is not given to us in narrative, but in a description. Locke and Rousseau have their own versions, both palpably implausible, but the first thing to note, before admiring Hobbes's version, is that all of these arguments, as arguments, are the same. They are the same because they have the same form. For a structuralist, at least, that is sufficient to establish an identity.

To understand what it means to "have the same form," let us examine a pair of children's board games, Winnie-the-Pooh and Treasure Island. Both are played on pasteboard fields designed to resemble their respective regions of the world: Pooh's has a stream and a bridge, woods, a house, a few fields, while the pirate realm is represented by seas and lagoons, an island, palm trees, ravines, lookout points, some jungle, a stretch of castaway beach, and so on. Through these landscapes, like a road which resembles a relaxed, even tangled, dressmaker's tape, runs a bright, clearly segmented path. Upon this path, counters of various colors and kinds are placed (a button will do if a counter is lost). These pieces stand for the characters that have been taken from their respective stories: Eeyore, Tigger, and Pooh in one set; Jim Hawkins, Long John Silver, and Ben Gunn in the other. There will be some point, probably a circle, marked START, and another, containing a honey pot or a chest of treasure, marked END. The players select their pieces (perhaps identifying with the characters and their roles in the original story). We are ready. Who shall go first? who shall roll the dice or spin the first spin?

The word "counter" is correctly chosen, because that's what we do when we play these games: we roll dice and add the number that turns up to the sum we have already amassed. This sum is dramatically displayed by the distance a piece has gone on the trail to the treasure; perhaps it has reached Coffin Cave just ahead of

Long John Silver, who, after all, has a wooden leg and ought to be lagging behind. A little subtraction (dare I say?) adds a bit of spice to the contest, or a player may be made to lose a turn when his piece falls into the Huffalump pit or is captured by cannibals. Embellishments or descriptive alterations do not make the slightest difference to the form: imagine, instead, a racetrack with six noble steeds ready to run as fast as the spinner will point them, neck and neck along competing columns of numbers—how exciting—six plus three plus two plus four plus five, galloping as fast as your favorite cliché, their manes streaming, their jockeys digging in their heels and using the whip, a fortune bet on the outcome, maybe the mortgages on several properties from the Monopoly board. I can keep a record of losses and victories—wins, places, shows— fast track or slow—rider names, weights, and numbers—farms and owners—dams and sires—positions in the starting gate. I can call the race in an excited voice. I can toast the victor and drop around his neck a horseshoe cut from colored paper. Still, a sum of only seven will lose to eleven every time, no matter what the horse is called, or the color of the jockey's silks. As far as the form goes, we might as well sit at a bar and roll dice for drinks. Even an ancient and much more complex game like pachisi, played with cowrie shells, states its nature in its name, which represents the game's highest throw: the number twenty-five.

Aristotle was the first to perceive clearly how statements became logically woven together in an argument. Nothing is more linear than the syllogism, or more like narrative in its nature. Aristotle saw how assertions (in his Greek) could be reduced to four subject/ predicate forms (all, none, some, and not), and how, with the help of a shrewdly placed and chosen middle term, such shapes could be validly linked to a conclusion. The discovery (one of the more momentous in the history of mankind's mind) required us to discard content and concentrate on structure, to remember, in short, that Winnie-the-Pooh and Treasure Island are the same game. Nevertheless, even students of logic are regularly seduced by arguments in striking costumes and propositions wearing beguiling perfume. The syllogism that runs "Movie stars lead glamorous lives, but glamorous lives don't last, so stars tend to twinkle once and die twice, the glamour going dead before they do," is more fascinating to most people than a simple old wheeze like "All men are mortal, some movie stars are men, so some movie stars are mortal"—an argument whose only interest is its caution.

Aristotle called the middle term the "cause" of the conclusion, and it was natural enough to identify the relation of premises to conclusion in an argument with the relation of cause to effect in physics. Thus the syllogism borrowed the idea of causality from the material world while the material world drew upon logic for the concept of necessary connection. The regress of events that threatened to be infinite, and therefore had to be terminated in a Prime Mover, Big Bang, or lightninglike *logos* called God, was the same sort of regress that endangered the syllogism with indeterminacy if every premise had in turn to have been the conclusion of some prior argument, and if there were no first principles or axioms or ultimate ideas.

The story of the state of nature, like any argument, pays off in the coins which have been fed into it. Its central process is one of pretended purification. Like a ship's hull, history must be scraped clean of encrustation—culturation—before its real shape can be appreciated. Since one cannot do this in fact, one must do it in one's head, in exemplary tales like that of Adam and Eve, or Gyges and his ring.

For John Locke the state of nature was essentially a state of peace; it was a fragile but genuine paradise. However, conflicts would inevitably arise, even between people of good will when their points of view sincerely contradicted and their interests genuinely clashed. If there were no just way of mediating these conflicts, a condition of peace would soon enough become a condition of war. Political structures are like blocks beneath the wheels of a truck parked on a steep slope. On the other hand, the snake in Rousseau's garden was society itself. The devil destroys the truth by organizing it. These organizations then multiply desires, create social classes, and foment disappointment, resentment, and strife.

Hobbes placed a different value on the natural condition, and belongs, with Freud, securely in Gyges's camp. The phrase "every man against every man" tolls through his text like a dirge.

Hereby it is manifest, that during the time men live without a common Power to keep them all in awe, they are in that condition which is called Warre; and such a warre, as is of every man, against every man. For WARRE, consisteth not in Battell onely, or the act of fighting; but in a tract of time, wherein the Will to contend by Battell is sufficiently known: and therefore the notion of *Time*, is to be considered in the nature of Warre; as it is in the nature of Weather. For as the nature of Foule weather, lyeth not in a showre or two of rain; but in an inclination thereto of many day together: So the nature of War, consisteth not in actual fighting; but in the known disposition thereto, during all the time there is no assurance to the contrary. All other time is PEACE.

Whatsoever therefore is consequent to a time of Warre, where every man is Enemy to every man; the same is consequent to the time, wherein men live without other security, than what their own strength, and their own invention shall furnish them withall. In such condition, there is no place for Industry; because the fruit thereof is uncertain: and consequently no Culture of the Earth; no Navigation, nor use of the commodities that may be imported by Sea; no commodious Building; no Instruments of moving, and removing such things as require much force; no Knowledge of the face of the Earth; no account of Time; no Arts; no Letters; no Society; and which is worst of all, continuall feare, and danger of violent death; And the life of man, solitary, poore, nasty, brutish, and short. [*Leviathan*, Pt. I, Ch. 13.]

Hobbes carries the dot-matrix theory of society back to its atomistic source. The leviathan he calls the State is built up like a photographic image. Each man is a dot, a body in motion. Each man is driven, willy-nilly, by desires, and everywhere seeks their satisfaction. The power over available means, which men need to dampen those drives, will be given up only when they realize the futility of going it alone. Civilization is therefore based upon the mutual surrender of rights, the ceding of individual sovereignty. Freud would say that it depends upon the sublimation of instincts.

So we begin our story in a state of war, where every man has a right to everything, and nothing is unjust because nothing is just, and we end it by establishing a power which is absolutely sovereign, and therefore in a state of peace. Narrative beginnings are necessarily unstable, whereas the endings of most every narrative are calm, resolved, steady.

The historical reality of the state of nature has always been a problem, and even a rationalist like Hobbes is tempted, now and then, by the idea of an actual and absolute starting point, just as others are seduced by utopian dreams—the narrative's ultimate, and triumphant, ending.

> It may peradventure be thought, there was never such a time, nor condition of warre as this; and I believe it was never generally so, over all the world: but there are many places, where they live so now. For the savage people in many places of *America*, except the government of small Families, the concord whereof dependeth on naturall lust, have no government at all; and live at this day in that brutish manner, as I said before. [*Leviathan*, Pt. I, Ch. 13.]

When beginnings are described in absolute and complete terms, it becomes difficult to find a fatal flaw or, amid the war of all, the small reign of reason, which can move matters off the mark. When Aristophanes said that we were once round and therefore that we *thought* we were perfect, he avoided the problem, since, clearly, we were not what we thought, and obviously full of false pride, and consequently in the wrong, and justly punished by our division; but we ought to have no such misapprehensions about any paradise that is truly a peaceable kingdom. Is a garden perfect if it may be improved by cutting down one tree? Paradise is a theological puzzle the way the Big Bang is a theoretical one. Why fall at all? Just in order to have a story? What made the Big Bang go boom? Do we begin with an instability raised to its highest power and end with a tranquillity so smoothly even everywhere energy cannot pilot-light a stove? If square one is impure, why call it square one? Are there going to be handicaps imposed before the race is run? Adam obeyed his wife, not God, but this result could scarcely have been a surprise. On the other hand, if square one is without blemish, why budge? Hobbes tries to have his cake remain as whole and untasted as when first baked, while eating it bit by bite from frost to crumb, but such a desire cannot be satisfied inside consistency.

It may seem strange to some man, that has not well weighed these things; that Nature should thus dissociate, and render men apt to invade, and destroy one another: and he may therefore, not trusting to this Inference, made from the Passions, desire perhaps to have the same confirmed by Experience. Let him therefore consider with himselfe, when taking a journey, he armes himselfe, and seeks to go well accompanied; when going to sleep, he locks his dores; when even in his house he locks his chests; and this when he knowes there bee Lawes, and publike Officers, armed, to revenge all injuries shall bee done him; what opinion he has of his fellow subjects, when he rides armed; of his fellow Citizens, when he locks his dores; and of his children, and servants, when he locks his chests. Does he not there as much accuse mankind by his actions, as I do by my words? [*Leviathan*, Pt. I, Ch. 13.]

What experience confirms (by counting our locks, our looks, our fears) is that society is at war with itself, as Rousseau suggested, not that nature necessarily is. But if nature is as warlike as Hobbes insists, we shall be as unable to release ourselves from its grip as we shall be powerless to prevent peace should we ever reach our absolute sovereign's final society.

6. LIFE IS LIKE THAT

Let us now imagine another game, one unlikely to be popular except with the kinky, which we might call Death March or, alternatively, Life Is Like That. The game gets going at a womb-shaped space on the playing board (discreetly rendered, of course, as if there were a sheet over the feet depicted in the stirrups, and we didn't begin in a puddle of amniotic fluid). At this point, a good roll of the dice may furnish us with a head start: hardy genes, moderate passions, an optimistic outlook, accurate senses, and a few brains; whereas a bad roll could send us limping, poor, blind, sickly, into the world. As in golf, in this game, low scores are the ones sought. The white pieces come from the best Boston families and are heavily favored to win. The black pieces are Ethiopians or Congolese and aren't given a chance. So, as the game goes on, the several players will experience various fates; a few will go to the best schools, most to the worst; many will endure every childhood illness, some suffer none; there will be those who will eat paint and be poisoned by its lead, those whom rickets will cripple and scurvy get; and, in the card pile, from which players often have to draw, there will be many more cards which say something like "Experience epileptic seizure due to mother's drug habit. GO FIVE SQUARES STRAIGHT AHEAD" than those that read: "Your father has given you a set of golf clubs for Christmas. LOSE A TURN."

The ghetto will kick a lot of kids along into middle age, or kill them right away, riddled while sitting on their front porch, beaten in an alley, stabbed in a bar. Others will be smoking at ten, and drinking, too, and hanging out at fast-food joints in their teens, speeding on speed, stuffed as a goose, drunk as a lord. So car crashes will erase a lot of players, as small wars will, overdoses, bad choices of career, falls in the tub, getting too sincerely mugged, contracting AIDS, being done in by despondency, cancer, colas, cigars. Failing at business, falling out of love, becoming bored by bodies and indifferent to ideas, aging at everything—memory going, beauty fading—vital fluids disappearing in a gurgle like water down a drain: none has been the fun that this game makes them. They are, in their petty details, the stuff of every story. Unhappy marriage? drop a decade of expectancy. Lost job? zip up six. Raise ungrateful kids? jump four. Lousy sex? cut out eight. Overweight? shorten by seven. Tense? tired? transferred to L.A.? made unwise investments? hit the skids? Watch the years blow away in the wind. So why not retire? but resting easy will cost you a couple. Take walks. Keep a pet. Have an interest. Bet on bingo. Stay off the streets. Eat out of tins. Good luck to all. The player to die last wins.

Let us consider another game, I suggested, but it was not truly "other," for all these games are quite the same. Death or treasure —praise or blame—cautionary or heedless—Huffalump or Market Crash—there are only plastic players, dice cups and spinners, play-mates or pirates, honey or money—even in what we want to call "real life" there is simply a series of steps or stages of achievement: standing, walking, talking, going to nursery school, making the grades, graduating, first from high school, then from college, get-ting a job, getting laid, getting married, going in debt, having kids; what are they? only colored squares and illustrated patches, pre-tended punishments, imaginary rewards.

I can insist on this essential identity, and make this dizzying deduction, if I can also persuade you to accept a separation be-tween the little elementary mathematics involved and counting's lurid embellishments—between "one" and what "one" is one of— between the shape of a sentence and its sense—between structure and texture, form and content—the joke and its versions, the tale and its telling—because, like man and society, I can regard the first term as the seed or source, some pure position, and the second term (everything that comes afterward) as a kind of encrustation (either by barnacles or by gems), as superficial, as cosmetic, the result of training and the minding of manners, as including what is now ever so commonly called "lifestyle."

We were without fire until Prometheus stole it for us; but the really important thing about this story, as with all the others, is that we *were* at all before we had fire or suffered our fall or signed our social contract; and that we are definable apart from sin, science, or society. We are wild animals who have been taught to jump through corporate hoops. We are honest rustics who have been corrupted by cynical city ways. Our id is deeply dark and wet within us like a hidden cistern. Mother and father, teachers and statesmen, athletes and idols of screen and guitar: none of them put that black well of restless wishes there. Civilization is a veneer—cheap and vulgar sometimes like aluminum siding, rich and costly like ivory and bird's-eye maple. We were once without sin, round as the round world, swollen with pride the way that fruit we stole was fat with juice, or we were once barely alive in a quarterless war, without helpmate or friend, ally or even a rational enemy, as full of fear as a field mouse, speechless as a stone, heartless as the wind. Once upon a time. By stages we have declined: from gold to silver, silver to bronze, bronze to iron, and thence to tin, until we are now made mostly of plastic. Or by steps we shall ascend: from the solidarity of tribe and family to the unity of the city-state, from neighborhood to nation, hence to the whole world, overcoming classes on the way, stifling economic strife, reaching an Eden in which ego will dance where id cooled its heels, and every will will give orders to itself that will be in harmony with every other order. So our history extends from what we were once upon a time toward what we shall become. Yet we can't have a story unless we have an identity. The pronoun "I" must sit like a cap on the same head for a whole life. Like the id, like every essence, like substance itself, the soul endures.

Another example. Suppose we related the myth, once more, concerning the pure realm of Forms, a paradise of principle and perfect law, of notions uncontaminated by notation or by any way of being "put" or "presented." And suppose we repeated how the Demiurge, Plato's creative god, made Time, the moving image of eternity, like a light lit in the sky, so that the history of the world could commence . . . once and for all, once upon a time. Suppose we told it, and have come to represent its end, when the souls of living things have reassembled in the radiantly angelic company of the Forms; when Time is no more because nothing moves, including the hands of the clock; at the end, when stasis takes over and concludes every story. What then? We shall have added only another great game to our fund of amusements, of things to say while huddled around a campfire on a dark and stormy night, of brave things to sing while the ship is sinking, of country tales to tell the way Boccaccio told them while the Black Plague was raging through the cities.

And we can make these differentiations: we can consider color apart from shape, the use of a word instead of its mention; we can study the motion of a bullet while indifferent to the bullet itself or the heart it enters; we can treat even the sorriest individuals as nonetheless ends-in-themselves, or play with frictionless systems; and it is often very useful to do so, to conceive of extents and extremes, of a pure poetry, for instance, or a world without hunger, to violate hitherto inviolate states to see if the wall falls instead of Humpty Dumpty, or the bubble bursts from a too intense spread of iridescence over its surface, or to estimate the degree of skill and level of emotion with which the first sin was committed.

To support what is after all the common narrative formula for life and its history seen as a sort of solid-state cinema—one frame following another like the topple of dominoes—is the apparently linear constitution of our languages (the Western ones, at any rate), because each letter, syllable, word, sentence, paragraph, or page pursues its fellow (even Volume Two seeks out its Volume One) like the units of a long parade, bands tootling one after another; and, when spoken, with each significant sound instantly replaced by a pointed pause or pregnant silence or still another meaningful noise, it resembles the way events disappear as the murderous metronome drones on, so the past won't clog the space of the present, a space that, like our silver screen, frees itself for the oncoming action and is always eager to push its occupant along in order to continue unabated the militant march of sound track and image. Thus conditions in the world, stages on life's way, states of human consciousness, the scatterings of memory, and all those uttered words seem to proceed in structural unity: a harmony as sequential and evanescent as music.

It is one of the lovelier illusions. Let us look back a moment at Hobbes and his language, which seems to unwind across the page in a continuous and dutiful line and seems to be presenting us with lively incidents from an old story. Yet the rules of English grammar, which determine word order and the direction of modification, require the reader to return, again and again, to what has gone before; to move the eye, that is to say, not at all like a stylus in a groove, but like a tailor's needle, loop after loop. When phrases are well turned, we linger over them, which interrupts the narrative; and when predicates lead us back to their subject, we find ourselves looking over our shoulder as we go, instead of straight ahead. "Hereby it is manifest," Hobbes declares, and we must carry that boast forward over an entire paragraph. What is manifest? That men are, when without a common power, in a condition of war. Hobbes halts his thought to tell us what war is in terms of what weather is. In short, any complex idea is like a territory to be traversed, not the way a number of ticks reach their tocks, but the way we crisscross a neighborhood or inhabit a building, holding the whole in our head as we walk along one walk, watching a florist wrap a bouquet or, through a window, a barber shave.

Again, when words rhyme or otherwise sing (as when he writes, "without a common Power to keep them all in awe") (*oh*'s bending about *eee*'s to reach *ah*'s), they form obdurate units like stones that disturb the smooth flow of a stream. When his sentences throw ahead of their arrival patterns of repetition and other rhetorical schemes ("no . . . Industry . . . no Culture of the Earth; no Navigation . . . no . . . building . . . no Instruments of moving . . . no Knowledge . . . no account of Time . . . no Arts; no Letters; no Society . . ."), they are creating blocks of prose with carefully articulated grids like the intermeshing streets of a city; and the very muscular movement of that prose, its gradual accumulation of force and decision ("And the life of man, solitary, poore, nasty, brutish, and short"), depends on our keeping the beat, retaining the sounds, feeling the accelerating absence of the verb, so that the successive conditions of solitude, poverty, nastiness, and brutishness are compounded, intermingled, caught up and forcefully squeezed into "short"—a word additionally appropriate in its concluding position because the fear of death, for Hobbes, is mankind's overriding emotion. Finally, the pungency of his style and the concision of its effects frequently depend upon an ironic balancing of one brief statement against a greater mass, a result he brilliantly achieves, finishing off the paragraph in which he defines war (the way we define conditions of our weather) as a continuing disposition to seek violent solutions, by saying, sourly, "All other time is Peace."

If we treat Hobbes's state of nature as a narrative, then we can abstract the tale from its telling the way he dissolves society into solitaries alone with their fears; but if Hobbes is mistaken and men must be defined in terms of communities of some kind, then it might be a similar mistake not to treat a style like his as seamless with its sense and at one with its occasion, just as wit is said to be wed to its manner and moment, unlike the joke, which will crack wise with anyone and try to find a buyer for its grin under almost any management; because Hobbes may have given us not really an argument to tussle with but a picture to contemplate—a picture that deploys its elements in an intellectual space—a picture whose effect has one cause called "the Whole," and one form called "Style," and one skill called "Art."

7. I (SPACIALLY) THINK, THEREFORE I (TEMPORALLY) AM

If narrative is a rhetorical strategy for arranging events in a serial order to suggest causal accountability and purposive direction within a circumscribed scheme (one with a beginning as well as an end); then exposition is a parallel device, one which deals with the exfoliation and orderly exposure of ideas, suggesting logical connection and descent from premises to conclusion within its own complete and consistent system; and its greatest modern exemplar is Descartes, the narrative philosopher *par excellence*, and one who realized that these two processes were not metaphysically innocent, but had the blood of ontology on their hands.

Not only does Descartes describe his discovery of the *cogito* as if it were a western isle, but in his *Discourse on Method* he composes the ideal narrative-writer's manual. I use the word "manual" because Descartes employs "making" as his model—making—as we might put together a bike from a box, or guess how to re-create in our own kitchen an elegant restaurant's dish. We analyze our problem, deconstructing it, identifying the kind and determining the quantity of every ingredient. These elements are then recombined in a specific order, so that the cook or the carpenter proceeds from the simple to the complex, reviewing his procedures to make sure he has not left out the salt or some essential nail.

Descartes (we discover) has his own state of nature, only the nature he is interested in is that of the mind. Once upon a time, there was a thought so clear and pure and undirected, it could be taken as indubitably true. It was not—this thought—a "Let there be light" but a "Let there be me." Descartes's paradise was also threatened by an evil demon; however, unlike frail Eve, who ate an apple from the tree of knowledge, Descartes became the apple of his own "I." He imagined away his body, so as to be free of the distractions of perception. Repeating Plato, he released himself from the diseases of desire and the irrational tyranny of passion so he might move only as the mind moves, step by step down no doubt golden stairs from the highest heaven of axiomatic truth to the most distant and particular conclusions that mark the proper extent and boundaries of its realm.

Descartes believed that we think the way we make, and that we understand something (like life in a plant or animal, for instance) when we can in fact construct it: gathering all the proper parts together, directing our actions according to a plan, then putting pieces in place, section by section, until the machine is finished—for, of course, if we can make any "it" this way (as Hobbes also maintained), "it" must be a machine.

Hobbes began with atoms, and by combining these and their motions into a kind of peaceable kingdom, he created what might be deemed molecules. Then, by grouping these, he manufactured cells; the cells united first to form plants, and later, with fancier and finer levels of organization, came animals of lower, then yet higher, constitutions, until finally man was achieved. Men became matter in motion, too, and joined in families, just like atoms clump into molecules; families led to clans and tribes; finally man evolved complex societies grand enough to claim statehood—states which were themselves solarlike systems, great masses in military motion.

Descartes's discovery of analytic geometry united the narrative world of matter and mechanics with the expository world of thought and theory, but in doing so it revealed the mind's bias: its need to represent every one of its operations in terms of a spatial model. Of course, this had always been the case, but the dominance of linear inference concealed it. Although the forms of the syllogism may have seemed to resemble temporal progressions, these proofs were accomplished by conceiving each term as a box —or pen—or class—or set—or place—into which particulars were put like silverware in its cloth-lined chest. The pens weren't used simply to keep cows. Other pens could be nested inside them. Our Venn diagrams demonstrate the spatial configuration of the syllogism, and we diagram sentences in terms of trees, boxes, ladders, rings. We map not only Ohio and circuits and the gross national product; we map the mind.

When geometry disappeared into algebra, algebra's Euclidean interior was disclosed. Our board games work within a field, and even the path which winds its narrative way gently o'er the lea is a line. The fact is "grasped." The mind is incapable of an entirely immaterial understanding (although a machine may be). It invariably and necessarily spatializes its "perception" of things.

If we enlarge our conception of connection, not only in terms of the incredibly complex collisions we may imagine might follow the Big Bang, but also in terms of a system of inference in which interrelated "wholes" comprise the premises; and therefore a system in which a multiplicity of factors may weigh in at once, not just in a line and one at a time like drops from a spigot, but in a downpour like rain from a cloud; consequently a system in which our feeling, for example, that "Robert is prompt" will proceed from our understanding of the totality of his nature, rather than from a coded set of properties pried from his personality; then we shall be "thinking" the way we should, all along, have been reading: carrying every concept forward as though it were a great wave hanging over our surfing attention and modifying every moment's meaning. And then returning the whole load to the beginning again. Though the novel may still be, as Stendhal said, a mirror dawdling down a road, we will no longer narrow the road to represent the speedy passage of time, but remember that what the mirror sees, it sees in terms of its own illusory but deep surround, and that there are two roads, really: the one we travel down as though life were like that, the dust behind us disappearing along with the barns, the farms, the trees; and that same road's image in the novel's wayward mirror—convoluted, multiple, inverted, simultaneous, continuous, pointless, cracked—that is to say, the way life is.

NATURE, CULTURE,
AND COSMOS

L et us imagine a world without language; and since I am going to insist that what we sometimes call the soul is simply the immediate source of any speech—the larynx of the *logos*—a world without words will be a soulless one as well. If there are rude hulks moving about such a virginal land who resemble man, they will be mulk mountynotty types indeed: Vico's gesturers, all hands and feet and face. To this world I want to give the ancient name of Nature—all too plurally significant to be anything but honorific. For its polar opposite, a world made wholly of words, of "words, words, words," in Hamlet's weary invocation of it, the title *Finnegans Wake* has already been nominated by its ambitious author, if it has not yet been conferred.

We tend to stand uneasily between unadulterated Nature on the one hand and total Culture on the other, as though on a teeter. We may not know much about this mute, rough thing which language has had no hand in smoothing out, since there has never been a moment, to our knowledge, when we have been without ourselves in this place, so that we are forced to infer it, to reach past our presence, as ubiquitous as it is, in order to figure out just what our absence might mean, what our silence might signify, what a world without figments might look like, for to imagine a world without language is also to imagine a world undisturbed by anybody's elaborated longings, a world untroubled by beliefs, concerns, conjectures, dreams—a cosmos without a cosmology.

Of course, it could also simply be the image of our innermost, uncivilized selves, if there's a patch domestication hasn't reached —a Calibaning consciousness: eye and ear and nose and tongue and teeth—naught else. Here is one cause of our uneasiness as we balance on the teeter: fear of the region of ourselves that lies even beyond our cultured cruelty and embraced deceits, an area so stony it cannot be spoken to, and which might break open one day to disclose what character of elemental heat?

Although there are those who believe that the natural world can't get along without them, that it depends from their attention like a tear from an eye; I think it is safer to assume that sometime before the blessed event of our arrival, and rather more than several days, the creation on which we are now perched like a bird on a branch would have taken place. What cosmologists today, with unintentional vulgarity, call the Big Bang would have scattered the seeds of itself long since into the space of Space. Perhaps after our own Big Bang has snuffed us out, trees will again refuse to fall in the forests; or perhaps everywhere, on the contrary, there will be the renewed bleeps of an unheard cacophany, the sound of the sea as solid as stones strewn along the beach. But at least it will be a world without theories, thoughts, beliefs, symbolic behavior. It will be a world without nonsense.

More than a numerical match for anything man manufactures, more than those native beads that precede his corruptions, more than coffin nails rolled from the finest leaf, more than the number of paper napkins that blot his slobber, more than the bricks of his buildings or the bolts of his machines, man makes mistakes, man falls into errors (the only real sin, according to the only real philosophers), man keeps and feeds and cossets his opinions even better than he does his pets—do they not purr at his approach, and snarl at the smell of others?—and like his pets they mostly sleep and eat, bark and shit.

Even after our arrival, an arrival possibly prefigured by the constitution, even destiny, of matter, there will be parts of the planet —dense and steamy jungles so full of life creation will seem no big bang but the simplest snap, or glacial desolations swept by bitter winds where lifelessness is epidemic—and each of these will strike us, perhaps, as bits of the original Nature peeking out through tears in the cultural fabric: the world as it was before we were shaped, what we like to call "the wilderness." In any case, the solar system, and the limitless immensities of outer space, those interstellar absences where so little is going on it has to be elemental, will look like Nature to our lengthened, rounded, and signal-gleaning instruments. Or maybe it will be when our submarines have hit deep seas that we shall feel we've reached the aboriginal.

Pretty clearly, though, Nature will be hard to find. Nature may really be extinct. In its place, not only for us but for every species who must suffer us, there is Culture to be found instead—Culture, with its classes and customs; Culture, with its conventions and its canons. One function of Culture, whatever else it comes to, is to obscure or replace Nature with itself, to surround man with man, because it does not seem that we can survive in a state of Nature as if we were a stone in a pudding. No, we land in that pudding like a blob of ink. We intermingle as we fear the races will. The horror Hobbes describes, that state of war which is his state of Nature, where life is "solitary, poore, nasty, brutish, and short," compels us, in order to escape it, to invent society, the state, the family, the kingdom, the cosmos. Of course, we neglect to notice that Hobbes's nature is another invention, its attributes obtained as much by rhythm and other elements of his rhetoric as by argument, his covenants are fictions, his leviathan an apocalyptic beast, while we complain of our present life that we find it lonely, mean, peopled by brutes, impoverished, miserable, yet bitterly brief, without apparently realizing we are simply repeating his famous lines, although they are now about an allegedly civilized society. The fact is that in a state of Nature, men might squabble over the last bite of meat, but wars would be unlikely; wars require societies, clans at the very least, disciplined killing; wars involve conflicts between organizations, and are fought with words, whatever other weapons are waved. Without words we cannot formulate the necessary lies. Without the necessary lies, there may be nothing we are willing to die for. If there is nothing we are willing to die for . . . then . . . by default . . . peace.

Eden was such a state of peace, a private neighborhood with walls and gates and its own police. Here, it was the snake who uttered the first words, and it was not to ask for a light. Eve was quite unclothed and noninviting, you remember, before words were found to dress her in nakedness and whistle to the phallus as if its name were Fido: "Up, boy!" When Adam and Eve ate of the apple, they became opinionated. Paradise was destroyed by doctrine. Soon speculators developed it, creating subdivisions, tracts, plots.

It is of no importance what the guilty doctrine was. Any doctrine will do. Thomas Hobbes, our momentary mentor in such matters, in a passage that deserves extended quotation, simply makes a little list.

And for that part of Religion, which consisteth in opinions concerning the nature of Powers Invisible, there is almost nothing that has a name, that has not been esteemed amongst the Gentiles, in one place or another, a God, or Divell; or by their Poets feigned to be inanimated, inhabited, or possessed by some Spirit or other.

The unformed matter of the World, was a God, by the name of *Chaos.*

The Heaven, the Ocean, the Planets, the Fire, the Earth, the Winds, were so many Gods.

Men, Women, a Bird, a Crocodile, a Calf, a Dogge, a Snake, an Onion, a Leeke, Deified. Besides, that they filled almost all places, with spirits called *Daemons:* the plains, with *Pan,* and *Panises,* or Satyres; the Woods, with Fawnes, and Nymphs; the Sea, with Tritons, and other Nymphs; every River and Fountayn, with a Ghost of his name, and with Nymphs; every house with its *Lares,* or Familiars; every man, with his Genius; Hell, with Ghosts, and spirituall Officers, as

Charon, *Cerberus*, and the *Furies*; and in the night time, all places with *Larvae*, *Lemures*, Ghosts of men deceased, and a whole kingdome of Fayries, and Bugbears. They have also ascribed Divinity, and built Temples to meer Accidents, and Qualities; such as are Time, Night, Day, Peace, Concord, Love, Contention, Vertue, Honour, Health, Rust, Fever, and the like; which when they prayed for, or against, they prayed to, as if there were Ghosts of these names hanging over their heads, and letting fall, or withholding that Good, or Evill, for, or against which they prayed. They invoked also their own Wit, by the name of *Muses*; their own Ignorance, by the name of *Fortune*; their own Lust, by the name of *Cupid*; their own Rage, by the name *Furies*; their own privy members by the name of *Priapus*; and attributed their pollutions, to *Incubi*, and *Succubae*: insomuch as there was nothing, which a Poet could introduce as a person in his Poem, which they did not make either a *God*, or a *Divel*. [*Leviathan*, Pt. I, Ch. 12.]

This list, which could be extended to include every subject that drew the interest of Bouvard and Pécuchet, might be made as lengthy as an encyclopedia, and as detailed as a dictionary.

Things happen their way. Let them. We shall explain things otherwise, to suit our fancy, maintain ourselves in power and privilege, conceal our fears and our ambitions, focus hate and keep resentments warm, gain some sexual, some social, some legal, some economic, advantage; meanwhile supplying ourselves (no matter how things, still going their way, turn out) with an ample stock of justifications, prognostications, and excuses, ad hoc hypothecations, ambiguously stated advice and other misdirections, canards of every color, beliefs so absurd that if we can induce them in our fellows, we can then be assured that they will swallow anything: Diet Coke and decaffeinated coffee, resurrection and the parting of the Red Sea. We shall systematically constrain the minds of our children to ensure that, though tight and small, they will have the right shape. External enemies will drive us together, internal enemies will explain our failures on every front, while our successes will spring from the well-deserved support of superior powers.

I frankly do not see how we can make an honest survey of our acts, our thoughts, our theories, over almost any slice of time without a rising sense of intellectual disgust. In every way equal to our history of rape, pillage, murder, and political oppression will be a history of ideas so craftily untestable, and so persistently unclear, and so tenaciously gripped, as to provoke the profoundest dismay. Admiration too, of course, and astonishment. At what? at how well men can live, living within illusion.

We frequently apologize for mankind's infatuation with the opera of ideas by pointing out how desperately we all require illusions: firstly of our lovers about ourselves, and for ourselves concerning them, while privately we trouble or amuse our inner eye by assuming the roles of phantoms. Without our myths, we say, we could not create or preserve the social order; we could not enable others, of course weaker than we, to establish an identity and choose wise goals. We need belief to bind us together a little better than baseball, and form a community of expectation that exceeds the lottery. How else could we persuade people to make the necessary sacrifices on occasion or daily to endure the unendurable. So we shall surround perhaps a poisoned well with legends of eternal youth, and lend to otherwise futile lives both hope and meaning. Before us all, there is the same great black hole in the ground, a yawning hollow, the boredom of the earth for our Being. We simply must erect a protective fence in front of this abyss.

The earth reflects this abyss in the night sky, so there we shall imagine heaven peeking warmly through the stars; there we shall construct our most glamorous confusions, cosmologies which defy the world's demise, and put Nature in a cage of words.

One virtue of Giambattista Vico's theory of history, at any rate according to the reading of his compatriot Benedetto Croce, is that it carefully separates material history, with its simple chronology, its routine of wars, plagues, earthquakes, pogroms, tyrannies, and famines, from that which represents the innermost movement of the human mind, and every invention of the human spirit. That is, over against a human history written as if it consisted of physical events in that realm I've called Nature, Vico places a history of culture. Language, of course, is the principal shaper of this cultural history. It is a history which advances as language advances, especially as it passes from that period when men gestured their desires and danced their desperations, through a time when they blazoned them on walls and shields and standards, wore totems like skins and skins like totems, and invented a language of tribal logos very much as our designers do now for Ford and General Motors (that far has the word *logos* fallen since God first said: "Licht und macht schnell!"), to the day they howled a vowel and growled a consonant and exchanged real caves for Plato's.

I sometimes think that Hobbes, Spinoza, and Freud were right. Inertia is the one real law. Sometimes called preservation, sometimes called equilibrium, sometimes called do-nothing. We'd stay in bed if someone would feed us. And we leave home looking back. Behind us are the soon-to-be-consummated tragedies of domesticity, and their queens and consorts: Medea, Electra, Clytemnestra, Antigone, and the rest; before us are the epics of the *Iliad* and the *Aeneid*; action and interrogation alternate; but while we swing between these poles of departure and return, reluctant change and unchanging reluctance, the rope tightens around our neck.

How beautifully Joyce pictures it in his brief tale of the prank-quean, a tale that capsulates Vico's eternal returns and the cycles of Joyce's own book, the cycles that turn round like Beckett's heroes will on their broken wheels, for we can wait for the end of our world anywhere now, any nearby bench will atomize as well as any wall, meadow, or church. We can begin to bleed from our nose and eyes while in or out of bed. We can be raped and riddled in a foreign country or on our own front porch. This borrowed cosmology, which no longer, in the Christian manner, imagines History as the shortest distance between our first Fall and our final Redemption; that is, as the marked accretions of Time, the crowding together of events that then darken it and make it palpable the way points may be imagined queuing in front of the Future, as if it were selling tickets, to compose a sentence of some length, if doubtful significance. The Christian line of Time resembles the line of Life, for both begin with a birth, descend unevenly toward death, and end, for the true believer, again, in a move which takes them out of the play, saves them from oblivion, and saves History from overcrowding.

The Viconian view treats history as if it were a cycle like the seasons, like the flooding of the Nile, like the paths of the planets and the movement of the stars. It treats history as if it were a thing, not an event. Things may be annihilated, but it makes no sense to speak of them as if they had just begun, had gone halfway, or were nearly over. We don't say: Hurry, the statue has just started. The world moves, according to Vico, like the brightly lit glass ball in the ballroom; its phases begin and end, but it revolves only to come round again. The pattern itself is a cultural invention. This moving image makes romantic a tawdry gym. Nevertheless, Vico's separation of historical mind from historical matter, which Croce applauded, allows us to see how much more important the invention of logic was, for example, than that drawn-out war on the Peloponnesus; how extraordinary even the creation of a new notation can be, like that which was finally devised for music; how like the discovery of the wheel is the Socratic conception of the soul—no longer shadow, blood, or breath, but a thoroughly abstract entity; how fundamental, in short, are the forms of the mind, how weak the so-called solid, simple facts.

That man must eat to live. That everyone must die. Really hard items. Dissolve into a dew, like Joyce's Anna Livia Plurabelle, do they? then evaporate entirely, only to be gathered together in soft clouds and driven against the mountains, where their rain enriches the rivers. The linear view of history is based upon the linear life of man, but where man's life draws an arc like an arrow's drooping path, the purpose of providence is to pull him out of his dive just in time. Vico's pagan view of history, however, sticks close to those rhythmical alternations that beat back and forth within life, and that seem to express long, slumberous lengths of Egyptian time and the continued quiet begetting of the generations, as well as the more tumultuous periodic conflagrations imagined by the Greeks.

So there is the stuttery voice of God, the clap of thunder, mutter in the mountains. The bomb drops, the ice cap cracks, and we hear the hundred letters of Joyce's lightning bolt punctuate the periodic appearances of the prankquean; we hear it as written on Finnegans' wind:

> It was of a night, late, lang time agone, in an auldstane eld, when Adam was delvin and his madameen spinning watersilts, when mulk mountynotty man was everybully and the first leal ribberrobber that ever had her ainway everybuddy to his love-saking eyes and everybilly lived alove with everybiddy else, and Jarl van Hoother had his burnt head high up in his lamphouse, laying cold hands on himself. And his two little jiminies, cous-ins of ourn, Tristopher and Hilary, were kickaheeling their dummy on the oil cloth flure of his homerigh, castle and earthenhouse. And, be dermot, who come to the keep of his inn only the niece-of-his-in-law, the prankquean. And the prankquean pulled a rosy one and made her wit foreninst the dour. And she lit up and fireland was ablaze. And spoke she to the dour in her petty perusienne: Mark the Wans, why do I am alook alike a poss of porterpease? And that was how the skirtmisshes began.

Countless cosmologies have been crowded in here, as if Joyce had hired a hall.

But that is the cruelty. We have to enter this labyrinthian fiction, with its arbitrary cosmos, its made-up laws, and its compacted lingo; we have to pull over our heads a cover of concepts and sleep like H. C. Earwicker himself the sleep of these syllables, before we can encounter the truth: that the world away from this work, the world we really eat and sleep and sweat and fight and screw in, is a fiction, too; but a fiction that fails to acknowledge its nature and is therefore and for that reason unreal; because the secret at the center of *Finnegans Wake* is written on a piece of paper which a hen, it's said, has scratched from a midden. Yes, the writer has woven our lies around us like binding lines of evidence. He convicts us of culture.

The prankquean has got God's goat for the third and last time. Here is how the skirtmisshes endupped:

> For like the campbells acoming with a fork lance of lightning, Jarl von Hoother Boanerges himself, the old terror of the dames, came hip hop handihap out through the pikeopened arkway of his three shuttoned castles, in his broadginger hat and his civic chollar and his allabuff hemmed and his bullbrag-gin soxangloves and his ladbroke breeks and his cattegut ban-dolair and his furframed panuncular cumbottes like a rudd yellan gruebleen orangeman in his violet indigonation, to the whole longth of the strongth of his bowman's bill. And he clopped his rude hand to his eacy hitch and he ordurd and his thick spch spck for her to shut up shop, dappy. And the duppy shot the shutter clup.

Whereupon the thunder punctuates the prose, and shortly Joyce concludes: "And that was the first peace of illiterative porthery in all the flamend floody flatuous world."

Nature is a lot like the blank page, the blank sky: there is a terrifying latitude to Nature, an immense indifference, which we symbolize by means of the sea and its implacable, impersonal, monotonous repetitions. If there is one thing we know about the world as it would be without us, it is the massive unconcern it has for us when we are present; for if we believe that the stars rule our lives, or that God's in his heaven, or that times return wearing the same face as the clock, or that certain disgusting objects are edible and some surely splendid ones are not, or that we ought to sacrifice virgins or use the elderly as bait for wild beasts, or circumcise ourselves or scar our cheeks, or kneel in front of tatty statues or wear a veil or feel that some people are base and unclean and others are like Shirley Temple . . . and so on until we reach leeks, as in Hobbes's little list; Nature would not lift a correcting hand, wrinkle a discriminating nose or raise a disapproving eyebrow. It lets us behave like fools; it lets us live among lies and think we're in a field of lilies; it lets us rape and call it marriage, enslave and call it soul-saving; it doesn't even go hoot when we call someone a godlike king or pope or saint or buddha. Not only that, but many civilizations, many systems of ideas, many philosophies and many works of art, many physical sciences and versions of psychology, many different sets of laws and views of politics and economics, can flourish and seem to sustain a society, allowing a people to reach what we think of as the highest cultural heights—the Greeks, the Egyptians, the Mayans, the Chinese, the Hindoos, Eng- lishmen, Bostonians, Southern belles—while contradicting one another so baldly, so continuously, so extremely, at almost every point, that we know most of them must be largely false—namely, every opinion but our own.

Although there has always been an honorable tradition in philos- ophy which holds that it is better not to believe at all than to believe badly—the list is long, from Socrates to Montaigne, from Nietzsche through Wittgenstein—philosophers have also been eager merchants of ideas. Still, they are wily. They commit only that part of the head where the hat rests. You cannot say, when you see one on the street, "Ah, there goes a person who believes that existence is a property." By the time we have reached ideology (where ideas are organized and administered by bureau clerks), another nature has been glued firmly over whatever is otherwise out there, so that Nature will now appear to support a history of point and purpose, to provide moralities for man which thoroughly demean him, and to offer status to the undeserving, and false hope to the trodden down.

The significance of cultural diversity is not that there are no universal truths, no objective morality, no general standards of taste; rather, it is that Nature is not their underwriter; it has no cosmology, no theology, perhaps no ontology of its own, nor is it made of Number, as the Pythagoreans suggested; and despite some suspicions to the contrary, Nature does not speak German. If we want walls on which to hang our values, we shall have to build them ourselves; but now the difference will be that we shall be beguiled by our cultural language only in the way *Finnegans Wake* beguiles us, and our standards supported the way *Finnegans Wake* supports its; for concerning fictions, as we know, many sorts of fine assessments can be made. Meanwhile, we shall enjoy all the advantages of doubt—a healthy, well-muscled mind among them. Who knows what we shall see when the mists of meaning lift? who knows how far we may be able to hear as ideological noise is reduced, all that white static cleared? Perhaps we shall even, now and then, receive the distant ding of the *Ding an sich* itself.

V

THE BABY
OR THE BOTTICELLI

We are to imagine a terrible storm like that which opens Verdi's *Otello*. The pavement of the *piazzetta* is awash. Saint Mark's pigeons are flying about, looking for land. The Venetian sun has gone down like a gondola in the lagoon. As we wade along in the dying light, a baby in a basket passes. It is being swept out to sea with the rest of the city's garbage. So is a large painting, beautifully framed, which floats its grand nude by us as if she were swimming. Then the question comes, bobbing like a bit of flotsam itself: Which one should we save, the tiny tot or the Tintoretto? the kid in the crib or the Canaletto?

It may be that during two thousand or more years of monsoons, tidal waves, and high water, this choice has not once actually presented itself; yet, undismayed, it is in this form that philosophers frequently represent the conflict between art and morality—a conflict, of course, they made up in the first place. Baby or Botticelli. What'll you have?

Not only is the dilemma an unlikely one; the choice it offers is peculiar. We are being asked to decide not between two different actions but between two different objects. And how different indeed these floating objects are. The baby is a vessel of human consciousness, if its basket isn't. It is nearly pure potentiality. It must be any babe—no one babe but babe in general, babe in bulk —whose bunk is boating by. Never mind if it was born with the brain of an accountant, inflicted with a cleft palate, or given Mo-

zartian talents: these are clearly irrelevant considerations, as are
ones concerning the seaworthiness of the basket, or the prospect
of more rain. One fist in this fight swings from the arm of an open
future against the chest of a completed past. . . .

. . . A completed past because we have to know the pedigree of
the painting or it's no contest. If it is the rosy nude who used to
recline behind the bar in Harry's, or just another mislaid entrant
in the latest Biennale, then the conditions of the case are fatally
altered and there is no real conflict of interest, though the blank
space behind the bar at Harry's will surely fill us with genuine
sorrow each scotch-and-water hour. It is not between infant and
image, then, that we are being asked to choose, but between some
fully realized esthetic quality and a vaguely generalized human
nature, even though it is a specific baby who could drown.

It is the moralists, of course, who like to imagine these lunatic
choices. It is the moralists who want to bully and beat up on the
artists, not the other way around. The error of the artists is indifference. Not since Plato's day, when the politicians in their grab for
public power defeated the priests, the poets, and the philosophers,
have artists, except for an occasional Bronx cheer, molested a moralist. Authors do not gather to burn good deeds in public squares;
laws are not passed by poets to put lying priests behind bars, nor
do they usually suggest that the pursuit of goodness will lead you
away from both beauty and truth, that it is the uphill road to
ruin. Musicians do not hang moralizing lackeys from lampposts as
though they were stringing their fiddles; moralizing lackeys do that.

On the other hand . . . We know what the other, the righteous
hand is full of: slings and arrows, slanders and censorship, prisons,
scaffolds, burnings and beatings. To what stake has Savonarola's
piety been bound by the painters he disgraced? Throughout history, goodness has done more harm than good, and over the years
moralists have managed to give morality a thoroughly bad name.
Although lots of bad names have been loaned them by the poets,
if the poets roast, they roast no one on the coals, only upon their
scorn, while moralists, to their reward, have dispatched who knows
how many thousands of souls.

The choice, baby or Botticelli, is presented to us as an example of the conflict between Art and Ethics, but between Art and Ethics there is no conflict, nor is this an instance, for our quandary falls entirely within the ethical. The decision, if there is one to make, is moral.

The values that men prize have been variously classified. There may be said to be, crudely, five kinds. There are, first of all, those facts and theories we are inclined to call true, and which, we think, constitute our knowledge. Philosophy, history, science, presumably pursue them. Second, there are the values of duty and obligation—obedience and loyalty, righteousness and virtue—qualities that the state finds particularly desirable. Appreciative values of all kinds may be listed third, including the beauties of women, art, and nature, the various sublimes, and that pleasure which comes from the pure exercise of human faculties and skills. Fourth are the values of self-realization and its attendant pleasures—growth, well-being, and the like—frequently called happiness in deference to Aristotle. Finally, there are those that have to do with real or imagined redemption, with ultimate justice and immortality. Some would prefer to separate political values like justice or freedom from more narrowly moral ones, while others would do the same for social values like comfort, stability, security, conditions often labeled simply "peace." But a complete and accurate classification, assuming it could be accomplished, is not important here. Roughly, we might call our goals, as tradition has, Truth, Goodness, Beauty, Happiness, and Salvation. (We can reach port, sometimes, even with a bad map.)

If we allow our classificatory impulse to run on a little longer, it will encourage us to list at least four customary attitudes that can be taken toward the relationship of these value areas to one another. First, one can deny the legitimacy or reality of a particular value group. Reckless pragmatists and some sophists deny the objective existence of all values except utility, while positivists prefer to elevate empirical truth (which they don't capitalize, only underscore) to that eminence. It is, of course, truth thinned to the thickness of a wire, which is fine if you want to cut cheese. The values

that remain are rejected as attitudes, moods, or emotions—subjective states of various sorts like wishing, hoping, willing, which suggest external objects without being able to establish them. I happen
to regard salvation values as illusory or mythological, since I deny
any significance to the assumptions on which they are grounded,
but other people may pick out different victims.

Second, we might accept the values of a certain sphere as real
enough, but argue that some or all of them are reducible to others,
even eventually to one. Reductionism is characteristic of Plato's
famous argument that virtue is knowledge; of Keats's fatuous little
motto, Beauty is Truth; of materialists and idealists equally. Rather
than reduce moral values to those of happiness, Aristotle simply
ignored them.

Third, we can try to make some values subordinate to others.
This is not the same as reduction. One might argue that artistic and
moral values are mutually exclusive, or unique, and yet support the
superiority of one over the other. There are, however, two kinds of
subordination. One asserts that X is more important than Y, so
that when one has to choose between them (baby or Botticelli),
one must always choose the baby. When designing buildings, for
instance, beauty regularly runs afoul of function and economy.
The other sort of subordination insists not only that X is more
important, or "higher" in value, than Y, but that Y should serve or
be a means to X: the baby is a model for the baby in the Botticelli.
The slogan Form follows function is sometimes so understood. I
take crude Marxism to require this kind of sacrifice from the artist.

Fourth, it is possible to argue, as I do, that these various value
areas are significantly different. They are not only different; they
are not reducible, but are independent of one another. Furthermore, no one value area is more important, abstractly considered,
than any other. In short, these various values are different, independent, and equal.

This does not imply that in particular instances you should not
choose one over the other and have good reasons for doing so; it is
simply that what is chosen in any instance cannot be dictated in

advance. Obviously, if you are starving, whether your food is served with grace and eaten with manners is less than essential. Should you skip dinner or lick the spilled beans from the floor? Should you choose to safeguard a painting or the well-being of its model? Should you bomb Monte Cassino?

That attachment to human life which demands that it be chosen over everything else is mostly humbug. It can be reasonably, if not decisively, argued that the world is already suffering from a surfeit of such animals; that most human beings rarely deserve the esteem some philosophers have for them; that historically humans have treated their pets better than they have treated one another; that no one is so essential he or she cannot be replaced a thousand times over; that death is inevitable anyhow; that it is our sense of community and our own identity which lead us to persist in our parochial overestimation; that it is rather a wish of philosophers than a fact that man be more important than anything else that's mortal, since nature remains mum and scarcely supports the idea, nor do the actions of man himself. Man makes a worse god than God, and when God was alive, he knew it.

Baby or Botticelli is a clear enough if artificial choice, but it places the problem entirely in the moral sphere, where the differences involved can be conveniently overlooked. What differences?

The writing of a book (the painting of a painting, the creation of a score) is generally such an exacting and total process that it is not simply okay if it has many motives; it is essential. The difference between one of Flaubert's broken amatory promises to Louise Colet and his writing of *Madame Bovary* (both considered immoral acts in some circles) is greater even than Lenin's willingness to board a train and his intended overthrow of the czar. Most promises are kept by actions each one of which fall into a simple series; that is, I meet you at the Golden Egg by getting up from my desk, putting on my coat, and getting into my car: a set of actions each one of which can be serially performed and readily seen as part of "going to lunch." I may have many reasons for keeping our date, but having promised becomes the moral one.

However, when I create a work of art, I have entered into no
contract of any kind with the public, unless the work has been
commissioned. In this sense, most esthetic acts are unbidden,
uncalled-for, even unexpected. They are gratuitous. And unlike
Lenin's intention to overthrow an empire (which can scarcely be
an intention of the same kind as mine to meet you for lunch,
involving, as it does, several years, thousands of folks, and millions
of rubles), my writing will, all along, be mine alone, and I will not
normally parcel out the adjectives to subordinates and the sex
scenes to specialists, or contract out the punctuation.

I have many reasons for going to the Golden Egg, then: I am
hungry; you are pretty; we have business; it is a good place to be
seen; I need a change from the atmosphere of the office; you are
paying, and I am broke—oh, yes . . . and I promised. All these
interests are easily satisfied by our having lunch. There is no need
to order them; they are not unruly or at odds.

So why am I writing this book? Why, to make money, to become
famous, to earn the love of many women, to alter the world's
perception of itself, to put my rivals' noses out of joint, to satisfy
my narcissism, to display my talents, to justify my existence to my
deceased father, to avoid cleaning the house; but if I wish to make
money, I shall have to write trash, and if I wish to be famous, I had
better hit home runs, and if I wish to earn the love of many women,
I shall have more luck going to work in a bank. In short, these
intentions do conflict; they must be ordered; none of them is particularly "good" in the goodie sense; and none is esthetic in any way.

But there is so much energy in the baser motives, and so little in
the grander, that I need hate's heat to warm my art; I must have
my malice to keep me going. For I must go, and go on, regardless.
Because making a work of art (writing a book, being Botticelli)
requires an extended kind of action, an ordered group of actions.
Yet these actions are not the sort that result, like a battle, in many
effects, helter-skelter: in broken bodies, fugitive glories, lasting
pains, conquered territories, power, ruin, ill will; rather, as a funnel
forms the sand and sends it all in the same direction, the many acts
of the artist aim at one end, one result.

We are fully aware, of course, that while I am meeting you for lunch, admiring your bodice, buying office equipment, I am not doing the laundry, keeping the books, dieting, or being faithful in my heart; and when I am painting, writing, singing scales, I am not cooking, cleaning house, fixing flats. The hours, the days, the years, of commitment to my work must necessarily withdraw me from other things, from my duties as a husband, a soldier, a citizen.

So the actions of the artist include both what he does and, therefore, what he doesn't do; what he does directly and on purpose, and what he does incidentally and quite by the way. In addition, there are things done, or not done, or done incidentally, that are quite essential to the completion and character of the work, but whose effects do not show themselves in the ultimate object or performance. As necessary as any other element, they disappear in the conclusion like a middle term in an argument. A deleted scene, for instance, may nonetheless lead to the final one. Every line is therefore many lines: words rubbed out, thoughts turned aside, concepts canceled. The eventual sentence lies there quietly, "Kill the king," with no one but the writer aware that it once read, "Kiss the king," and before that "Kiss the queen." For moralists, only too often, writing a book is little different from robbing a bank, but actions of the latter sort are not readily subject to revisions.

The writer forms words on a page. This defaces the page, of course, and in this sense it is like throwing a brick through a window; but it is not like throwing a brick through a window in any other way. And if writing is an immense ruckus made of many minor noises, some shutting down as soon as they are voiced, then reading is similarly a series of acts, better ordered than many, to be sure, but just as privately performed, and also open to choice, which may have many motives too, the way the writing had. Paintings and performances (buildings even more so) are public in a fashion that reading and writing never are, although the moralist likes to make lump sums of everything and look at each art as if it were nothing but a billboard or a sound truck in the street.

If we rather tepidly observe that a building stands on its street quite differently from a book in its rack, must we not also notice

how infrequently architects are jailed for committing spatial hanky-
panky or putting up obscene façades? Composers may have their
compositions hooted from the hall, an outraged patron may assault
a nude, a church may be burned to get at the God believed to be
inside, but more often than not it is the *littérateur* who is shot or
sent to Siberia. Moralists are not especially sensitive to form. It is
the message that turns their noses blue. It is the message they will
murder you for. And messages that are passed as secretly as books
pass, from privacy to privacy, make them intensely suspicious. Yet
work which refuses such interpretations will not be pardoned either. Music which is twelve-toned, paintings which are abstract,
writing which seems indifferent to its referents in the world—these
attacks on messages themselves—they really raise the watchdog's
hackles.

In life, values do not sit in separate tents like harem wives; they
mix and mingle rather like sunlight in a room or pollution in the
air. A dinner party, for example, will affect the diners' waists, delight or dismay their palates, put a piece of change in the grocer's
pocket, bring a gleam to the vintner's eye. The guests may be
entertained or stupefied by gossip, chat, debate, wit. I may lose a
chance to make out, or happily see my seduction advance past
hunt-and-peck. The host may get a leg up in the firm whose boss
he's entertaining; serious arguments may break out; new acquaintances may be warmly made. And if I, Rabbi Ben Ezra, find myself
seated next to Hermann Göring, it may put me quite off the quail
—quail that the *Reichsmarschall* shot by machine gun from a
plane. There should be no questions concerning the rabbi's
qualms. It would be a serious misjudgment, however, if I imagined
that the quail was badly cooked on account of who shot it, or
believed that the field marshal's presence had soured the wine,
although it may have ruined the taste in my mouth. It might be
appropriate to complain of one who enjoyed the meal and laughed
at the fat boy's jokes. Nevertheless, the meal will be well prepared
or not, quite independently of the guests' delightful or obnoxious
presence, and it would be simpleminded to think that because

these values were realized in such close proximity, they therefore should be judged on other than their own terms—the terms, perhaps, of their pushier neighbors.

The detachment it is sometimes necessary to exercise in order to disentangle esthetic qualities from others is often resented. It is frequently considered a good thing if moral outrage makes imbeciles of us. The esthete who sees only the poppies blowing in Flanders fields is a sad joke, to be sure, but the politicized mind is too dense and too dangerous to be funny.

I have been mentioning some differences between moral acts as they are normally understood (keeping promises, saving the baby) and what might be called artistic ones (dancing the fandango, painting the Botticelli), and I have been drawing attention to the public and private qualities of the several arts lest they be treated *en bloc*. Finally, I have suggested that values have to be judged by sharply different standards sometimes, though they come to the same table. However, my dinner party differs from Petronius' banquet in another essential: it is "thrown" only once. Even if the evening is repeated down to the last guest's happy gurgle, the initial party can be only vaguely imitated, since you can't swallow the same soup twice (as a famous philosopher is supposed to have said). The events of my party were like pebbles tossed into a pond. The stones appear to shower the surface of the water with rings, which then augment or interfere with one another as they widen, although eventually they will enlarge into thin air, the pond will become calm, and the stones' effects will be felt only after eons, as they lie, slowly disintegrating, on the bottom.

Art operates at another level altogether. Petronius' story does not fling itself like a handful of stones at the public and then retire to contemplate the gradual recession of its consequences, but occurs continually as readers reenact it. Of course these readings will not be identical (because no reading is written or automatically becomes a printed part of the text), but the text, unless it has been mutilated or reedited, will remain the same. I shall recognize each line as the line I knew, and each word as the word that was. The letter abides and is literal, though the spirit moves and strays. In short, the mouth may have an altered taste, but not the soup.

For this reason the powers of events are known to be brief, even when loud and unsettling, and unless they can reach the higher levels of historical accounts—unless they can reach language—the events will be forgotten and their effects erased. Accounts, too, can be lost or neglected, so those texts that are truly strong are those whose qualities earn the love and loyalty of their readers, and enlist the support and stewardship of the organizations those readers are concerned with and control (schools, societies, academies, museums, archives), because the institutions encourage us to turn to these now canonical texts again and again, where their words will burn in each fresh consciousness as if they had just been lit.

Moralists are right to worry about works of art, then, because they belong to a higher level of reality than most things. Texts can be repeated; texts can be multiplied; texts can be preserved; texts beget commentaries, and their authors energize biographers; texts get quoted, praised, reviled, memorized; texts become sacred.

The effects of a text (as every failed commission on pornography has demonstrated) cannot be measured as you measure blows; the spread of a text cannot be followed like the course of an epidemic; there is no dye that can be spilled upon the ground to track the subtle seepages of its contamination. Texts are not acts of bodies but acts of minds; for the most part, then, they do not act on bodies as bodies act, but on minds as minds do.

Most religions do not gather their followers about God, as they pretend, or attract the faithful to the high ideals they claim to serve and defend: no—these believers have sold their souls to a book, and sit inside a text as though it were a temple, and warm themselves with the holy, unmistaken, and enduring Word. They protect the Word; they preach the Word; the blade of their sword is made mostly of the Word; and any other word is suspicious, likely to be an enemy bent on endangering the authority of whatever's gospel.

The position I am trying to defend is not that literature has no relation to morality, or that reading and writing, or composing, or painting, aren't also moral, or possibly, immoral acts. Of course they can be. But they are economic acts as well. They contribute to their author's health or illness, happiness or melancholy. They fill libraries, concert halls, museums. And much more. The artistic value of a book, however, is different from its economic value, and is differently determined, as is its weight in pounds, its utility as a paperweight or doorstop, its elevating or edifying or life-enhancing properties, its gallery of truths: new truths, known truths, believed truths, important truths, alleged truths, trivial truths, absolute truths, coming truths, plain unvarnished truths. Artistic quality depends upon a work's internal, formal, organic character, upon its inner system of relations, upon its structure and its style, and not upon the morality it is presumed to recommend, or upon the benevolence of its author, or its emblematic character, when it is seen as especially representative of some situation or society.

As I have already suggested, values may reinforce one another, or interfere with their realization in some thing or person. The proximity of Herr Göring may put me off my feed. Perhaps I ought to be put off. Perhaps the chef should have poisoned the quail. Perhaps each of the guests should have left in a huff. And the housemaid and the butler grin as they quaff champagne in the kitchen, grin so little bones appear between their open teeth. How's the pâté no one invited would eat? Deelish.

Wagner's works are not wicked simply because he was; nor does even the inherent vulgarity deep within the music quite destroy it. Frost's poetry seems written by a better man than we've been told he was. In fact, we are frequently surprised when an author of genius (like Chekhov) appears to be a person of some decency of spirit. The moral points of view in works of art differ as enormously as Dante's do from Sophocles', or Shakespeare's from Milton's. Simply consider what we should have to say if the merit of these writers depended at all upon their being correct, even about anything. In any case, Balzac sees the world quite differently than Butor does; Goethe and Racine cannot both be right; so if being right mattered, we should be in a mess indeed, and most of our classics headed for the midden.

How many of us are prepared to embrace the cuckoo-clock concepts of Blake and Yeats? Or perhaps Pound? How about Kipling? D. H. Lawrence? The Marquis de Sade?

If author and art ought not to be confused, neither should art and audience. If we were to say, as I should prefer, that it is the moral world of the work which ought to matter to the moralist, not the genes of the author's grandfather, or the Jean who was a long-time lover, or a lean of the pen holder toward the political right or left, we ought also to insist that the reactions of readers aren't adequate evidence either. If Wagner's anti-Semitism doesn't fatally bleed into his operas and, like a bruise, discolor them, and if Balzac's insufferable bourgeois dreams don't irreparably damage his fictions, then why should we suppose the work itself, in so much less command of its readers than its author is of the text, will communicate its immoral implications like a virus to the innocents who open its covers?

To be sure, authors often like to think of their works as explosive, as corrupting, as evil. It is such fun to play the small boy. Lautréamont asks Heaven to "grant the reader the boldness to become ferocious, momentarily, like what he is reading, to find, without being disoriented, his abrupt and savage path through the desolate swamps of these somber and poison-filled pages." Yet this is an operatic attitude; reading is never more than reading, and requires a wakeful understanding—that is all. Certainly we should like to think that we had written some "poison-filled pages," but no luck. Even chewing them won't make you sick, not even queasy. And if you feel the least bit odd afterward, it's the ink.

If the relation of morality to art were based simply on the demand that art be concerned with values, then almost every author should satisfy it even if he wrote with his prick while asleep. (Puritans will object to the language in that sentence, and feminists to the organ, and neither will admire or even notice how it was phrased.) Henry Miller's work has been condemned, but Henry Miller is obsessed with ethical issues, and his work has a very pronounced moral point of view. *Madame Bovary* was attacked; *Ulysses* was forbidden entry into the United States; *Lady Chatterley's Lover* was brought to court, where they worried about signs of sodomy in it; *Lolita*, of course, was condemned; and, as Vonnegut has said (who also has suffered such censorship), so it goes. How long the list would be, how tiresome and dismaying and absurd its recital, if we were to cite every work that has been banned, burned, or brought into the dock.

It is simply not possible to avoid ethical concerns; they are everywhere; one is scarcely able to move without violating someone's moral law. Nor are artists free of the desire to improve and instruct and chastise and bemoan the behavior of their fellow creatures, whether they call themselves Dickens, D. H. Lawrence, or Hector Berlioz. Céline is so intensely a moral writer that it warps his work. That is the worry. "There are still a few hatreds I'm missing," he wrote. "I am sure they exist." Hate, we mustn't forget, is a thoroughly moralized feeling.

It is the management of all these impulses, attitudes, ideas, and emotions (which the artist has as much as anyone) that is the real problem, for each of us is asked by our aims, as well as by our opportunities, to overcome our past, our personal aches and pains, our beloved prejudices, and to enlist them in the service of our skills, the art we say we're loyal to and live for. If a writer is extended on the rack of love, let pain give the work purpose, and disappointment its burnished point. So the artistic temperament is called cold because its grief becomes song instead of wailing. To be a preacher is to bring your sense of sin to the front of the church, but to be an artist is to give to every mean and ardent, petty and profound, feature of the soul a glorious, godlike shape.

It is actually not the absence of the ethical that is complained of, when complaints are made, for the ethical is never absent. It is the absence of the *right* belief, the *right* act, that riles. Our pets have not been fed; repulsive enthusiasms have been encouraged, false gods pursued, obnoxious notions noised about; so damn these blank and wavy paintings and these hostile drums, these sentences that sound like one long scratch of chalk.

Goodness knows nothing of Beauty. They are quite disconnected. If I say "shit" in a sentence, it is irrelevant what else I say, whether it helps my sentence sing or not. What is relevant is the power of certain principles of decorum, how free to be offensive we are going to be allowed to be. When the dowager empress of China, Cixi, diverted funds intended for the navy to construct a large and beautiful marble boat, which thousands now visit at the Summer Palace in Beijing, she was guilty of expropriation. If her choice had been a free one, she would seem to have chosen to spend her money on a thing of peace rather than on things of war (a choice we might applaud); in fact, we know she simply spent the money on herself. She cannot have chosen the beauty she received, because beauty is beyond choice. The elegant workmanship which went into the boat, the pleasure and astonishment it has given to many, its rich and marvelous material, are serendipitous and do not affect the morality of the case.

When a government bans nonobjective art, it is because its very look is threatening; it is its departure from the upright, its deviationism, that is feared—a daub is a dangerous breach of decorum. Finally, when the Soviet authorities decided to loosen their restrictions on the publication of books and the holding of performances, this was not suddenly a choice of art over politics on their part; it *was* politics, and had to do with such issues as the freedom of information, the quashing of the Stalin cults, the placation of certain opponents, and so on, not with art. They knew what the novels in the drawers were about.

I do happen to feel, with Theodor Adorno, that writing a book is a very important ethical act, consuming so much of one's life; and that, in these disgusting times, a writer who does not pursue an alienating formalism (but rather tries to buck us up and tell us not to spit in the face of the present, instead of continuing to serve this corrupt and debauched society although it shits on every walk and befouls every free breath), is, if not a pawn of the system (a lackey, we used to say), then probably a liar and a hypocrite. (Shit cannot sing, you say? perhaps; but by the bowels, shit sells.) It is a general moral obligation to live in one's time, and to have a just and appropriate attitude toward it (to spit upon it if need be), not to live in the nineteenth century or to be heartless toward the less fortunate or to deny liberty and opportunity to others, to hold on to stupid superstitions, or fall victim to nostalgia.

But good books have been written by bad people, by people who served immoral systems, who went to bed with snakes, by people who were frauds in various ways, by schemers and panderers. And beautiful books have been written by the fat and old and ugly, the lonely, the misbegotten (it is the same in all the arts), and some of these beautiful books are, like Juan Goytisolo's, ferociously angry, and some of them are even somewhat sinister like Baudelaire's, and some are shakingly sensuous like those of Colette, and still others are dismayingly wise, or deal with terror tenderly, or are full of lamentable poppycock. (I am thinking most immediately of Pope's *Essay on Man*.)

I think it is one of the artist's obligations to create as perfectly as he or she can, not regardless of all other consequences, but in full awareness, nevertheless, that in pursuing other values—in championing Israel or fighting for the rights of women, or defending the faith, or exposing capitalism, supporting your sexual preferences or speaking for your race—you may simply be putting on a saving scientific, religious, political mask to disguise your failure as an artist. Neither the world's truth nor a god's goodness will win you beauty's prize.

Finally, in a world which does not provide beauty for its own sake, but where the loveliness of flowers, landscapes, faces, trees, and sky are adventitious and accidental, it is the artist's task to add to the world's objects and ideas those delineations, carvings, tales, fables, and symphonic spells which ought to be there; to make things whose end is contemplation and appreciation; to give birth to beings whose qualities harm no one, yet reward even the most casual notice, and which therefore deserve to become the focus of a truly disinterested affection.

There is perhaps a moral in that.

SIMPLICITIES

1

Junichiro Tanizaki wrote that we "Westerners are amazed at the simplicity of Japanese rooms, perceiving in them no more than ashen walls bereft of ornament." What he wrote is certainly true about Americans. We are amazed. Often, furthermore, we deeply approve; for simplicity—severity even—plainness—are pioneer virtues still held in high esteem by us, if rarely practiced now. Indeed, the simple, in our covered-wagon days, was directly connected, as a tool might be, to the hand and what the hand made. This simplicity implied less skill than it demanded determination, and it emerged from coarse necessity the way the vegetables we grew in the dirt near our farmhouse kitchen did: products equally of effort and rough chance, as crude as our first fence, and cultivated no farther than you would dig a well—not an inch beyond the reach of water.

The shelters we built were like the ground we broke and the implements we made—plain as their names: house, field, food, cloth, plough—simple as the simple liberties we enjoyed, though these were not freedoms from Nature, certainly, since Nature hemmed us in and made life hard; nor from thieves or Indians or illness, dangers common and recurrent as nighttime; but from society, from other people's profiteering regulations, from laws we didn't like, servitude, and our own past failures, from the exasperating complications of a civilization caught in the toils of Time, tied down by custom and privilege.

In a land whose very features were unfamiliar, where even the rules of life were strangers, where the past had been abolished so that everyone could feel they were starting life as equals from a line of opportunity which was the same for all; in such a land, with such a task, you had to learn to depend on yourself, to make a religion, as Emerson did, out of "self-reliance" and become a handyman, a "jack-of-all-trades," as it was put. But it was also true that when you did need others, you desperately needed them—to form a posse, raise a roof, to bridge a stream—nor did you have the time or training to divine obscure intentions or engage in elaborate ritual games in order to discover whether another person was a friend or an enemy, a worker or a wastrel, dependable or weak, an honest man or a rustler; so you wanted to know immediately "how the land lay," and the frank and open countenance was consequently prized, as were the looks of a man who had worked long and hard in the wind and sun, who appeared to fear God (for you were often beyond the reach of any other law), who had the confidence that came from overcoming many obstacles, who "put on no airs," "wore his heart on his sleeve," was entirely "up front," and, as the salacious saying is now, "let it all hang out"—presumably his (his wife's) wash. Nowadays, even a candid, blunt, abrasive boss can be admired because he has been "straight" with you, letting you know "where you stood."

The simple, like the straight and the plain, is relatively featureless. It reduces the number of things with which you have to cope. After all, when crossing the country by covered wagon, you took winding trails only when rivers and mountains made the circuitous the shortest way. And in the Bible, didn't God promise to make the crooked straight and the rough places plain? We liked the land we settled to be level, well-drained, free of rock. We often preferred the companionship of animals because they couldn't talk at all and could be expected to act within their species as if in a cage. It was the body which dealt with the day's difficulties. It was the body which built, which ploughed, which planted, and which, on occasion, danced and sang and played. The body baked. The body begot. It was not the brain.

So our breath was supposed to be too short for long sentences. Democracy didn't encourage subordination, not in people or in any part of their speech, whether it was to fancy words or flattering phrases or complicated clauses. Honesty was suspicious of endless ramifications. Adverbs that didn't contribute to their action were needless frills. If it didn't matter to the bite of the blade what the color of the ax's handle was, you didn't write it down or say its name. Events were the chief ingredient in stories, and the main thing was not to dawdle but to offer up the verb and then get on with it. Ideas fuddled you far worse than alcohol. Theories couldn't thread a needle. You read a bit from the Good Book of an evening because, otherwise, God might blight your wheat. And you went to the Sunday Meeting for the society of it, and for the same wary reason you read. What's more, there was always another row to hoe.

How different this simplicity was from the sort praised by the subtle Tanizaki, and how misled we Westerners were when we admired an innocence we thought was our own. Those ashen walls, with their unadorned surfaces, the candles that lit them, the unpretentious wood that framed the windows, the plain mats that softened and warmed the floor, were there to receive the indefinite wavers of the flame, to grow uneven with revelation and conceal-ment, to move, as if alive, inside their planes and provoke the profoundest contemplation.

While the walls of the American settlers existed to keep out the cold and be forgotten . . . existed to keep out the vast space of the prairie, which lay around every cabin like an endless sea . . . existed to keep out the high sky you could fall into like a pit.

The traditional Japanese room might give out onto a garden of gravel, a small raked space with one or two stones, which stood for a world or any mountain, each tame as a household bird. What of the planks whose grain will emerge only after years of timidity and suspicion, the mats that greet each footstep with a whisper which they pass among their fibers? and what of the corners in such a room, carved from darkness, where perhaps a thread of gold gleams from the flank of an otherwise invisible lacquer chest, where the dimmest hint of an ardent desire may lie wrapped in alternating layers of shadow and silk so that an additional breath bends the candle flame? These conditions, these qualities, speak to us not of simplicity, not in our sense, but of the indirect and devious, and suggest—there is the word!—they suggest that these plain surfaces and impassive features are screens on which one reality plays while another lurks behind them, and may move, when it moves, in metaphysical earnest.

One kind of simplicity is reached, then (we cannot say "achieved"), when skills and means and time and energy are minimal. It is the sort of simplicity which looks not at the causes of things but only at their effects. Who cares, it says . . . who cares what drove the nail if now its head rests in the right place? When the larder holds only a bit of ground corn, a corn cake is what we shall have. Two "I do"s shall marry a couple as well as any cathedral ceremony.

Another sort of simplicity is reached by removal and erasure, by denial and refusal. It begins with features already played upon by the artist, with surfaces into which the candle's flicker has been cut, and dark corners created with charcoal, so there need never be an actual niche or a real lantern, but only a steady, indifferent glare of light; for absences will have to be understood to be as solidly in place as any wooden headrest, waiting the head that will sleep. It begins by looking at decoration as if it were a disease, as a form of social mold, a sign of spiritual decay, another case of the showy bad taste of some nouveau riche, or the loud cosmetics of a whore. Beneath these excrescences, these layers of gilt, these scabs of fashion, is an honest beam, more richly grained and more interesting than all these distracting carvings; beneath this powder and this cream is a natural beauty who might again send the Achaeans against Troy; behind these nervous variations is a mighty theme; let us hear it. Just one time. So cleanly, so clearly, we cannot be confused, nor any flaw be disguised. We want to grasp the lines, follow the form, find the true source of our sensation. Then, when real simplicity has returned, when the essential has been restored to disclose its few rightful properties, we may let fall upon it the pale light of our mind; we may shadow it with the darkness that lives in a few of our own thoughts; we may allow to cross it the slow movements of our meditations.

Let us reconsider, for a moment, the simple objects that our ancestors made: a plain wooden bowl, for example, hollowed from a sawed round of tree trunk. A chisel bites into the heart of that wood, eats into the center of its rings of yearly growth, so that shortly a spoonful of milk could be placed in it, and then a cup's worth, although there will be bark remaining around the rim. The rind is peeled off, needless bulk is cut away, and by continued gnawing at the core, the tools of the carpenter create a basin we can begin to recognize as a bowl. Or perhaps hot coals burn the hollow in it. Its interior should be smooth enough to let liquids slosh, a spoon to scoop, a larger one to ladle, and it should rinse out easily. The wood must be hard and dense so that warm soup won't penetrate its fibers. Beyond this, little needs to be done. For the utilitarian, the means cease the moment the end is reached. A little sand will scour the bowl; a little seasoning will secure the grain. If it were a size to conveniently stack—that would be a plus. Our sentences should similarly fly to the mark, deposit their message, and disappear, as if a pigeon were to become its poop, so when any one of us looked up to complain because our shoulder had been stained, there'd be no bird there.

Then why did we ever worry about the exact slope of the hollow our tools had chipped, the precise sheen of the wood, the slim line and smooth run of the rim? We certainly should have cared about how sturdily the dish sat, and how its sides widened so the soup could cool; but why were we concerned about the match of its rings, the quality of the grain in the base and bowl, the shape of the shadows which crept from beneath its sides?

This bowl is ceasing to be simple. Hardship forces the makeshift upon us; primitive conditions produce primitive results; urgent needs aren't choosy; indeed, the sharp teeth of need close like a trap on any victim; but when circumstances are no longer as straitened as they once were and a bit of leisure, some small level of satisfaction, has been reached, the mind can let go of the plough's handle, can turn aside from its single thought and transform its lust into a little love.

The bowl has ceased to be simple. A word like "perfection" has us by the ear. Now we are seeking a smoothness, an evenness, an achievement in its completion that will take us days—months— beyond an efficient use of our time. We become obsessed (is it suddenly or slowly?) by geometry, by geometry's deceptive simplicities, its lucent beauty, and we see how the bowl is but a nest of circles whose circumferences are steadily shrinking and whose diameters contract.

The bowl is a celebration of complexity. We've had to set several versions aside in order to start over, trying to improve its proportions, passing before our mind's demanding eye, as though they were bathing beauties, images of other utensils whose alluring features may help us with the one we're composing. What is this resulting bowl, then, whose shaping requires the failure of so many others, which devours this base and that rim, accepts a surface, adapts a form, distorts a tendency—acquiring qualities the way an actor takes on personalities in order to realize a role? what is this object whose making is directed by memory as much as by the pots that are broken when they fail to satisfy, or the bowls that are burned as kindling when the wind turns cold, or the words that are sent away from the sentence they were to serve in, and linger near it like disconsolate shades? what is this thing built so solidly of ghosts?

How reluctantly, in the United States, have we come to recognize that civilization is refinement; that it requires leisure, judgment, taste, skill, and the patient work of a solitary mind passing itself, as though it were both a cleaner and a cleansing cloth, back and forth across an idea, back and forth until the substance of it— wood or marble or music, in syllables seeking their place in some song—back and forth until the matter of it begins to gleam deeply from its buried center, deeply where thought and thing are one,

and therefore not solely from its surface, where a glitter may sometimes be glibly emitted, a glitter that comes just after a bit of light
has struck, a glitter, a glit, before the beam has bounded off—a
glitter, a glit—a spark, after which there will be only the light that
has gone.

Apart from the simplicity associated with the pioneer spirit of
America, we developed, also very early, a simplicity of a second
sort, though certainly in some sympathy with the first: this was
exemplified by the distilled designs, the purified life and even purer
dreams, of a sect called Shakers (so named because of their custom
of dancing during their religious services, and of being frequently
and literally moved by their love of God). They were separatists,
forming withdrawn and self-sustaining communities. They were
pacifists like the Quakers (another name signifying uncontrolled
movement), and believed in equality and in the actual, rather than
the rhetorical, Brotherhood of Man. They were celibate and endeavored to live a life free of sexual tension and gender competition. They were undogmatic, preferring to follow their faith rather
than preach it, drawing communicants not by argument and pro-
paganda but by shining example. Since Shakers did not breed, they
were never guilty of corrupting their children with their principles,
and converts came to them entirely out of free choice and when in
possession of a presumably mature mind.

"When a World's Fair was held several years ago in Japan," June
Sprigg, a student of the Shakers, writes, "one of the most popular
features was an exhibit of Shaker furniture. Chairs without carving, tables without knickknacks, the simplicity of Shaker stoves and
baskets, even the white walls and bare wood floors—all these made
sense to the Japanese, who recognized and appreciated the same
simplicity based on spiritual principles that characterize traditional
Japanese culture."

I wonder if the visitors to the fair saw how directly the Shakers
translated moral qualities into principles of craftsmanship: spare,
straight, upright, plain, simple, direct, pure, square, tight, useful,
orderly, unaffected, neat, clean, careful, correct. For every chair

there was a peg on the wall from which it would hang while the floor was thereby more swiftly swept, and every peg was perfect. Since the chair was hung by its heels, as it were, what dust there was would settle on the bottom of the seat and not on the side where one sat. Beds folded up into the wall, and drawers drew out of anywhere. A sewing box might be fitted into a rocker, shutters slid up and down instead of swinging out into the room, and boxes were invariably nested. Every space was made of appointed places, and the tools that cleaned those hard-to-reach corners were hooked alongside a horsehair sieve sometimes, or a fluted tin mold for maple sugar.

Yet the Shakers used only the finest maple, the truest oak and clearest pine, the best slate. Grooves and pegs which were internal to a piece, and therefore never seen, were finished as finely as if they would live their whole lives out-of-doors. Drawers not only slid out smoothly; they said they slid, in the look of them, in the shush of their sliding; and the ingenious nesting of things, the creation of objects which did double duty, the ubiquitous ledges and holders and racks and pegs, spoke of order, and neatness, and fit—the Godliness of Utility; for though their chairs were stiff and forthright, their tables were wide and unencumbered, and their solutions to problems quite evidently inspired by necessity; there was nothing humble about their materials, pure and as prized as silver and gold. There was nothing humble about the days of careful labor that obviously went into them. There was nothing humble and spare about houses with double doors and double stairs—one for each sex. Nor is there anything humble about a building built to stand a thousand years, or in some handmade things so supremely finished they provoke us to exclaim: "Handmade, maybe, but what careful fingers, what holy hands!" There is nothing humble about perfection.

And the hidden joints, the concealed beds, the matched grains, the boxes which live their carefully concealed lives in other boxes: these are habits of the High Baroque.

Unlike pioneer simplicity, which was perforce crude and incomplete, Shaker simplicity spoke eloquently about its moral ideals. Every room was as much God's place as a church. Every object was, in its fealty to spirit, in its richness of refinement, in its strenuous demands on occupants and employers, a symbol of Divinity and Divine Law.

2

Simplicities, in short, are not all the same. When, in her masterpiece called "Melanctha," a story of black people and the problems of love, Gertrude Stein resorts to the plainness of the pioneer style, she does so to render the rhythms of black Baltimore speech, and to convey the handmade quality of such talk as it struggles to express powerful and complex feelings through the most ordinary of words and by the social patterns implicit in its echoes, rhymes, and repetitions.

> Melanctha told Rose one day how a woman whom she knew had killed herself because she was so blue. Melanctha said, sometimes, she thought this was the best thing for herself to do.
>
> Rose Johnson did not see it the least bit that way.
>
> "I don't see Melanctha why you should talk like you would kill yourself just because you're blue. I'd never kill myself Melanctha just 'cause I was blue. I'd maybe kill somebody else Melanctha 'cause I was blue, but I'd never kill myself. If I ever killed myself Melanctha it'd be by accident, and if I ever killed myself by accident Melanctha, I'd be awful sorry."

Although Ernest Hemingway's style gets some of its substance from Gertrude Stein (it is even more deeply indebted to Sherwood Anderson), its aim is less complex than hers. He borrows a bit of machismo from the pioneer, some of his ostentatious simplicity from the Shaker, and sharpens this by means of a selectivity which is severe and narrow. If Adolph Loos, architecture's enemy of orna-

ment, felt we should sweep walls free and wipe planes clean,
Hemingway's purpose was to seize upon the basics right from
the beginning and therefore be in a position to give an exact description of "the way it was." He would remove bias and cliché,
our conception of how things had always been, our belief in how
things ought to be, and replace them with the square-shouldered
resoluteness of reality.

> Out through the front of the tent he watched the glow of the
> fire when the night wind blew on it. It was a quiet night. The
> swamp was perfectly quiet. Nick stretched under the blanket
> comfortably. A mosquito hummed close to his ear. Nick sat
> up and lit a match. The mosquito was on the canvas, over his
> head. Nick moved the match quickly up to it. The mosquito
> made a satisfactory hiss in the flame. The match went out.
> Nick lay down again under the blankets. He turned on his side
> and shut his eyes. He was sleepy. He felt sleep coming. He
> curled up under the blanket and went to sleep.

Brevity may serve as the soul for wit, but it is far from performing
such a service for simplicity. The economy of most of Hemingway's
writing is only an appearance. To shorten this passage, we could
have encouraged the reader to infer more, and said: "The fire
brightened when the night wind breathed upon it. The swamp was
as quiet as the night." If images, implications, and connectives are
allowed, a condensation can be sought which is far from simple.
"A mosquito sang in his ear so he sat and lit a match." Matches do
go quickly out. No need to mention that. Moreover, Nick could be
put to sleep far less redundantly. But Hemingway needs to state
the obvious and avoid suggestion, to appear to be proceeding step
by step. He needs the clumsy reiteration. It makes everything seem
so slow and simple, plain, even artless, male.

Hemingway's search for the essential was characteristically
American; that is, it was personal; he sought a correct account of
his own experience, because anything less would be fraudulent and
insincere. The simplifying came prior to the writing; it was to be

built into the heart and the eye, into the man—hunting or fishing, running with the bulls, going to war, mastering his woman. On the whole, Hemingway's work has not held up very well, and that is perhaps because he didn't see or feel any more than he reports he felt or saw, because the way it was was really only Heming's way.

According to Democritus, the atom was so simple it could not be divided, and that simplicity, Plato thought, was the source of the soul's immortality. Only if you had parts could you come apart, and only if you came apart could you decay and die and disappear. Change itself, Parmenides argued, depended upon such minuscule divisions, but it required, in addition, the space to come apart in, for when separation occurred, something (which was a swatch of Nothing, in most cases) had to fill the breach in order to ensure that the cut would continue and not heal around the knife. So the atom remained an atom because it was a plenum and contained not even a trace of the real agent of decay: empty space.

Behind the search for the simple is a longing for the indivisible, the indestructible, the enduring. When a noun is reified, its elements fuse. It obtains an Essence. It becomes One, Primitive, Indefinable. Or, rather: any definition will be analytic. "God is good" is a version of "God is God." A rose is a rose. Business is business. And that is that.

These ultimate simples were invisible, not because they were very, very small, but because they were very, very pure. Purity is a property of simplicity. It is often what is sought in seeking the simple. Atoms had no qualities. Atoms had nothing to say to the senses. Atoms were geometries. They had shapes; you could count them; they weighed; they fell through the Void like drops of rain; they rebounded; they combined; and when these combinations came undone, they remained as unaffected by their previous unions as any professional Don Juan.

Visibility is impurity. Invisibility belongs to the gods, to the immaculate Forms, to the primeval seeds. It is not morally pure, ethereal spirits but those ghosts clotted with crime who hang about like frozen smoke in the still air. The soul, as a penance, is encumbered with flesh. Thought is brought to us in terms that can't help but demean it, as if our sincerities were written in neon. Sin and sensation together veil the truth. Simplicity serves the essential, so the simple style will stick to the plainest, most unaffected, most ordinary words; its sentences will be direct and declarative, following the basic grammatical forms; and to the understanding, it will seem to disappear into its world of reference, more modest than most ministers' wives, and invisible as a perfect servant.

Memory, too, is a polluter. The purity of the maid lies not in an untorn hymen, which is simply a symbol, but in the fact that she brings to her husband's embrace the memory of no other arms. The purity of the maid guarantees the purity of her husband's line: that his son is his; no uncertified seed has fertilized her first, been there ahead of him to father the future with a past. A fair maid has no past. Her husband will form her, as though her breasts grew beneath his hands. So she shall wear white as a sign she is unsullied, suitable, and as ready as a turkey to be carved.

The ultimate simples which the early philosophers revered were near enough to numbers as to make the move from Materialism to Idealism a small step. The logician, in an exactly similar fashion, seeks the supreme, unfactorable unit to begin with, and to that unit he then applies his intuition of the first fundamental logical operation, namely addition. One, and then one more. One. And one. And one. Adam did no less. Like Roman numerals or a prisoner's day. One. And one. Bars, mars, nicks, accumulating in the direction of an unapproachable infinity. Others argue that anything either Is (like a light switch, On) or it Isn't (like a light switch, Off); that a yes or a no suffices. To build a machinelike mind. Plato's Demiurge lets the right triangle flop about like a stranded fish, and in that way it forms squares, cubes, and other polyhedrons, or it spins itself into a cone (for a cone is a triangle revolving like a door), while this shape, pivoting on its peak, will turn itself, in turn, into a sphere. With every essential figure drawn and every atom formed, the remainder of the universe is easy.

At one extreme, then, we find mathematicians, logicians, and those quantitative scientists who shave with Occam's razor; whose concepts have one (and only one) clear meaning; whose rules are unambiguous, and conclusions rigorously drawn; while, on the other hand, there are the pious craftsmen who think with their hands, reverence their materials, and build their own beds.

Simple as the simple is, and basic as butter is to French cuisine, it never seems to be nearby or abundant but has to be panned, like silver or gold, from a muddy stream. Surfaces have to be scrubbed, disguises divested, impurities refined away, truths extracted, luxuries rejected, seductions scorned, diversions refused, memories erased. Because if some things in life are simple, quite a lot is not; quite a bit is "buzzing, blooming confusion." There is, of course, deception's tangled web. There are the many mysteries of bureaucracy, the flight path of bees, the concept of the Trinity; there are the vagaries of the weather, the ins and outs of diplomacy, business, politics, adultery; there is poetry's indirection, the opacity of German metaphysics, the ornamentation of Baroque churches, and the cast of the Oriental mind.

Simplicity is not a given. It is an achievement, a human invention, a discovery, a beloved belief.

In contrast to the bubbling stew we call our consciousness (and to reprise), there are the purities of reason, which require clear rules of inference and transparent premises; there are the invisible particles of matter, those underlying elements out of which the All is made Universal by the Few; there are nascent conditions of existence, unsullied by use or age or other kinds of decay; there are definitions brief and direct as gunshots; there are modes of being that streamline the soul for its afterlife flights. Consequently, beneath simplicity itself, whenever it serves as an ideal, lie moral and metaphysical commitments of considerable density. There are Hume's simple impressions. There are Leibnitz's monads. There are Lucretius' jumpy atoms. Yet we do not behold the simple simply. If our gaze is direct, its object open, our climb to the mountain's top is circuitous, the path perilous. If the foundations of Reality are simple, the grounds of Simplicity are complex.

Those who champion simplicity as a way of life are aware of the political and moral statement they are making. Gustav Stickley, who contributed so substantially to the Arts and Crafts Movement in America around the turn of the century, certainly was. For him, simplicity was not a Spartan lunch of caviar and champagne, or a lazy day sunning on the deck of the yacht. In his first collection of *Craftsman Homes*, Stickley writes:

> By simplicity here is not meant any foolish whimsical eccentricity of dress or manner or architecture, colonized and made conspicuous by useless wealth, for eccentricity is but an expression of individual egotism and as such must inevitably be short-lived. And what our formal, artificial world of today needs is not more of this sort of eccentricity and egotism, but less; not more conscious posing for picturesque reform, but greater and quieter achievement along lines of fearless honesty; not less beauty, but infinitely more of a beauty that is real and lasting because it is born out of use and taste.

For Stickley, his movement's heroic figure was an Englishman, Edward Carpenter, whose writings he much admired and frequently cites. *England's Ideal* (which is the title of one of Carpenter's books) appears to be agrarian, anticolonial, puritan, roundhead, and reformist. Our labor should not be a stranger to all that sustains us; our culture should be of our own contriving, and not something we have purchased in a shop; the true character of life ought not to be shamefully concealed; the head must have a hand, both to help it and to hold it in check. Possessions, in particular, are like unwanted immigrants—the first family to arrive is soon followed by boatloads of their relatives. Carpenter is vivid:

> It cannot be too often remembered that every additional object in a house requires additional dusting, cleaning, repairing; and lucky you are if its requirements stop there. When you abandon a wholesome tile or stone floor for a Turkey carpet, you are setting out on a voyage of which you cannot see the

end. The Turkey carpet makes the old furniture look uncomfortable, and calls for stuffed couches and armchairs; the couches and armchairs demand a walnut-wood table; the walnut-wood table requires polishing, and the polish bottles require shelves; the couches and armchairs have casters and springs, which give way and want mending; they have damask seats, which fade and must be covered; the chintz covers require washing, and when washed they call for antimacassars to keep them clean. The antimacassars require wool, and the wool requires knitting-needles, and the knitting-needles require a box, the box demands a side table to stand on and the carpet wears out and has to be supplemented by bits of drugget, or eked out with oilcloth, and beside the daily toil required to keep this mass of rubbish in order, we have every week or month, instead of the pleasant cleaning-day of old times, a terrible domestic convulsion and bouleversement of the household.

Of course, for the person who does not hear the Turkey carpet call for a stuffed couch, or rejects its demands for a walnut-wood table, or refuses to fill the table's polishing requirements, or the bottle's for a shelf, as if they were medical prescriptions; for such a person the growing snowball of belongings will never overtake and amalgamate the needs of the sagging seat or soiled cover; because the simplest thing to do with dust is never to disturb it, while wear can be watched with the same interest accorded to a sunset, and juxtapositions of hilarious quaintness or stylistic jar can often be appreciated as accurate images of the condition of life. Simplicity carries at its core a defensive neatness that despairs of bringing the wild world to heel and settles instead on taming a few things by placing them in an elemental system where the rules say they shall stay. Corners full of cupboards, nooks full of crannies, built-in shelves, seats, and drawers, deny each corresponding desire for change, for adjustment. They may begin as conveniences, but they end as impositions. It is their insistence that every function has its

implement, every implement its place, every place its station, and
every station its duties, as they wish the world does, and had,
and did.

Labor-saving devices like the sewing machine, Carpenter argues,
only provide more time for fashioning frills and flounces. Economy, like purity, like neatness, is one of simplicity's principal ingre-
dients. We must be frugal with what we have when what we have
(of premises or provisions) is so limited; but we need to be frugal
whether our possessions are many or few, because frugality is inherently virtuous. In describing economy's consequences, Carpenter does not conceal the religious implications but records them,
albeit with a saving smile.

> For myself I confess to a great pleasure in witnessing the
> Economics of Life—and how seemingly nothing need be
> wasted; how the very stones that offend the spade in the gar-
> den become invaluable when footpaths have to be laid out or
> drains to be made. Hats that are past wear get cut up into
> strips for nailing creepers on the wall; the upper leathers of old
> shoes are useful for the same purpose. The under garment
> that is too far gone for mending is used for patching another
> less decrepit of its kind, then it is torn up into strips for ban-
> dages or what not; and when it has served its time thus it
> descends to floor washing, and is scrubbed out of life—useful
> to the end. When my coat has worn itself into an affectionate
> intimacy with my body, when it has served for Sunday best,
> and for week days, and got weather-stained out in the fields
> with the sun and rain—then faithful, it does not part from
> me, but getting itself cut up into shreds and patches descends
> to form a hearthrug for my feet. After that, when worn
> through, it goes into the kennel and keeps my dog warm, and
> so after lapse of years, retiring to the manure-heaps and pass-
> ing out on to the land, returns to me in the form of potatoes
> for my dinner; or being pastured by my sheep, reappears upon
> their backs as the material of new clothing. Thus it remains a

friend to all time, grateful to me for not having despised and thrown it away when it first got behind the fashions. And seeing we have been faithful to each other, my coat and I, for one round or life-period, I do not see why we should not renew our intimacy—in other metamorphoses—or why we should ever quite lose touch of each other through the aeons.

Just suppose, though, that carelessness is the way of the world; that natural selection proceeds by means of an immense waste; that survival is hit or miss and fitness is genetic. Suppose that the deepest of energy's rhythms are random, and that nature may conserve matter but callously use up each of its particular forms. Suppose that order is only a security blanket; that there are no essences; that substance is another philosophical invention like soul and spirit and ego and the gods, like mind and will and cause and natural law. Suppose that life will run every which way like a dispersed mob; that the words for life are "proliferation" and "opportunism," and that ends are absent and meaning too, purposes pointless and pointlessness the rule: what will simplicity explain in such a case? what will it justify? how will its economies console? its purities protect? its neatness regulate?

So many simplicities! How is one to know where one is? what one has? We sometimes admire the naive directness of the primitive painter, failing to notice that what is attractive is often what is not there, rather than what is; and the simplicity we associate in the United States with the Shakers can be found in the mystically inspired Piet Mondrian, as well as in other artists for whom purity of color, line, and shape represents a holiness otherwise out of reach, although what each reaches is obscured behind a different mist; then there is the meditative simplicity of someone like Tanizaki, which seems to require only a cleared space, a bare screen, a benevolent silence, into which he can cast shadows like so many heavy sacks, or project a dance of light and mind, or provoke the mosquito into speaking, or prevail on the moon to wane; perhaps nearby we can place the duplicitous simplicity of the drape or curtain behind which plots may be planned, or bring out the bland expression that lids a kettle of seething rage, or maybe we can unfold a calm screen, like a newspaper held in front of our breakfast face, behind which caresses unscheduled by any passion can continue themselves to their self-canceling conclusion; while finally we must find a spot beside the psychological essentialism of a writer like Hemingway, or alongside the ontological researches of a painter like Bashō, where we can put the expressive simplicities of such minimalists as Samuel Beckett and Mark Rothko, who brood upon their motifs like Cézanne on his mountain, or Flaubert on his Bovary, until any silly little thing, so intensely attended to— as words often are, as symbols are, as bodies, as beliefs—until any ugly old tatter, attended to, touched by concern, becomes as full of the possible as an egg, an embryo, a soft explosion of sperm; and we stare at the striations of a stone, for instance, as at a star, as if time itself wore every scar the stone does, as if the rock were that world of which the poet so often speaks—that world made cunningly; that world held in the palm of the hand; that flower, wooden bowl, or grain of sand, of which the poet so often speaks—speaks to another world's inattentive ear.

"Limitations of means determines style." That is the pat answer to many a talk-show question. "With one hand tied behind my back . . ." is the common boast. The simple can be a show of strength; it can place a method or a bit of material under significant stress so as to see what it is capable of, what its qualities can achieve. In the small and simple atom is a frightful force, a heat equivalent to a nation's hate, if it is unanimously released, as meaning in a lengthy sentence sometimes waits to the last syllable to explain itself, or a life of persistent disappointment bursts suddenly down the barrel of a gun, years of pent-up letdowns set loose.

Simplicity can be a boast—"See how I deprive myself"; it can be an emblem of holiness, a claim to virtues that might otherwise never be in evidence: the peasant-loving prince, the modest monarch, unspoiled star, humble savior, rich man's downcast door. But most of all it is a longing: for less-beset days, for clarity of contrast

and against the fuddle of grays, for certainty and security, and
the deeper appreciation of things made possible by the absence
of distraction, confusion, anxiety, delay. Simplicity understands
completeness and closure, the full circle, something we can swing
a compass round, or—to hammer out the line—get really straight.

What it does not understand so well is exuberance, abundance,
excess, gusto, joy, absence of constraint, boundless aspiration,
mania, indulgence, sensuality, risk, the full of the full circle, variation, elaboration, difference, lists like this, deviousness, concealment, the pleasures of decline, laughter, polyphony, digression,
prolixity, pluralism, or that the devil is the hero in the schemeless
scheme of things. If our North Pole is Samuel Beckett and our
South Pole is Anton Webern, our equator is made by François
Rabelais with Falstaff's belt.

Thinking now of how complex simplicity is, perhaps we have an
answer (though I do not remember previously posing any question). Before the buzzing, blooming abundance of every day, facing the vast regions of ocean and the seemingly limitless stretch of
empty space; or—instead—wincing at the news in the daily papers
(you had not thought the world—as wide as earth, water, and air
are—could contain so much crime, such immense confusion, this
daunting amount of pain); or—instead—reading the novels of
Henry James and James Joyce and Melville and Mann, or living in
Proust or traveling in Tolstoy, you are again impressed by immen-
sity, by the plethora of fact, by the static of statistics and the sheer
din of data, by the interrelation of everything, by twists and turns
and accumulations, as in this sentence going its endless way; yet as
one proceeds in science, as one proceeds through any complex
esthetic surface, as one proceeds, the numerous subside in the
direction of the few (the Gordian knot is made, it turns out, of a
single string), the power of number grasps vastness as though each
Milky Way were the sneeze of a cicada; so that slowly perhaps,
steadily certainly, simplicity reasserts itself. The simple sentence is
achieved.

Thinking, then, of how simple complexity turns out to be, I can understand, when we began with a bowl chipped from a bit of wood, how its innocence drew suitors. Simplicity disappeared the way a placid pool is broken when a bit of bread brings a throng of greedy carp to boil, or when the mind turns plain mud or simple wood into moving molecules, those into atoms orbiting alarmingly, these into trings, trons, and quarks, until the very mind that made them gives up trying to calculate their behavior. At such times, and in such times as these, don't we desire the small garden into which we can carry our battered spirit, or perhaps a small room at the top of some tower, a hut in a forest, a minibike instead of a Toyota, a bit of smoked salmon on an impeccable leaf of lettuce, a small legacy from a relative long forgotten whose history is no burden and no embarrassment? only one servant?

Tanizaki explains to us how the high shine of lacquerware (whose surface under electric light is so harsh and vulgar) becomes softly luminous in the candlelight it was meant for; how the voluminous folds of a lady's garment may hide her body from us, only to permit her to seduce us with her wit. He allows us to see that the simplest step is nevertheless a step in a complex series, a series whose sum is simple. Cultures are both complex and simple, the way the world is. Having reached that world, with the poet's help, from a grain of sand, and found that stretch of sand peopled with every sort of sunbather, we must remember to disembody bather and sand again, to simplify the beach and its sighing surf, so that now we watch the water run up that sand, as full of foam as ale is, only to slow and subside and slip back into the sea again, leaving a line at each wave lap—a line as pure as a line by Matisse, a line as purely sensuous as the outline of some of those bathers, lying on a beach one grain of which we'd begun with, when we said we could see the world in a bit of grit.

THE MUSIC OF
PROSE

To speak of the music of prose is to speak in metaphor. It is to speak in metaphor because prose cannot make any actual music. The music of prose has the most modest of inscriptions. Its notes, if we could imagine sounding them, do not have any preassigned place in an aural system. Hence they do not automatically find themselves pinned to the lines of a staff, or confined in a sequence of pitches. Nor is prose's music made of sounds set aside and protected from ordinary use as ancient kings conserved the virginity of their daughters. In the first place, prose often has difficulty in getting itself pronounced at all. In addition, any tongue can try out any line; any accent is apparently okay; any intonation is allowed; almost any pace is put up with. For prose, there are no violins fashioned with love and care and played by persons devoted to the artful rubbing of their strings. There are no tubes to transform the breath more magically than the loon can by calling out across a lake. The producers of prose do not play scales or improve their skills by repeating passages of De Quincey or Sir Thomas Browne, although that might be a good idea. They do not work at *Miss iss ip pi* until they get it right. The sound of a word may be arbitrary and irrelevant to its meaning, but the associations created by incessant use are strong, so that you cannot make the sound *m o o n* without seeming to mean "moon." By the time the noun has become a verb, its pronunciation will feel perfectly appropriate to the mood one is in when one moons, say, over a girl, and the "moo" in the mooning will add all its features without feeling the least discomfort. In music, however, the notes are allowed to have their own way and fill the listeners' attention with themselves and their progress. Nonmusical associations (thinking of money when you hear do-re-me played) are considered irrelevant and dispensable.

In sum, prose has no notes, no scale, no consistency or purity of sound, and only actors roll its *r*'s, prolong its vowels, or pop its *p*'s with any sense of purpose.

Yet no prose can pretend to greatness if its music is not also great; if it does not, indeed, construct a surround of sound to house its meaning the way flesh was once felt to embody the soul, at least till the dismal day of the soul's eviction and the flesh's decay.

For prose has a pace; it is dotted with stops and pauses, frequent rests; inflections rise and fall like a low range of hills; certain tones are prolonged; there are patterns of stress and harmonious measures; there is a proper method of pronunciation, even if it is rarely observed; alliteration will trouble the tongue, consonance ease its sounds out, so that any mouth making that music will feel its performance even to the back of the teeth and to the glottal's stop; mellifluousness is not impossible, and harshness is easy; drum roll and clangor can be confidently called for—lisp, slur, and growl; so there will be a syllabic beat in imitation of the heart, while rhyme will recall a word we passed perhaps too indifferently; vowels will open and consonants close like blooming plants; repetitive schemes will act as refrains, and there will be phrases—little motifs—to return to, like the tonic; clauses will be balanced by other clauses the way a waiter carries trays; parallel lines will nevertheless meet in their common subject; clots of concepts will dissolve and then recombine, so we shall find endless variations on the same theme; a central idea, along with its many modifications, like soloist and chorus, will take their turns until, suddenly, all sing at once the same sound.

Since the music of prose depends upon its performance by a voice, and since, when we read, we have been taught to maintain a library's silence, so that not even the lips are allowed to move, most of the music of the word will be that heard only by the head and, dampened by decorum, will be timorous and hesitant. That is the hall, though, the hall of the head, where, if at all, prose (and poetry, too, now) is given its little oral due. There we may say, without allowing its noise to go out of doors, a sentence of Robert South's, for instance: "This is the doom of fallen man, to labour in the fire, to seek truth *in profundo*, to exhaust his time and impair his health and perhaps to spin out his days, and himself, into one pitiful, controverted conclusion"; holding it all in the hush of our inner life, where every imagined sound we make is gray and no more material than smoke, and where the syllables are shaped so deeply in our throats nothing but a figment emerges, an *eidolon*, a shadow, the secondhand substance of speech.

Nevertheless, we can still follow the form of South's sentence as we say it to ourselves: "This is the doom of fallen man. . . ." What is?

	. . . to labour in the fire . . .
	. . . to seek truth *in profundo* . . .
	. . . to exhaust his time . . .
and	. . . [to] impair his health . . .
and perhaps	. . . to spin out his days . . .
and	. . . [to spin out] himself . . .

"into one pitiful, controverted conclusion." That is, we return again and again to the infinitive—"to"—as well as to the pileup of "his" and "him," and if we straighten the prepositions out, all the hidden repeats become evident:

. . . to labour into one pitiful, controverted conclusion . . .
. . . to seek truth in one pitiful, controverted conclusion . . .
. . . to exhaust his time in one pitiful, controverted conclu-
    sion . . .
. . . [to] impair his health [obtaining] one pitiful, controverted
    conclusion . . .

. . . to spin out his days into one pitiful, controverted conclusion . . .
. . . [to spin out] himself into one pitiful, controverted . . .

To labour, seek, exhaust, impair, spin out . . . what? Work, truth, time, health, days, himself. Much of this tune, said sotto voce in any case, doesn't even get played on any instrument, but lies inside the shadow of the sentence's sound like still another shadow.

So South's prose has a shape which its enunciation allows us to perceive. That shape is an imitation of its sense, for the forepart is like the handle of a ladle, the midsections comprise the losses the ladle pours, and the ending is like a splashdown.

This is the doom of fallen man, to labour in the fire,
to seek truth *in profundo*,
to exhaust his time
and impair his health
and perhaps to spin out his days,
and himself,
into one pitiful, controverted conclusion.

In short, one wants South to say: "pour out his days . . ." "in two one pit eee full, conn trow verr ted conn clue zeeunn . . ." so as to emphasize the filling of the pit. However, "spin" does anticipate the shroud which will wrap around and signify "the doom of fallen man."

In short, in this case, and in a manner that Handel, his contemporary, would approve, the sound (by revealing the spindle "to" around which the sentence turns and the action that it represents is wound) certainly enhances the sense.

However, South will not disappoint us, for he plays all the right cards, following our sample with this development: "There was then no pouring, no struggling with memory, no straining for invention. . . ." We get "pour" after all, and "straining" in addition. The pit is more than full; it runneth over.

Often a little diction and a lot of form will achieve the decided

lilt and accent of a nation or a race. Joyce writes "Irish" throughout
Finnegans Wake, and Flann O'Brien's musical arrangements also
dance a jig. Here, in O'Brien's *At Swim-Two-Birds*, Mr. Shanahan
is extolling the virtues of his favorite poet, that man of the pick and
people, Jem Casey:

> "Yes, I've seen his pomes and read them and . . . do you
> know what I'm going to tell you, I have loved them. I'm not
> ashamed to sit here and say it, Mr. Furriskey. I've known the
> man and I've known his pomes and by God I have loved the
> two of them and loved them well, too. Do you understand
> what I'm saying, Mr. Lamont? You, Mr. Furriskey?
> Oh that's right.
> Do you know what it is, I've met the others, the whole lot
> of them. I've met them all and know them all. I have seen
> them and I have read their pomes. I have heard them recited
> by men that know how to use their tongues, men that couldn't
> be beaten at their own game. I have seen whole books filled
> up with their stuff, books as thick as that table there and I'm
> telling you no lie. But by God, at the heel of the hunt, there
> was only one poet for me."

Although any "Jem" has to sparkle if we're to believe in it, and even
though his initials, "JC," are suspicious, I am not going to suggest
that "Casey" is a pun on the Knights of Columbus.

> "No 'Sir,' no 'Mister,' no nothing. Jem Casey, Poet of the
> Pick, that's all. A labouring man, Mr. Lamont, but as sweet a
> singer in his own way as you'll find in the bloody trees there of
> a spring day, and that's a fact. Jem Casey, an ignorant God-
> fearing upstanding labouring man, a bloody navvy. Do you
> know what I'm going to tell you, I don't believe he ever lifted
> the latch of a school door. Would you believe that now?"

The first paragraph rings the changes on "known" and "loved,"
while the second proceeds from "know" and "met" to "seen" and

"heard," in a shuffle of sentences of the simplest kind, full of doubled vowels, repeated phrases, plain talk, and far-from-subtle rhyme, characteristics that lead it to resemble the medieval preacher's rhythmic prose of persuasion. It is the speech, of course, of the barroom bore and alcoholic hyperbolist, a bit bullyish and know-it-all, even if as empty of idea as a washed glass, out of which O'Brien forms an amusing though powerful song of cultural resentment.

It is sometimes said that just as you cannot walk without stepping on wood, earth, or stone, you cannot write without symbolizing, willy-nilly, a series of clicks, trills, and moans; so there will be music wherever prose goes. This expresses an attitude both too generous and too indifferent to be appropriate. The sentence with which Dreiser begins his novel *The Financier*, "The Philadelphia into which Frank Algernon Cowperwood was born was at his very birth already a city of two hundred and fifty thousand and more," certainly makes noise enough, and, in addition to the lovely "Philadelphia," there are "Algernon" and "Cowperwood," which most people might feel make a mouthful; but the words, here, merely stumble through their recital of facts, happy, their job done, to reach an end, however lame it is. Under different circumstances, the doubling of "was" around "born" might have promised much (as in Joyce's paradisal phrase "when all that was was fair"); however, here it is simply awkward, and followed unnecessarily by another "birth," the reason, no doubt, for Dreiser's mumpering on about the population. After another sentence distinguished only by the ineptness of its enumeration ("It was set with handsome parks, notable buildings, and crowded with historic memories"), the author adds fatuousness to his list of achievements: "Many of the things that we and he knew later were not then in existence —the telegraph, telephone, express company, ocean steamer, or city delivery of mails." "We and he" do ding-dong all right, but rather tinnily. Then Dreiser suffers a moment of expansiveness ("There were no postage-stamps or registered letters") before plunging us into a tepid bath of banality whose humor escapes even his unconscious: "The street-car had not arrived, and in its place were hosts of omnibuses, and for longer travel, the slowly developing railroad system still largely connected with canals." It makes for a surreal image, though: those stretches of track bridged by boats; an image whose contemplation we may enjoy while waiting for the streetcar to arrive.

"Bath of banality" is a bit sheepish itself, and brings to mind all the complaints about the artificiality of alliteration, the inappropriateness of rhyme in prose, the unpleasant result of pronounced regular rhythms in that workaday place, the lack of high seriousness to be found in all such effects: in short, the belief that "grand" if not "good" writing undercuts its serious and sober message when it plays around with shape and the shape of its sounds; because, while poetry may be permitted to break wind and allow its leaves to waltz upon an anal breeze, prose should never suggest it had eaten beans, but retain the serious, no-nonsense demeanor of the laboring man in *At Swim-Two-Birds*.

Some tunes are rinky-dink indeed, and confined to the carnival, but I get the impression that most of these complaints about the music of prose are simply the fears of lead-eared moralists and message gatherers, who want us to believe that a man like Dreiser, who can't get through three minutes of high tea without blowing his nose on his sleeve, ought to model our manners for us, and tell us truths as blunt and insensitive, but honest and used, as worn shoes.

What they wish us to forget is another kind of truth: that language is not the lowborn, gawky servant of thought and feeling; it is need, thought, feeling, and perception itself. The shape of the sentence, the song in its syllables, the rhythm of its movement, is the movement of the imagination too; it is the allocation of the things of the world to their place in the world of the word; it is the configuration of its concepts—not to neglect them—like the stars, which are alleged to determine the fate of we poor creatures who bear their names, suffer their severities, enjoy their presence of mind and the sight of their light in our night . . . *all right* . . . *all right* . . . *okay*: the glow of their light in our darkness.

Let's remind ourselves of the moment in *Orlando* when the

queen (who has, old as she is, taken Orlando up as if he were a perfumed hanky, held him close to her cleavage, and made plans to house him between the hills of her hope) sees something other than her own ancient figure in her household mirror:

> Meanwhile, the long winter months drew on. Every tree in the Park was lined with frost. The river ran sluggishly. One day when the snow was on the ground and the dark panelled rooms were full of shadows and the stags were barking in the Park, she saw in the mirror, which she kept for fear of spies always by her, through the door, which she kept for fear of murderers always open, a boy—could it be Orlando?—kissing a girl—who in the Devil's name was the brazen hussy? Snatching at her golden-hilted sword she struck violently at the mirror. The glass crashed; people came running; she was lifted and set in her chair again; but she was stricken after that and groaned much, as her days wore to an end, of man's treachery.

Where shall we begin our praise of this passage, which, in *Orlando*, is merely its norm? And what shall we observe first among its beauties? perhaps, in that simple opening sentence, the way the heavy stresses which fall on "mean-," "while" (and equally on the comma's strong pause), "long," "win-," "months," "drew," and finally "on" again, make those months do just that (the three *on*'s, the many *m*'s and *n*'s don't hurt, nor does the vowel modulation: een, ile, ong, in, on, ou, on), or the way the river, whose flow was rapid enough reaching "ran," turns sluggish suddenly in the middle of the guggle in that word. Or maybe we should admire the two *and*'s which breathlessly connect a cold, snowy ground with shadowy rooms and barking stags; and then, with confidently contrasting symmetry, how the three semicolons trepidate crashing, running, lifting, while enclosing their two *and*'s in response. Or should we examine, instead, the complex central image of the figure in the glass, and the way the two clauses beginning with "which" are diabolically placed? or the consequent vibration of the sentence from the public scene of Orlando in embrace to the queen's personal shock at what she's seen out the open door, thanks to her "magic" mirror. Nor should the subtle way, through word order mainly, that Virginia Woolf salts her prose with a sense of the era—her intention quite serious but her touch kept light in order to recall the Elizabethan period without parody—be neglected by our applause.

It is precisely the queen's fear of spies and murderers which places the mirror where it can peer down the corridor to the cause of her dismay—that is the irony—but it is the placement of the reasons ("which she kept for fear of spies always by her," etc.) between the fragments of the perceptions ("through the door," "a boy," and so on) that convinces the reader of the reality of it. It is not enough to have a handful of ideas, a few perceptions, a metaphor of some originality, on your stove, the writer must also know when to release these meanings; against what they shall lean their newly arrived weight; how, in retrospect, their influence shall be felt; how the lonely trope will combine with some distant noun to create a new flavor.

What is said, what is sounded, what is put in print like a full plate in front of the reader's hungry eye, must be weighed against what is kept back, out of view, suggested, implied. The queen, in her disappointed rage, has fallen to the floor, but we are told only that she was lifted and put back in her chair again. And nothing will henceforth be the same in the last, morose moments of her life. On account of a kiss caught by a mirror through a door kept ajar out of fear of another sort of assault.

In music, sounds form phrases; in prose, phrases form sounds. The sentence fragment almost immediately above was written to demonstrate this, for it naturally breaks into units: "On account of a kiss/caught by a mirror/through a door kept ajar/out of fear of another/sort of assault." These shards, in turn, can be subdivided further: "On account/of a kiss. . . ." Certain pieces of the pattern act like hinges: "kiss/caught" "door/kept," for instance, while possessives play their part, and the grammatical form that consists of an article and a noun ("a count/a kiss/a mirror/a door/a jar/a nother/a sault") stamps on the sentence its special rhythm.

Words have their own auditory character. We all know this, but the writer must revel in it. Some open and close with vowels whose prolongation can give them expressive possibilities ("Ohio," for instance); others are simply vowel heavy (like "aeolian"); still others open wide but then close sharply ("ought"), or are as tight-lipped as "tip," as unending as "too," or as fully middled as "balloon." Some words look long but are said short (such as "rough" and "sleight"); some seem small enough but are actually huge ("otiose" and "nay"). A few words "whisper," "tintinnabulate," or "murmur," as if they were made of their meanings, while "Philadelphia" (already admired) is like a low range of hills. Some words rock, and are jokey, like "okeydokey." Or they clump, like "lump" and "hump" and "rump" and "stump," or dash noisily away in a rash of "ash/mash/bash" or "brash/crash/smash/flash" or "gnash/lash/hash/stash/cash" or "clash/trash/splash/potash/succotash." Vowel changes are equally significant, whether between "ring," "rang," and "rung," "scat" and "scoot," "pet" and "pat," "pit" and "pot," or "squish" and "squooze."

The Latinate measures of the great organist Henry James find an additional function for the music of prose. Here all it takes is a parade of the past tense ("he had") down a street paved with negations.

> He had not been a man of numerous passions, and even in all these years no sense had grown stronger with him than the sense of being bereft. He had needed no priest and no altar to make him for ever widowed. He had done many things in the world—he had done almost all but one: he had never, never forgotten. He had tried to put into his existence whatever else might take up room in it, but had failed to make it more than a house of which the mistress was eternally absent.

If some men are has-beens, poor Stransom (in James's judgment) is a had-not-been. The passage is crammed with loss: "bereft," "widowed," "failed," "absent," in addition to the doubling of "sense," "no," "never," in succeeding sentences, and the gloomy repetition of the past tense, particularly "been" and "done." Our hero, we cannot help but hear, is a transom. He only looks on. But the music of the passage ties terms together more firmly than its syntax: "being," for instance, with "bereft," "done" with "one," "never" with "ever," and "what-" with "ever" as well. Each sentence, all clauses, commence with poor Stransom's pronoun, or imply its presence: "he had, he had, he had" trochee along like a mourning gong.

Musical form creates another syntax, which overlaps the grammatical and reinforces that set of directions sometimes, or adds another dimension by suggesting that two words, when they alliterate or rhyme, thereby modify each other, even if they are not in any normally modifying position. Everything a sentence is is made manifest by its music. As Gertrude Stein writes:

> Papa dozes mamma blows her noses.
> We cannot say this the other way.

Music makes the space it takes place in. I do not mean the baroque chamber, where a quartet once competed against the slide of satin, the sniff of snuff, or the rustle of lace cuffs; or the long symphonic hall full of coughing, whispered asides, and program rattle; or the opera house, where the plot unfolding on the stage plays poorly against the ogling in the boxes and the distractions in the stalls; or even the family's music room, where heavy metal will one day leave its scratches like chalk screech on the windowpanes —none of these former or future pollutions of our pleasure; but again in that hall of the head (it holds so much!) where, when the first note sounds behind the lids, no late arrivals are allowed to enter, and when the first note sounds as if the piano were putting a single star down in a dark sky, and then, over there, in that darkness, another, the way, for instance, the 1926 sonata of Bartók begins, or a nocturne of Chopin's, slowly, so we can observe its creation, its establishment of relation; because we do see what we hear, and the music rises and falls or feels far away or comes from close by like from the lobe of the ear, and is bright or dim, wide or thin, or forms chains or cascades, sometimes as obvious as a cartoon of Disney's, splashy and catchy, and sometimes as continuous and broad and full as an ocean; while at other times there is only a ding here and a ping there in a dense, pitchlike lack of action, and one waits for the sounds to come back and fill the abyss with clangor, as if life were all that is.

And when we hear, *we* hear; when we see, and say: "Ah! Sport!" *we* see; our consciousness of objects is *ours*, don't philosophers love to say? and though we share a world, it is, from the point of view of consciousness, an overlapping one: I see the dog with delight, you with fear; I see its deep, moist eyes, you its cruel wet mouth; I hear its happy panting, you its threatening growl; and I remember my own loyal pooch, and you the time a pug pursued you down the street; so we say the same word, "dog," yet I to welcome and you to warn, I to greet and you to cringe; and even when we think of what our experience means and ponder the place of pets in the human scheme, thus sharing a subject, as we have our encounter, we will pursue our problem differently, organize it in dissimilar ways, and doubtless arrive at opposite ends.

But I can shape and sound a sentence in such a way my sight of things, my feeling for what I've seen, my thoughts about it all, are as fully present as the ideas and objects my words by themselves bear. D. H. Lawrence, for instance, in that great chapter of *Sea and Sardinia* called "The Spinner and the Monks," does not simply tell us he saw two monks walking in a garden.

> And then, just below me, I saw two monks walking in their garden between the naked, bony vines, walking in their wintry garden of bony vines and olive trees, their brown cassocks passing between the brown vine-stocks, their heads bare to the sunshine, sometimes a glint of light as their feet strode from under their skirts.

Anyone can put a pair of monks in a garden and even hang around to watch their no-doubt sandaled feet flash, but Lawrence is a whole person when he perceives, when he repeats, when he plans his patterns; so that, just as he himself says, it is as if he hears them speaking to each other.

> They marched with the peculiar march of monks, a long, loping stride, their heads together, their skirts swaying slowly, two brown monks with hidden hands, sliding under the bony vines and beside the cabbages, their heads always together in hidden converse. It was as if I were attending with my dark soul to their inaudible undertone. All the time I sat still in silence, I was one with them, a partaker, though I could hear no sound of their voices. I went with the long stride of their skirted feet, that slid springless and noiseless from end to end of the garden, and back again. Their hands were kept down at their sides, hidden in the long sleeves and the skirts of their robes. They did not touch each other, nor gesticulate as they walked. There was no motion save the long, furtive stride and the heads leaning together. Yet there was an eagerness in their conversation. Almost like shadow-creatures ventured out of their cold, obscure element, they went backward and forwards in their wintry garden, thinking nobody could see them.

And we go to and fro here, too, as the sentences do, passing between vowel and idea, perception and measure, moving as the syllables move in our mouth, admiring the moment, realizing how well the world has been realized through Lawrence's richly sensuous point of view.

They clothe a consciousness, these sounds and patterns do, the consciousness the words refer to, with its monks and vines, its stilled observant soul, its sense of hearing them speak as well as seeing them striding along together, the quality of mystery and community the passage presents by putting them in the light of a late winter afternoon.

And I noticed that up above the snow, frail in the bluish sky, a frail moon had put forth, like a thin, scalloped film of ice floated out on the slow current of the coming night. And a bell sounded.

A beautiful, precise image, translucent itself, is carried forward by an arrangement of *f*'s and *l*'s, *o*'s and *u*'s, with such security their reader has to feel he's heard that bell even before it sounds.

Suddenly the mind and its view have a body, because such sentences breathe, and the writer's blood runs through them, too, and they are virile or comely, promising sweetness or cruelty, as bodies do, and they allow the mind they contain to move, and the scene it sees to have an eye.

The soul, when it loves, has a body it must use. Consequently, neither must neglect the other, for the hand that holds your hand must belong to a feeling being, else you are caressing a corpse; and that loving self, unless it can fill a few fingers with its admiration and concern, will pass no more of its passion to another than might a dead, dry stick.

The music of prose, elementary as it is, limited as it is in its effects, is nonetheless far from frivolous decoration; it embodies Being; consequently, it is essential that that body be in eloquent shape: to watch the mimsy paddle and the fat picnic, the snoozers burn and crybabies bellow . . . well, we didn't go to the beach for that.

THE BOOK AS A CONTAINER OF CONSCIOUSNESS

"So! You've written a book! What's in it?"

When Hamlet was asked what he was reading, he replied, "Words, words, words." That's what's in it.

Imagine words being "in" anything other than the making mouth, the intervening air, the receiving ear. For formerly they were no more substantial than the rainbow, an arch of tones between you and me. "What is the matter, my lord?" Polonius asks, to which Hamlet answers, "Between who?" twisting the meaning in a lawyerlike fashion, although he might have answered more symmetrically: Pages, pages, pages . . . that is the matter . . . paper and sewing thread and ink . . . the word made wood.

Early words were carved on a board of beech, put on thin leaves of a fiber that might be obtained from bamboo and then bound by cords, or possibly etched in ivory, or scratched on tablets made of moist clay. Signs were chiseled in stone, inked on unsplit animal skin stretched very thin and rolled, or painted on the pith of the papyrus plant. A lot later, words were typed on paper, microfilmed, floppy-disked, Xeroxed, faxed. As we say about dying, the methods vary. Carving required considerable skill, copying a lengthy education, printing a mastery of casting—in every case, great cost—and hence words were not to be taken lightly (they might have been, indeed, on lead). They were originally so rare in their appearance that texts were sought out, signs were visited like points of interest, the words themselves were worshiped; therefore the effort and expense of writing them was mostly devoted to celebrating the laws of the land, recording community histories, and keeping business accounts.

These marks, each and every one, required a material which would receive them, and a space where they might spread out, since they were becoming visible for the first time, made formerly from air and as momentary as music. They were displacing themselves from their familiar source: the lips, teeth, tongue, the mouth, from which they normally emerged on their journey to an ear; for words were once formed nearly as easily as breathing, heard without effort, taken in automatically, along with their normal surroundings, which were also essential to their understanding—the tone and timbre of the speaker's voice, a scowl or smile crossing the face like a fox across a clearing, inflections accompanied by gestures as well as confirmed or contradicted by the posture of the body—and shaped into sentences made, as Socrates suggested, by the soul who felt them first, thought them, brought them forth like symptoms of an inner state, and was responsible for them, too, accountable because the psyche itself was their author and knew well the consequences of the word when accurately aimed, when deployed like a phalanx, armored and speared.

Before there was writing and paper and printing, before words remained in the trail left by their maker like the ashes of a fire or the spoor of a deer, another sort of stability had to be achieved; since it would scarcely do the speaking soul much good or the listener any harm if words were no more felt than a breeze briefly touching the cheek, or no more remembered than the distant ding of cattle bells, or no more noticed than the sounds of breathing, those soft sighs that are with us always, next our ear like a pillow. As we know, many of language's earliest formations have a mnemonic purpose. They made play with the materialities of speech, breaking into the stream of air that bore their sounds—displaying speed and vehemence, creating succession—and working with the sounds, the ohs and ahs themselves, possibly because, like the baby's babbling, it was fun, and a fresh feat for a new life, but more practically because when the sense of a sentence or a saying was overdetermined and the words connected by relations other than the ideas they represented by themselves, then they were more firmly posted up in memory and might like a jest be repeated, and like a jingle, acted on, leading to the casting of a vote or the purchase of bread, to the support of the very cause that the sentence, wound like that snake around one of Eve's limbs to beguile her, had slyly suggested.

When cast in lead, carved in bark, billboarded by a highway, up in lights, words had a palpability they had never had before; nor did they need all the machinery of rhyme and rhythm and phrasing, of rhetoric's schemes or poetry's alliterations, since they could be consulted again and again; they could be pored over; they could be studied, annotated, lauded, denied. For Plato, though, the written word had lost its loyalty to the psyche, which had been its source, and Phaedrus could hold beneath his cloak a roll on which another's words were written, words which Phaedrus thought he might soon pronounce, allowing them to seem his, performing passions and stating beliefs not necessarily held or felt by him, handing his conscience over to a ghost, practicing to be a president.

Although the written word made possible compilations of data, subtleties of analysis, persistence of examination, and complexities of thought which had hitherto seemed impossible, it contributed to the atrophy of memory, and, eventually, by dispelling the aura of the oral around words, to the absence of weight, consequence, and conviction as well.

Except that poets and prophets and canny politicians continued to write as if they spoke for the soul, and to this end their sentences sometimes still sang in a recognizable voice. However, the displayed word was almost immediately given fancier and fancier dress; calligraphic sopranos soon bewitched the eye; creatures, personalities, events, and other referents, were pictured alongside language to amplify it, dignify it, illuminate it, give it the precious position it deserved. In fact, so unchecked and exuberant was this development of the visual that writing was often reduced to making headlines or composing captions.

Add radio to print and the word became ubiquitous. It overhung the head like smoke and had to be ignored as one ignores most noise. It was by loose use corrupted, by misuse debased, by overuse destroyed. It flew in any eye that opened, in any ear hands didn't hide, and became, instead of the lord of truth, the servant of the lie.

Readers were encouraged to race like a motorcar across the page, taking turns on two wheels, the head as silent as an empty house, eager for the general gist, anxious to get on. Rarely did a reader read in the old-fashioned, hesitant, lip-moving way—by listening rather than by looking, allowing the language fastened on the page its own performance; for then it would speak as though souled, and fly freely away into the space of the mind as it once had in the rarer atmospheres of the purely spoken world.

New notations confound old orders and create essential changes. They are not simply, as Hobbes mistakenly thought, "poor unhandsome though necessary scaffolds of demonstration." They become a part of the process they describe, the relations they denote. Zero came into being when we learned to circumnavigate its absence. Now we know Nothing is this convincing hole in "O." Given a new and supple symbol system, mathematicians make astonishing strides. Descartes's discovery of analytic geometry is based upon a new way of representing points, lines, and figures in a matrix of numbers. The alphabet helps make the mind, and language becomes not only the very vehicle of thought but much of its cargo. Music bursts forth into its modern form when signs that facilitate sight-reading emerge from neumes, and when the voice learns it must do more than merely rise and fall to please. As a consequence of the miracle of the modern scale, the composer could take down imagined music. Similarly, more than memory is served when objects are reduced to reproducible, transmissible, dots. The image is now as triumphant as money, as obnoxious as the politician's spiel, as ignored as other people's pain, as common as the cold.

In sum: there is the observed word, watched as you might an ant or an interesting bird; and there is, of course, the spoken word as well, since we still make conversation, go to plays, and look on in a contrived night while movie stars enunciate clichés as if such commonplaces were the only language; but, in addition, there are the silent sounds we make within the hall of our head when we talk to ourselves, or take any prose or poetry seriously enough to perform it, to listen with our brains, whether to a writing written when singing it was standard, as here, in this wonderful bit of early Middle English, dealing with one of the seven sins:

> The greedy glutton is the fiend's manciple. For he sticketh ever in the cellar or in the kitchen. His heart is in the dishes; his thought is all on the cloth; his life in the tun; his soul in the crock. Cometh forth before his Lord besmutted and besmeared, a dish in his one hand, a bowl in his other. Babbleth with words, and wiggleth as a drunken man that mindeth to fall, beholds his great belly; and the fiend laugheth that he bursteth.

or in this delicious bit from Jeremy Taylor, one of English prose's greatest masters, about the difficulty of dying:

> Take away but the pomps of death, the disguises and solemn bugbears, the tinsel, and the actings by candlelight, and proper and fantastic ceremonies, the minstrels and the noise-makers, the women and the weepers, the swoonings and the shriekings, the nurses and the physicians, the dark room and the ministers, the kindred and the watchers; and then to die is easy, ready, and quitted from its troublesome circumstances.

These are lines composed for the pulpit and delivered to the ear as honesty ought. Nearer to our time, there is now and then prose whose performance is only hoped for, bidden but rarely achieved, like any of Proust or James or Joyce.

> I call her Sosy because she's sosiety for me and she says sossy while I say sassy and she says will you have some more scorns

while I say won't you take a few more schools and she talks
about ithel dear while I simply never talk about athel darling
she's but nice for enticing my friends and she loves your style
considering she breaksin me shoes for me when I've arch trouble and she would kiss my white arms for me so gratefully but
apart from that she's terribly nice really, my sister . . .

Beginning with the breath, first broken into audible elements,
then made visual as a hawk is admirable, soaring on similar air,
and concluding in the inhibited movements of the inner voice,
each of our three languages is made of more or less extended strips
of signs, ribbons of words like the spool which makes up Krapp's
last tape, and, geometrically speaking, is reducible to lines of variable lengths. It might be prudent simply to remind ourselves that
the spaces which poetry requires to distance verses and lines from
one another are operative elements in the verbal path, which, in
that sense, remains equally unbroken whether prose or poetry is in
question.

It is natural to suppose that the splitting up of the printed line
(composed of alphabet blocks and blocklike spaces), as well as the
arrangement of these lengths in rows on the plane of the page and
the subsequent piling of pages one upon another to form the material volume of the text, which the book's case will then retain and
protect, are all the most normal and modest of conventions, as, of
course, the sounds and letters are (indeed, it constitutes a perfectly
Euclidean lesson in spatial construction, beginning with points,
assembling their numbers into lines, combining the lines to form
planes, and, by stacking these, eventually achieving volume); and
that there is nothing about the book as a material entity, neither in
its pages, nor in its lines, nor in its principles of manufacture, that
is essential to the meaning and nature of its text, no more than the
shelf that holds the spices is a spice itself or adds to their piquancy
or savor.

Even if sounds once wonderfully mimicked the various kinds of
things and creatures that populated nature, and even if ancient

hieroglyphs depicted their referents as faithfully as the most vulgar bourgeois painter, by now these resemblances have been forgotten and are no longer relevant, because it is the sheerest accident, as far as sense goes, that "book" and "look," "hook" and "crook," "brook" and "spook," "nook" and "cook," share twin *o*'s, like Halloween eyes, and terminate in *k* as does "kook" and "rook." Moreover, the relation between "hoot" and the owl's, "toot" and the train's, "soot" and smudge, "loot" and L.A., is perfectly arbitrary, could be anything at all, except that frequently used words tend to be short, and coarse words Anglo-Saxon.

So one is inclined by common sense and local practice to consider the book as a simple vehicle for the transportation of texts, and no more does the meaning of a text change when clapped between unaccustomed covers than milk curdles when carried by a strange maid.

However, as Whitehead suggested, common sense should find a wall on which to hang itself. That the size of type, the quality of paper, the weight of what the hands hold, the presence and placement of illustration, the volume's age, evidence of wear and tear, previous ownership and markings, sheer expense, have no effect upon the reader and do not alter the experience of the text is as absurd as supposing that *Aïda* sounds the same to box or gallery, or that ice cream licks identically from cone or spoon or dish or dirty finger.

But, Mr. Obvious objects, the meaning of the text cannot change unless the text changes. Any reaction to that meaning is certainly dependent upon external factors, including one reader's indigestion and another reader's mood; however, the text remains the text, regardless of print, paper, and purse strings, unless you alter the words and their procession.

Three basic errors must be made before Mr. Obvious's view can begin to sustain itself. First, the nature of the word must be misunderstood; next, the concept of "text" will require an overly narrow definition; and third, the metaphysical problems every book embodies will have to be resolutely ignored. Only in this way, for

Mr. Obvious, can a book remain . . . well . . . a book, what else? Furthermore, for Mr. Obvious again, the future of the book will have to seem doubtful, since new technologies have surpassed it in density of data, convenience of use, ease of reference, immediacy of communication, complexity of relation. Computers, with their keys, screens, codes, and disks, their facile methods of manipulation, their memories and hyperspaces, will do it in.

Let us consider the word, first, in terms of the ontology of its composition. This will be the same, in a way, as considering any larger units, whether they be phrases, paragraphs, pages, volumes, or sets.

The words that I am reading now, for instance, in order that I may speak them in your presence are not words in the full sense; they are, first of all, marks on an otherwise unmarked page, then sounds undulating in a relatively quiet space; however, these marks and these sounds are but emissaries and idols themselves, what logicians call tokens, of the real English words—namely "now," namely "reading," namely "am," namely "I," namely "that," namely "words," namely "the"—or what logicians refer to as the Language Type. If this were not so, then, if I were to erase the word "word" from this paragraph's opening clause—"the words that I am reading now"—or if I were to fall firmly silent in front of the w and refuse to go on; then there'd be no more "word" for word, written or spoken, like that momentarily notorious expression "dibbit ulla rafiné snerx," which was said once—just now—written hardly at all, given this temporary body only to disappear without ever gaining a soul, that is to say, a significance.

To be precise, we do not write words or speak them either. We use their tokens, or stand-ins. Each hand, each voice, is unique; each stamp, each line of print, is somewhat less so, though they form the same message, ACCOUNT OVERDRAWN, on the checks of hundreds of congressmen, in the headlines of the papers, in the accusations of impropriety by their constituents. But the Language Type is the same whatever the ink, the cut of the stamp, the font, the accent, tone of voice. At this level a word is more than its meanings; it is also a group of rules for its spelling and pronunciation, as well as a set of specifications which state its grammatical class and determine its proper placement and use in the normal sentence. That is, if my recent paragraph's opening had been: "I that am words reading the," we should recognize the tokens—"the" is still "the" there, as far as its marks mean and its sounds sign, but we should have trouble assigning them their Language Types, for "the" is not where "the" belongs, articling up to something.

Precisely the same distinction—that between type and token—can be made concerning sentential forms, since an assertion's shape is only embodied by a proposition and is not so enamored of its momentary location and job description that it can't serve somewhere else, even at the same time, or find that its fate is fastened to the tokens in whose sentence it is, for the nonce, displayed. Rhetorical schema are equally abstract and repeatable. The difference is that forms are displayed while meanings are signified.

So let us journey into Plato's country for a moment, and speak of the Pure Type, not merely a linguistic one, and of a Pure Rhetorical Schema, a Sentential Form. Although "*mot*" means "word" and "wort" means "word" and "parole" means "word" and "word," to be fair, means "*logos*" means "*verbo*," and so on, from tongue to tongue, the pure Word they each depend on, and which constitutes their common core, has no rules for its formation, since it escapes all specific materiality, has, in fact, never been written, never spoken, never thought, only dreamed during our extrapolations, envisioned solely by great Gee'd Geist, large R'd Reason, or the high-sided M of Mind.

This progression—from verbal token to Language Type and from that Type to unspoken Idea—has always seemed to some philosophers to be eminently reasonable, while it appears to others as an example of Reason capitalized, another case of reification, and, like Common Sense before, leading us astray. But imagine for a moment that all the tokens of a particular Language Type have been removed from past or present use, as the Führer wished to do with Jewish names. Even so, we would be able to generate tokens once again, since we should still have a definition, know the word's part of speech, and understand its spelling. Indeed, only intellectually is it possible to separate the spelling of a word from the word itself. To show how a word is spelled, one writes the word. However, if the Language Type were also removed, the word would at once disappear, and disappear for good, because the Pure Type has no material instantiation. It is a limit. Which means that words have a special kind of nonspecific or floating residence, because our belief even in a Pure Type depends on there being at least one material instance (or the rules for making such an instance) in existence. Which is as true of the book as of the word, for, in a way, the book itself isn't "in" any one example of its edition, either, although at least one copy has to be about, or the printer's plates, along with the outline for its manufacture.

In any case, something interesting happens when we examine an extended text from the point of view of these distinctions. *Madame Bovary*, for instance, has been translated into many languages, but does this feat mean there is a Pure, un-French *Madame B*, one beyond any ordinary verbal exactness or lyrical invention? Clearly *Madame Bovary* is confined to its language, and that language is not merely French in some broad, undifferentiated sense, but is Flaubert's so particularly that no other hand could have handled the studied pen of its composition. In short, as we rose, somewhat dubiously, from the token to the Pure Type, we now, more securely, mark the descent from a general language like French to the specific style of an artist like Flaubert or Proust. With their native tongue they speak a personal language, and may even, as in the case of Henry James, have a late as well as an early phase.

They achieve this individuality of style, as we shall see, by being intensely concerned with the materiality of the token, whether of word or sentence form or larger rhetorical scheme, although a text may be notable for its ideas or particular subject matter as well. In doing so, they defy the idea that the relation between token and type is purely arbitrary. By implication, they deny that a book only hauls its passengers.

Words really haven't an independent life. They occupy no single location. They are foci for relations. Imagine an asterisk made by innumerable but inexactly crisscrossing lines: that's one image of the word. Tokens take on meanings as well as contribute their own by the way they enter, then operate in and exit from, contexts. The Pure Type may sit like a sage on its mountaintop, pretending it is a Holy Thing, but the Language Type is dependent in great part upon the history of use that all its tokens have, for the oddity is that if the word is not the token, it is nevertheless the token that does the word's work; that suffers age and becomes archaic; that undergoes changes, usually vulgar, in its meaning and even grammatical condition; that finds itself, if highborn, among hoi polloi or other ruck, if an immigrant, suddenly surrounded by the finest families, or rudely plopped into metaphors, hot as pots of wash, there to be stained by the dyes of strangers.

If the word is an accretion formed from its history of use, then when it scrapes against another word, it begins to shave the consequences of past times and frequent occasions from its companion, as well as being shorn itself. We can imagine contexts which aim to reduce the ambiguous and rich vagueness of language and make each employed term mean and do one and only one thing (Gertrude Stein says she aimed at this effect for a time, and insisted that when words were so primly used, they became nearly unrecognizable); and there are certainly others whose hope is to employ the entire range of any word's possibilities, omitting not even its often forgotten roots (as Joyce does in *Finnegans Wake*). The same token can indeed serve many words, so that, while the word "steep," set down alongside the word "bank," will withdraw a few meanings from use, it may take an adjective like "muddy" to force the other "banks" to fail. Differentiation and determination are the goals of great writing: words so cemented in their sentential place they have no synonyms, terms so reduced to single tokens they

lose their generality; they survive only where they are, the same
size as their space, buried words like buried men:

> Though grave-diggers' toil is long,
> Sharp their spades, their muscles strong,
> They but thrust their buried men
> Back in the human mind again.

All our lines of language are like the rope in a tug of war: their
referential character pulls them one way, in the direction of things
and the material world, where "buried men" are covered corpses,
no otherwise than fossil bones; while the conceptual side of our
sentences drags them toward a realm of abstraction and considers
them in their relation to other ideas: those, first of all, that define
terms and tell us most matter-of-factly what it is to be buried, but
only word for word; secondly, associations that have been picked
up over time and use, like dust on travel clothes, and which shadow
each essential sense to suggest, in this case, that death in one life
is life in another; and, thirdly, those connections our own memories make—for instance, if these lines remind us of a few of Edwin
Muir's, and link us suddenly with a land frozen into flooring, a
place whose planks are crossed, let's say, by a miller's daughter one
cold winter's day, in another country and in another poem, and
where the implications for the buried are quite otherwise than
those suggested by Yeats.

> But they, the powerless dead,
> Listening can hear no more
> Than a hard tapping on the sounding floor
> A little overhead
> Of common heels that do not know
> Whence they come or where they go
> And are content
> With their poor frozen life and shallow banishment.

Our own awareness, too, is always being drawn toward its objects, as if it were being sung to by sirens, at the same time that it's

withdrawing, in the company of the cautious self-regarding self, into the safe citadel of the head; unless, of course, desire is doing the driving, for then the same sensation that is sharply focused on the being of another (an exposed chest, a piece of moist cake) will find itself inside of hunger's stomach.

These brief considerations should be sufficient to suggest that the word may be troubled by the same ontological problems which plagued Descartes (and all of us who inherited his hobbies): there are two poles to the person which are pulling the person apart, namely mind—meaning and mathematics—inside the circle of the self, and body—spatial location and mechanics—within the determined realm of things. A book is such a bodied mind. Descartes described these spheres (in the way, it seemed to him, accuracy required) as so separate, so alien from each other (for consciousness is no-thing, is no-where, and its reasoning powers, if we confine ourselves to those, are correctly exercised in free souls like ourselves in precisely the same way, just as mathematical proofs proceed, not in consequence of coercion, but from rational rule; whereas matter is unfree, fixed, almost entirely engaged in occupancy, and a tribute to cause and effect)—indeed, as so opposed in every character and quality—that we might naturally wonder how self and world could combine, meet, or merely hail each other if they are at such ontological odds; and we have seen, as I have said, how bodylike the book is, how mindlike the text, and if Descartes's critics complained that he had made of us a ghost in a machine, we might now understand the text as thought slipped warmly between cold sheets, elusive as a spirit, since its message cannot be injured by ripping up its pages or destroyed by burning its book. Dog-earing can do no damage to the significance of the sign, according to the Cartesian division; nor can the cruel reader's highlight pen clarify obscurity, a check mark change a stress, or an underline italicize a rhyme. This bifurcation of reality can be made persuasive, yet does our experience allow us to believe it?

Of course we continue to call them copies, as if there were an exemplar still and every book were but a vassal of its Lord, an

Adam to its Maker. This medieval scheme is gone; nor are books copied piecemeal anymore, the way translators seize on a huge work of Herman Wouk's, turning it, chapter by chapter, into several forms of Japanese; rather, the book is an object of mass production like a car (there is no first Ford), and both language and printing confer upon it a redoubtable generality to accompany its spiritual sameness. Like citizens in our country, all copies are truly equal, although this one, signed by the author, is somewhat more valuable; and this one, from the original edition, is to be preferred to all subsequent impressions; and this one, bound beautifully and illustrated by Picasso, is priceless (see, it's wrapped in tissue); and this one, dressed in vulgar colors and pretending to be a bosom, not a book, like a whore flaunting its contents while ashamed of its center, asks to be received as nothing but an object, a commodity for learning or for leisure use, certainly not as a holy vessel, a container of consciousness, but instead as a disposable duplicate, a carbonless copy, another dollar bill, and not as a repository for moments of awareness, for passages of thought—states which, we prefer to believe, make us most distinctly us.

Descartes endeavored (it was a futile try) to find a meeting point for mind and matter, a place where they might transact some business, but consciousness could not be moored to a material mast like some dirigible, and his famous gland could not reside in both realms at once, or be a third thing, neither one nor tuther, not with realities so completely contrary. Yet if he had looked inside his *Cogito* instead of pursuing its *ergo* to its *sum*, he would have found the simple, unassuming token, made of meaningless ink as its page is of flattened fibers, to which, in a formal yet relaxed way, were related both a referent in the world and a meaning in the mind. It was not that world; it was not that mind. Both had to happen along and find their union in the awareness of the reader.

Normally, we are supposed to say farewell to the page even as we look, to see past the cut of the type, hear beyond the shape of the sound, feel more than the heft of the book, to hear the bird sing whose name has been invoked, and think of love being made through the length of the night if the bird's name is the nightingale; but when the book itself has the beauty of the bird, and the words do their own singing; when the token is treated as if it, not some Divine intention, was holy and had power; when the bird itself is figured in the margins as though that whiteness were a moon-bleached bough and the nearby type the leaves it trembles; and when indigo turbans or vermilion feathers are, with jasmines, pictured so perfectly that touch falls in love with the finger, eyes light, and nostrils flare; when illustrations refuse to illustrate but instead suggest the inside of the reader's head, where a consciousness is being constructed; then the nature of the simple sign is being vigorously denied, and the scene or line or brief rendition is being treated like a thing itself, returning the attention again and again to its qualities and its compositon.

> If it's ever spring again,
>> Spring again,
> I shall go where went I when
> Down the moor-cock splashed, and hen,
> Seeing me not, amid their flounder,
> Standing with my arm around her;
> If it's ever spring again,
>> Spring again,
> I shall go where went I then.

What is this as-if "if"? It is as if the tokens were rebelling against their simple dispensable utilitarian status; it is as if they were appealing to the meanings they ostensibly bear by saying, "Listen, hear how all of me helps you, for I won't let you merely declare your intention to return to a place and a time when you saw the moor-cock amorous with his hen and held your own love fast in tribute to him, but I shall insist that my very special music become meaning too, so that none of me, not a syllable of my substance, shall be left behind like an insignificant servant, because, as you can hear and see and feel, I am universal too, I am mind, and have ideal connections."

Yet it is only a longstanding philosophical prejudice to insist on the superiority of what are called the "higher" abstract general things, for they feel truly ghostly, orphaned, without even a heaven to make a shining mark on, and beseech the material world to give them a worthy home, a residence they may animate and make worthwhile; they long to be some-thing, to be some-place, to know the solidity and slow change of primal stuff, so they—these ideas, these designs—will rush into the arms of Thomas Hardy's lines and, instead of passing away into one realm or other, will remain and be repeated by us, revisited as the poet revisits that meadow full of springtime: "I shall go where went I when." Like a kite, the poem rises on the wind and longs to be off, yet the line holds, held by the page—though pulling to be away, required to remain.

> Wandering through cold streets tangled like old string,
> Coming on fountains rigid in the frost,
> Its formula escapes you, it has lost
> The certainty that constitutes a thing.

This stanza of Auden's describing "Brussels in Winter" discloses what rhymes do: they mate; they mate meanings on the basis of a common matter. On the basis of an accidental resemblance argue common blood. Through this absurd connection, they then claim equivalent eloquence for the mute as for the vocal.

> Only the old, the hungry and the humbled
> Keep at this temperature a sense of place,
> And in their misery are all assembled;
> The winter holds them like an Opera-House.

Rows of words become the frozen scene, while the scene is but the sounds the syllables align.

> Ridges of rich apartments loom to-night
> Where isolated windows glow like farms,
> A phrase goes packed with meaning like a van,

> A look contains the history of man,
> And fifty francs will earn a stranger right
> To take the shuddering city in his arms.

Rhymes ball their signs like snow, then throw for fun the hard-packed contents of the fist at the unwary backside of a friend, who will nonetheless laugh when he receives the blow.

It was Emerson who wrote:

> He builded better than he knew;—
> The conscious stone to beauty grew.

The stone is carved by the consciousness of the carver. That way consciousness achieves the dignity of place, and the stone overcomes its cold materiality and touches spirit.

The oscillation of interest between "thing" and "thought" inside the sign is complemented by a similar vibration in consciousness, inasmuch as we are eager to lose ourselves in our experience, enjoy what Nietzsche called a Dionysian drunkenness, and become one with what we know; but we are also anxious to withdraw, observe ourselves observing, and dwell in what Nietzsche said was a dream state but I prefer to imagine is made of the play of the mind, an Apollonian detachment, the cool of the critical as it collects its thoughts within the theater of the head.

The book contains a text. A text is words, words, more words. But some books want to be otherwise than cup to coffee at the diner's anonymous counter. That's what I've so far said. They want to be persons, companions, old friends. And part of their personality naturally comes from use. The collector's copy, slipcased and virginal, touched with gloves, may be an object of cupidity but not of love. I remember still a jelly stain upon the corner of an early page of *Treasure Island*. It became the feared black spot itself, and every time I reread that wonderful tale, I relived my first experience when, my morning toast in a negligent tilt, I saw Blind Pew approaching, tapping down the road, and Billy Bones, in terror of what he might receive, holding out a transfixed hand. I licked the dab of jelly from the spotted page.

I scribbled many a youthfully assured "shit!" in my earliest books, questioning Pater's perspicacity, Spengler's personality, or Schopenhauer's gloom (even if marginally), but such silly defacements keep these volumes young, keep them paper playthings still, in their cheap series bindings and pocket-book-colored covers, so that now they are treasures from a reading time when books were, like a prisoner's filched tin spoon, utensils of escape, enlargements of life, wonders of the world—more than companions; also healers, friends. One is built of such books, such hours of reading, adventures undertaken in the mind, lives held in reverential hands.

In a book bin at the back of a Goodwill store in St. Louis, I come upon a copy of *The Sense of Beauty*. By what route did Santayana's first work reach this place? We scarcely wonder what wallet has previously enclosed the dollar bill we're on the brink of spending, but I at least get romantic about the vicissitudes of such voyages, about hurt spines, dust, thumbprints on certain sheets, wear and tear, about top edges that have faded, and feel that some texts age like fine wine in their pages, waiting for the taste of the right eye, the best time. Pure texts have no such life. Only their tokens, and the books that keep them safe, wallow in the world.

Decorations did not always dirty the word by disgracing its depth and subtlety with lazy loops, silly leaves and flowers, poorly imagined scenes, or with characters as crudely drawn as most comics. Nor were banal texts invariably embarrassed by leather bindings, complex enclosing borders, and initial letters as elaborately tacky as a Christmas tree. The better matches were reminders of the Book's ideal: to realize within its covers a unity of type and token, the physical field supplying to its pastured words the nutrients they need to flourish, and actually making the text serve the design of a beautiful thing, while that object itself becomes something of a symbol, enlarging on the significance of the text and reminding the reader where his imagination belongs—on that page where "a phrase goes packed with meaning like a van."

If, then, the miseries of metaphysics are to be found in author, book, and reader, as well as in the whole unheeding world, and if, as its geometry suggests, a book is built to be, like a building, a body for the mind, we might usefully peer into that head where the text will sometime sound and see what elements need to be combined to complete its creation and its containment of a consciousness.

Clearly, the epistemological passage begins with the kind of awareness of the world and its regulations which the writer of our text achieves. When a thing is seen, it says its name and begs to be perceived as fully and richly as possible, because sensing of any kind transforms its innocent object, as Rilke so often wrote, into an item in consciousness: that stone jug, standing on a trestle table, gray as the wood, its lip white with dried milk; or the old mill whose long stilled wheel showers every thought about it with the tossed fall of its working water; or the worn broom, dark with oil and dust, leaning now like a shadow in a corner, quietly concerned about who will take hold of it next; and birdcall, of course, and the smell of anciently empty dresser drawers, the coarse, comforting feel of dark bread between the teeth—would any of these qualities be realized: rage in a face, print on a page, valley filled with fog, would these? the dissolve of cheese into its toast and the tongue's thoughtful retrieval of it, would that? or a cricket's click, your tentatively touched thigh, slow coast of skin, calm water, or the cat's contented sigh, would they? without the valiantly alert observer, dedicated to the metamorphosis of matter into mind, with the obligation to let nothing escape his life, never to let slip some character of things: the way wood wears at corners, or rust grows rich, lamps stand on carpets, and whistles trail away at the end of an expelled breath, a little like the affection they sometimes invite; it would all be missed, our own speech too, the complexity of an animal's posture or a sock's sag, that wrinkle beneath the eye which wasn't there last Saturday, each gone, along with the momentary and ineffable softness of cloth a fat bus driver has all day sat on, the lost expression of faces surprised in a mirror, surprised to see they are not themselves, and—my god—all those clouds . . . if they were not first brought, as treasures are, into some sensory fulfillment.

Our ideal writer will naturally understand that experience is everywhere toned by our mood, soothed or inflamed by immediate feeling, and that these emotions are modified by what we see or think or imagine, so that sometimes new ones will emerge. I take an emotion to be a perception of the relation of the self to other things: fear or hate when they threaten me or mine, jealousy when I am faced with loss, envy when I wish I had someone else's talent, luck, or favor, love when I identify my own well-being with another's, then more generally, loneliness as a recognition that I am not sought or valued by my environment, alienation when I believe I have no real relation to the world, happiness when sufficiently deluded, melancholy when I see no possibility of improvement in my affairs, and so on. About these judgments a person may be correct or mistaken. And our ideal writer will be right about hers, able to empathize with those of others, and be adept at measuring how feeling deforms things or how cannily it makes most of its assessments.

Thought is another essential character in consciousness, going on sometimes at a tangent to perception or in indifference to emotion (as philosophers like to brag it ought), though, if I am right about one of the functions of awareness, each and every element is cognitive; and it is a fortunate person, indeed, who has feelings the head trusts, and perceptions his other faculties can count on. I can feel persecuted and be deceived; I can see snakes and be D.T.'d; I can believe in my project of squaring the circle and be deluded; and we do know people who can't get anything right, who marry wrong, who embrace a superstition and call it faith, whose perceptions lack clarity, color, and depth, and who have never once heard the horn in the forest. Such a person might very well wish to possess the character of a good sentence.

For the most part, our formal thought goes on in words: in what we say to ourselves, in the *sotto voce* language I have already spo-

ken of. Plainly, a meditative person will need the data his perception furnishes and the support which sound emotions lend; but he
will, in addition to the disciplines of logic, mathematics, and the
scientific method, need to possess a rich vocabulary, considerable
command of it, and the fruit (in facts and their relations, in words
and theirs) of much skilled and careful reading, because reading is
the main way we discover what is going on in others; it is the
knothole in the fence, your sight of my secrets, my look at what
has been hidden behind your eyes, since our organs are never
shared, cannot be lent or borrowed. In order to be known, we
speak. Even to ourselves.

We must notice our drives, our desires, our needs, next, although they are always calling attention to themselves. They put
purpose in our behavior, position the body in the surf, urge us to
overcome obstacles or make hay while the sun shines. And whatever we desire, Hobbes says, we call good, and whatever we are
fearful of and loathe, we insist is bad, avoiding it even if at cost.
These are cognitions, too, and we discover, when we realize our
aims, whether we were right to want to go home again or were
once more disappointed in the pie, the place, the conversation,
and the trip.

Finally, in addition to our passions, purposes, and perceptions,
the skills and deftness of our brains, there is what Coleridge called
the esemplastic power—that of the creative imagination. As I am
defining it, the imagination is comparative, a model maker, bringing this and that together to see how different they are or how
much the same. The imagination prefers interpenetration. That's
its sex. It likes to look through one word at another, to see streets
as tangled string, strings as sounding wires, wires as historically
urgent words, urgent words as passing now along telephone lines,
both brisk and intimate, strings which draw, on even an everyday
sky, music's welcome staves.

Having read the classics closely, the inner self with honesty, and
the world well—for they will be her principal referents—the writer
must perform the second of our transformations: that of replacing

her own complex awareness with its equivalence in words. That is, the sentence that gets set most rightly down will embody, in its languid turns and slow unfolding, or in its pell-mell pace and pulsing stresses, the imperatives of desire or the inertia of a need now replete; it will seize its subject as though it were its prey, or outline it like a lover, combining desire with devotion, in order to sense it superbly, neglecting nothing its nature needs; it will ponder it profoundly, not concealing its connections with thought and theory, in order to exhibit the play, the performance, of mind; and it will be gentle and contemplative, if that is called for, or passionate and rousing, if that's appropriate, always by managing the music, filling each syllable with significance like chocolates with cream, so that every sentence is a bit of mindsong and a fully animated body made of muscle movement, ink, and breath.

Lastly, as if we had asked Santa for nothing yet, the adequate sentence should be resonant with relations, raise itself like Lazarus though it lies still upon the page, as if—always "as if"—it rose from "frozen life and shallow banishment" to that place where Yeats's spade has put it "back in the human mind again."

How otherwise than action each is, for even if—always "even" —always "if"—I preferred to pick the parsley from my potatoes with a knife and eat my peas before all else, I should have to remember that the right words must nevertheless be placed in their proper order: i.e., parsley, potatoes, and peas . . . parsley, potatoes, and peas . . . parsley, potatoes, and peas.

That is to say, the consciousness contained in any text is not an actual functioning consciousness; it is a constructed one, improved, pared, paced, enriched by endless retrospection, irrelevancies removed, so that into the ideal awareness which I imagined for the poet, who possesses passion, perception, thought, imagination, and desire and has them present in amounts appropriate to the circumstances—just as, in the lab, we need more observation than fervor, more imagination than lust—there is introduced patterns of disclosure, hierarchies of value, chains of inference, orders of images, natures of things.

When Auden, to return to him, "Lullaby"'s this way:

> Lay your sleeping head, my love,
> Human on my faithless arm;

he puts a most important pause—"my love"—between "head" and "human," allowing the latter to become a verb, and then, by means of an artfully odd arrangement, resting the *m*'s and *a*'s and *n*'s softly on the *a*'s and *m*'s and *r*'s.

Of course we can imagine the poet with a young man's head asleep on an arm which the poet knows has cushioned other lovers equally well, and will again; and we can think of him, too, as considering how beautiful this youth is, and pondering the fleeting nature of his boyish beauty, its endangerment now calmly ignored:

> Time and fevers burn away
> Individual beauty from
> Thoughtful children, and the grave
> Proves the child ephemeral: But in
> my arms till break of day
> Let the living creature lie,
> Mortal, guilty, but to me
> The entirely beautiful.

Yet it is scarcely likely that Auden's contemplating mind ran on just this way, making in that very moment the pun on "lie," or creating that delicious doubled interior rhyme "but to me/The entirely," which so perfectly confirms the sentiment. It's probable that the poet, passion spent, looked down on his lover in a simple sog of sympathy. Later, he recalled his countless climbs into bed, in sadness at their passing, perhaps, but with a memory already resigned, recollecting, too, certain banal routines, in order, on some small notebook's handy page, to cause a consciousness to come to be that's more exquisite, more—yes—entire, and worthy of esteem, than any he actually ever had, or you, or me.

What the poem says is not exceptional. This midnight moment will pass, this relationship will die, this boy's beauty will decay, the poet himself will betray his love and lie; but none of that fatal future should be permitted to spoil the purity of the poet's eye as it watches now, filled with "every human love." Nor can we compliment Auden's art by repeating Pope, that what it says has been "ne'er so well express'd," because that formula misses what has so beautifully been given us: a character and quality of apprehension.

Sentences, I've said, are but little shimmied lengths of words endeavoring to be similar stretches of human awareness: they are there to say I know this or that, feel thus and so, want what wants me, see the sea sweep swiftly up the sand and seep away out of sight as simply as these sibilants fade from the ear; but such sentences present themselves in ranks, in paginated quires, in signatures of strength; they bulk up in the very box that Cartesian geometry has contrived for it, to stand for the body that has such thoughts, such lines that illuminate a world, a world that is no longer their author's either, for the best of writing writes itself, as though the avalanche, in falling from the side of its mountain, were to cover the earth like paint from a roller rather than sweeping it clean or crushing objects like old sweethearts in its path.

How wrong it is to put a placid, pretty face upon a calm and tragic countenance. How awful also to ignore the essential character, the profounder functions, of the container of consciousness— to think of it even as a box from which words might be taken in or out—for I believe it is a crime against the mind to disgrace the nature of the book with ill-writ words or to compromise well-wrought ones by building for them tawdry spaces in a tacky house. "The book form," Theodor Adorno writes,

> signifies detachment, concentration, continuity: anthropological characteristics that are dying out. The composition of a book as a volume is incompatible with its transformation into momentary presentations of stimuli. When, through its appearance, the book casts off the last reminder of the idea of a text in which truth manifests itself, and instead yields to the primacy of ephemeral responses, the appearance turns against

the book's essence, that which it announces prior to any specific context . . . the newest books [have] become questionable, as though they have already passed away. They no longer
have any self-confidence; they do not wish themselves well;
they act as though no good could come of them. . . . The
autonomy of the work, to which the writer must devote all his
energies, is disavowed by the physical form of the work. If the
book no longer has the courage of its own form, then the
power that could justify that form is attacked within the book
itself as well. ["Bibliographical Musings," translated by S. W.
Nicholson, *Grand Street*, 39: 136–7.]

It remains for the reader to realize the text, not only by reachiev-
ing the consciousness some works create (since not all books are
bent on that result), but by appreciating the unity of book/body
and book/mind that the best books bring about; by singing to themselves the large, round lines they find, at the same time as they
applaud their placement on the page, their rich surroundings, and
everywhere the show of taste and care and good custom—what a
cultivated life is supposed to provide; for if my meal is mistakenly
scraped into the garbage, it becomes garbage, and if garbage is
served to me on a platter of gold by hands in gloves, it merely
results in a sardonic reminder of how little gold can do to rescue
ruck when ruck can ruin whatever it rubs against; but if candlelight
and glass go well together, and the linens please the eye as though
it were a palate, and one's wit does not water the wine, if one's
dinner companions are pleasing, if the centerpiece does not block
the view and its flowers are discreet about their scent, then whatever fine food is placed before us, on an equally completed plate,
will be enhanced, will be, in such a context, only another successful element in the making of a satisfactory whole; inasmuch as
there is nothing in life better able to justify its follies, its inequities,
and its pains (though there may be many its equal) than in getting,
at once, a number of fine things right; and when we read, too, with
our temper entirely tuned to the text, we become—our heads—we

become the best book of all, where the words are now played, and we are the page where they rest, and we are the hall where they are heard, and we are, by god, Blake, and our mind is moving in that moment as Sir Thomas Browne's about an urn, or Yeats's spaded grave; and death can't be so wrong, to be feared or sent away, the loss of love wept over, or our tragic acts continuously regretted, not when they prompt such lines, not when our rendering of them brings us together in a rare community of joy.

A NOTE ON THE TYPE

The text of this book was set in Electra, a typeface designed by W. A. Dwiggins (1880–1956). This face cannot be classified as either modern or old style. It is not based on any historical model, nor does it echo any particular period or style. It avoids the extreme contrasts between thick and thin elements that mark most modern faces, and it attempts to give a feeling of fluidity, power, and speed.

Composed by Dix!, Syracuse, New York
Printed and bound by R. R. Donnelley & Sons,
Harrisonburg, Virginia
Designed by Peter A. Andersen